TYING FLIES THE
PARALOOP WAY

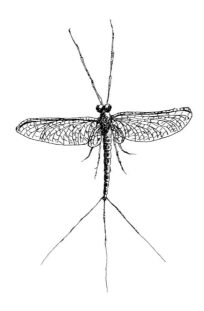

TYING FLIES THE
PARALOOP WAY

IAN MOUTTER

SWAN·HILL
PRESS

Half title page illustration: A blue-winged olive, an upwinged fly

Illustration opposite: A midge fly

First published in the UK in 2001
by Swan Hill Press, an imprint of Quiller Publishing Ltd

British Library Cataloguing-in-Publication Data
   A catalogue record for this book
   is available from the British Library

ISBN 1 904057 00 4

Typeset by Rowland Phototypesetting Ltd, Bury St Edmunds, Suffolk
Printed in Hong Kong

Swan Hill Press
an imprint of Quiller Publishing Ltd
Wykey House, Wykey, Shrewsbury, SY4 1JA, England
E-mail: info@quillerbooks.com
Website: www.swanhillbooks.com

This book is dedicated with love to my
mother and father, Vera and Bill Moutter,
who always supported and encouraged me
in my fishing interest.

From those days at Edgeley's Pond to today.
Thank you.

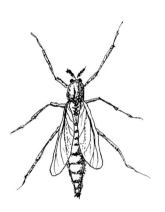

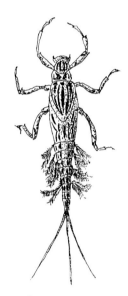

Nymph of an upwinged fly

Contents

INTRODUCTION: How to Use This Book   11

   1. Tools and Equipment   17
   2. Materials   28
   3. Tying a Basic Paraloop Fly   52
   4. Techniques Used When Tying Paraloop Flies   61
   5. Traditional Dry Flies Paraloop-Style   83
   6. Tying Emerger Patterns Using the Paraloop Method   100
   7. Tying Buzzer Patterns Using the Paraloop Method   114
   8. Tying Spent Winged Flies Using the Paraloop Method   124
   9. Tying Wet Flies Using the Paraloop Method   137
  10. The Paraloop in the Hands of Others   140
  11. Adding a Little Sparkle to Paraloop Flies   154
  12. The Paraloop and Its Future   159

APPENDIX I.   Gallery   162
APPENDIX II.   Common Problems Encountered When Tying Paraloop Flies   176
APPENDIX III. Glossary   178
APPENDIX IV.   Materials Used   181
APPENDIX V.   Useful Addresses   182

               Bibliography   188
               Index   189

Spinners in flight

Preface

Imagine a method of tying artificial flies which can be applied to dry flies, whether they be traditional or of new design. A method that is equally, if not more, useful when tying emerger patterns, which includes completely new ways to imitate this important stage for the fly fisher in the life cycle of a fly. Imagine it can be used to tie spent-winged flies, providing a unique and effective wing profile, and for additional seasoning throw in buzzers and wet flies. Such a method is the Paraloop. This book explains the development of the technique, from when I first became aware of it to today, when it can be applied to many different forms of artificial flies. The tying sections of the book are presented so

that they can be used as a bench-side manual, making it easy to apply the techniques described while sitting tying the flies. All the techniques required for tying each fly are described in detail, and many can be applied to flies other than Paraloop flies.

In the early part of 1997 I was driving from Edinburgh to my home in the Borders. The day was cloudy and very wet, a day that would, in the local vernacular, be described as 'dreich'. As I drove along my thoughts turned to how it was possible to tie certain flies. This may seem a strange subject to many people, but to those blessed – or perhaps inflicted – with a love for fly fishing and tying their own flies, it is, I can

The Author teaching casting with the double-handed rod.

assure you, quite reasonable. Close to home, at a point where the road changes from straight to bends, a notorious black spot for road accidents, it occurred to me that it would be possible to get a particular profile of fly if adjustments were made to a well-established fly tying method, the parachute fly. Quite why this idea should reveal itself at this time is a mystery to me, but it did. This was the first clue to what I was eventually to call the Paraloop Method. Darkness had fallen by the time I arrived home and I went immediately to my tying bench, forgetting the rumblings of my empty stomach. In the next few hours I tied numerous patterns, based on this simple thought. Looking at the results it was clear that the idea worked. Not only did it work, but it also provided a profile I had often wanted in my flies and had only been able to achieve by cutting off the hackle on the underside. Since that time the method has developed and extended into many other forms. Wet flies and dry flies, buzzers (hatching midges) and emergers, spinners and spent, can all be tied using the basic technique and its further developments.

I had foolishly thought at the time that the method was a new and original innovation. Accordingly I sent actual patterns and a description of the method to many knowledgeable tyers around the world. All agreed that they had not seen it before. All, that is, except one. I had sent examples of the flies to Hans Weilenmann in Holland and Hans told me of a similar technique he had seen used in the USA. In fact he was even able to describe the method and to give me a name, Jim Cramer. I was able to contact Jim and yes, he did indeed use a form of what I had

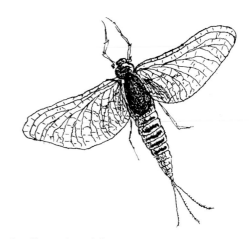

Small upwinged fly

named the Paraloop. He was also able to give me the names of two other fly dressers, Ned Long and Bob Quigley, who also use the technique in many different ways. In fact there were at least two other names for it, the Hackle Stacker and the Pullover technique. So once again it seems there is nothing new in fly tying and my foolish presumption was brought soundly back to earth. There is in this book a chapter on the Paraloop (or Hackle Stacker/Pullover) in the hands of other tyers, including Jim and Ned, which I hope you enjoy. That I was not the originator of the method is of no consequence, other than a slight nip to my ego. I was happy to learn that others used the method and hungry to see how. My personal use of the Paraloop has developed far beyond the original sample flies tied on that first day and would appear to extend far beyond anything published to date.

How to Use This Book

When deciding what format to use for this book, it was clear that it should appeal to the experienced and less experienced fly tyer alike. As a result, certain sections will appear somewhat elementary to more experienced tyers. I would like to ask them to accept that this is necessary in a practical, hands-on publication of this type. The book does, however, assume that the reader is able to attach thread to the hook and to complete a whip finish either by hand or using a whip-finishing tool. I believe there is much here to satisfy the curiosity and abilities of fly tyers at all levels of skill and experience. The book has a great deal more to offer than just 'how to tie certain patterns'. Much of what is described and illustrated can be applied to all aspects of fly tying, not just to Paraloop flies.

The practical tying sections of the book are designed to be used as a bench-top manual, ideally to be open while tying. The instructions are backed up with clear illustrations and photographs, each one including a full step-by-step tying sequence. I hope that these instructions are straightforward enough for everyone to follow, including the less experienced fly tyer. When following the illustrated sequence of a particular tying, it is advisable to stick to the instructions from the first step to the very last. This may seem to be an altogether obvious point to make, but if you are like me, you may often 'follow instructions' without actually doing so! A brief glance at a photograph of a fly and invariably I think I completely understand what to do to tie it. I usually find myself surprised at how my attempt does not turn out exactly as planned, or in fact anything like that intended. In the case of the instructions in this book, I guarantee that if you start at step one and follow each step as described, you will achieve the desired result. Each set of tying instructions has been tested and followed to ensure that they are an accurate description of the actual tying of every fly.

The choice of materials is very important and I recommend that those indicated are used. A fly which includes a floating dubbing will act very differently when fished to one with a sinking dubbing. If a pattern calls for the rear of the fly to be tied using a sinking dubbing and the front with a floating dubbing, there is a reason. Similarly in the choice of hooks, if a very light wire dry-fly hook is prescribed, then the make suggested, or its equivalent, is an important part of the fly. A hook comparison table is included, which suggests alternative sources of hooks where possible. The weight and size of hook is elemental in how a fly will perform when on or in the water. In such cases, the reasons are invariably to allow the fly to sit in or on the water in a certain way and this is fundamental to the pattern. Whilst fish are not always particular in what they eat, there are times when it is absolutely imperative that the artificial fly imitates the real one, and in some cases the exact stage of development that the fish are feeding on. By following the instructions here, the flies will prove highly successful; not following them will almost certainly ensure an element of disappointment.

The first two chapters deal with the materials, equipment and tools necessary to complete the fly patterns described later. Every tool required is explained and its use made clear. For many tyers this will be their first introduction to the use of a gallows tool. The development of the Paraloop has resulted in many a gallows tool being wiped down and used after years of collecting dust. The use of the gallows tool is covered in detail, as it is, I believe, an essential piece of equipment for tying successful Paraloop flies. It is true that Paraloops can be tied without it, but to complete each method successfully, a gallows tool is necessary. On a few occasions, when demonstrating tying Paraloop flies, I have had people say that they are well able to tie the flies without one. In each case, where they have had the opportunity to try, they have agreed that its use is preferable and for some materials essential. Its importance will become obvious when actually tying the flies described. The length of what I refer to as the 'hackle brush' makes it imperative that the post is held tight, to ensure that an acceptable hackle is wound.

There are a couple of pieces of equipment I use and recommend that are not available to buy. They are simple to make, however, taking only a few minutes, and they require available materials – full instructions, including illustrations, are included. The most important of these is what I call the 'neck breaker'. I consider this

tool essential, as it makes tying Paraloop flies easier and more comfortable.

Each material is described and the reasons for its use explained. There is also a comprehensive list of suppliers from around the world in the appendix. Each material has been tried and tested, both for the tying qualities it offers and for practical fishing purposes. I have often found fly patterns described in fly fishing publications that are so impractical when it comes to actually fishing, I can only suspect that the authors describing them have never really fished with them. I would like to sing the praises of Richard Walker in this context. He always instigated a very thorough testing of a fly before allowing the details to be published. This is just one of the areas for which he stands as a positive example to all of us who endeavour to contribute to the world of fly fishing. Over the years these 'dodgy' flies have included sinking dry flies, 'helicopter specials' (you know the type, the fly that spins so much it turns your leader into a bit of springy braided nylon), flies dressed so heavily that the chances of any fish being hooked are minimised

A typical Paraloop fly. Note the lack of hackle below the hook shank.

– what I call 'release and release' flies, the next step up from 'catch and release' perhaps. Every fly described in this book has been tried and tested around the world with excellent results. The dry flies float, the wet flies sink. Those designed to sit within the surface of the water do so. None spin the leader; put simply they are eminently fishable.

One of the major features of a Paraloop fly is that the hook is ideally placed for hooking the fish, a sign of good fly tying which is not always apparent. It is this hooking ability which I and others have found makes a Paraloop fly excellent to fish with. More fish are hooked and more fish stay on. Why is this? It is my belief that the lack of hackle under the shank results in easier and more effective hooking. More often than not the fish hook themselves. I have also found this with parachute flies, for example the excellent Klinkhamar style and the funnel-like tyings of Aimé Deveaux, the remarkable French fly dresser. I am sure that you will find this to be the case too. Flies can be dressed heavily hackled to be fished in fast, rough water and still leave the point of the hook clear.

Paraloop flies can be fished in all types of water and examples are given throughout the book of when and where to fish them. One of the problems we anglers have is that we lack confidence in anything new at the far end of our tackle. There is little doubt that we love to acquire new equipment, in fact it could truthfully be said that acquiring tackle is one of the attractions of the sport. There are few anglers who do not enjoy loitering, with or without intent, in a good tackle shop. Arthur Ransome expressed this most eloquently when he wrote that fishermen find their pleasure on rivers, lakes and in tackle shops. When it comes to tying on a fly, however, we tend to stick to those proven patterns that have served us over the years and which we will probably always use. In fact, I can become a little twitchy if I have a new pattern on the end of my leader which has not proved itself. When fishing, we need to feel confidence in the flies that we use. Without this confidence it is doubtful that we will fish as well as we can. Each fly described in these pages will work in the right circumstances. Try them! I am sure some will find their way into your essential fly box.

The Klinkhamar.

Paraloop flies will not cover all fishing situations, far from it, but at the right time and place they will more than prove themselves.

What is it that makes Paraloop flies special? Put simply it has to be the profile when on or in the water. With no hackle below the hook shank the fly sits low. It is this factor which has made parachute flies so successful, and it is the same with Paraloops. The Paraloop is without question more flexible than the parachute fly, allowing more variation and options. It could be seen as a natural progression of the parachute fly. The variety of techniques based around the Paraloop Method can be found throughout this book, including some wholly new concepts, such as the 'open loop' emergers and Paraloop spent spinners. Each technique is described in full, and I am confident that discerning fly tyers and fly fishers will recognise the qualities each one has to offer.

The tying section of the book proper kicks off from chapter 3. This chapter describes the basic Paraloop Method. It is essential that readers understand the method, as it forms the basis for all future tyings. For this reason, each aspect of the basic technique is covered in great detail. It could be said that chapter 3 is the very foundation of the whole book. The basic Paraloop tying can be used to tie any number of fly patterns; the patterns shown here are there simply as examples. Once you are familiar with the technique, the basic Paraloop Method can be used to tie whatever simple hackled pattern you wish using it as an alternative when tying traditionally hackled flies. All the flies illustrated in the book can be classed as imitative patterns and the fly or flies being imitated will be named.

Chapter 4 covers standard techniques well known to experienced tyers and special techniques developed for the tying of Paraloop flies. This chapter has been placed after chapter 3 because to understand some of the techniques described, it is necessary to have at least some knowledge of the tying of a basic Paraloop fly. Like chapter 3 it is vital to read and understand these techniques before proceeding to the next chapters. The techniques described here will be referred to throughout this book. Paraloop flies

A typical funnel-like tying of Aimé Deveaux, the French fly tyer.

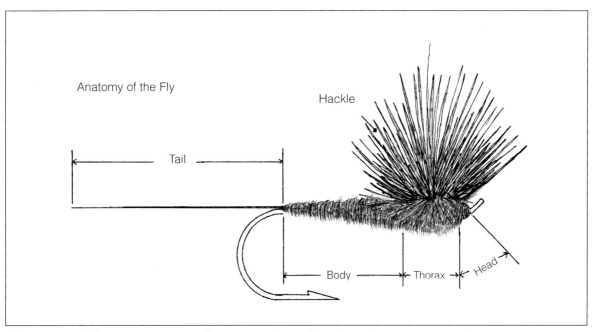

Anatomy of the Fly

Hackle

Tail

Body — Thorax — Head

The anatomy of the Paraloop fly is in the main similar to that of most fly patterns, as can be seen.

can be tied without using all the techniques described here, but using them as explained will result in a far better tied fly, which will do exactly what you expect of it. The techniques described in this chapter give control in the tying of a fly. The same fly tied using the methods described here will behave very differently when on the water from one which has not had these techniques applied. Put simply the techniques are used to achieve a certain result and that result is what is required of the fly.

When a specific technique is referred to, other than in the initial tying of the Paraloop fly in chapter 3, its reference will be made with two numbers in brackets separated by a slash. For example (3/3) refers to chapter 3, section 3. This method of cross-referencing will be used throughout the book when further information can be obtained in another chapter.

Chapters 5–9 describe the use of the Paraloop in tying a variety of different types of flies, from well-known traditional patterns, to new concepts. Each pattern is described and illustrated clearly, with step-by-step tying sequences. Each form of fly has its own chapter: traditional dry flies, emerger patterns, buzzer patterns (midge pupa), spent-wing patterns and wet flies. How

and when to fish each fly is explained, including what the fly is meant to be imitating. It is in these chapters that the variety and flexibility of the method become apparent. As a basic technique, the Paraloop Method is a useful and important addition to any fly tyer's repertoire. These chapters take the Paraloop beyond that, providing a flexibility and usefulness found in very few other methods. The tying sequences used for each fly are those I considered at the time to be the most appropriate for each pattern. If any reader prefers to change the sequences, feel free. I find most flies can be tied using different sequences of material application and undoubtedly some procedures are better than others. If a sequence is changed, take care to keep to the dimensions and materials recommended, as changing these will fundamentally affect the fly and how it can be used.

As I explained in the preface, I had originally believed the Paraloop Method of tying flies to be a new concept, but found it was not the case. There are a number of tyers in the USA who have been using the method, in various forms, for many years and developing it amongst themselves. As it is my intention that this book should be the definitive book on the Paraloop, I have, accordingly, asked a couple of these tyers to provide material for a chapter. In chapter 10 you will find their contributions plus a contribution from a Scottish tyer. It is fascinating how things develop in the hands of others; the tyings included here are imaginative and extremely well thought out. It is clear that the contributors have much more to offer than can be conveyed within a single publication. Their knowledge and skill are very much apparent. What is clear though is how flexible the Paraloop Method is when in the hands of skilled and imaginative tyers.

Chapter 11 takes the methods used in previous chapters and explains how to add a bit of extra sparkle to Paraloop flies. The use of reflective synthetics is explained and how, when and where to add them to maximise their effect. Various materials are highlighted and their properties and uses described.

The final chapter summarises the develop-ment of the Paraloop to date, and the possibilities for future tyings. Like all good methods it will continue to evolve and become an essential tool in the skill box of more and more fly tyers.

There is a photographic gallery of flies, complete with tying menus, all using the Paraloop Method of tying in some way or another, and the book ends with a list of common problems, a glossary of terms and useful information on such matters as where to buy the materials used and where to find more details of Paraloop tyings.

I do hope you enjoy this book. Every effort has been made to maintain the integrity of the information it contains. Similarly the same effort has gone into making it easy to follow. I hope you find it achieves the goal of being a practical guide, with a little extra spice added to make it all the more enjoyable. Tight lines and may your thread never break.

1 Tools and Equipment

To complete the flies described in this book successfully you will require a number of tools. For those readers who are experienced fly tyers, most, if not all, of these tools will be part of your existing equipment. For those readers who are just setting out into the world of fly tying, or those who are relatively inexperienced, I will list each tool and explain its use. The purpose of some of them will be obvious, others not so. I will therefore take the liberty of assuming that readers have no knowledge of fly tying tools at all. For this I again beg the patience of the more experienced reader.

The list can appear a little daunting to those readers just starting fly tying, who may imagine that great expense will be incurred. Let me reassure you. It is not necessary to spend large

sums on these items. Like most things you can always spend more if you wish. The latest version of this, the high-tech version of that, the super deluxe special, will always be available to those wishing to invest that extra bit of money. As a complete sucker for the best in tools and equipment, I am probably the last to talk, but it *is* easy to purchase the necessary tools for very little outlay. Go to your local fishing tackle shop which deals in fly tying equipment, take the list and ask them to quote you a price, emphasising that you do not want to spend over a certain amount. You will probably be surprised at how little it will cost. After you have gained some experience, upgrade your kit as you require or desire.

These are the tools and equipment you will need:

 fly-tying vice
 gallows tool
 'neck-breaker'
 scissors
 hackle pliers
 bobbin holder
 dubbing needle
 dubbing brush
 whip-finishing tool if required
 hair stacker
 view board
 overhead lamp or other light source
 bobbin threader, half hitcher, craft knife and cigarette lighter

1. The Vice

A vice is essential in fly tying; it is our third hand, firmly fixed to a work surface. There may be a few people reading this who will disagree

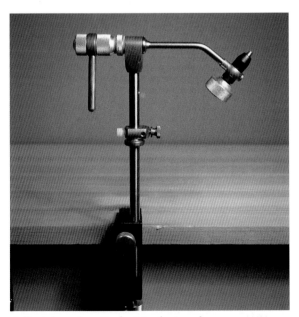

A fly-tying vice attached to the bench.

with that statement. They may well point out that some tyer here or there ties all his flies using just his hands. Yes, I have seen that and it can be impressive and briefly entertaining. However, I have yet to see a fly tied without a vice that is superior to one tied with one. The qualities of a good vice are very simple. First, it must hold a hook firmly, not allowing it to move during tying. Secondly, the vice itself must not inhibit tying. Some vices have so many nuts and bolts on the head section that they can cause problems when manipulating materials, especially when using small hooks. Thirdly, the locking and releasing mechanism should be straightforward and simple to use. Finally, and not wholly essential, the jaws should ideally rotate, enabling the fly to be turned upside down. One does not need to pay a lot for a vice that fits these criteria. One can be acquired for pocket change or if you want to spend the money, the price of a small used car. I use this example because at one time my vice cost *more* than my car; it was, however, a very cheap car!

There are two ways in which a vice can be held stable. It is either fixed to a table with a clamp or slotted into a free-standing, heavy pedestal base. Which one to use? Well that is up to you. If you tie your flies on the best table in the house, then use a pedestal base; it will save damaging the table. If not then use a clamp. Most good vices can use both a pedestal and a clamp and it can sometimes be handy having both. On the whole I prefer to use a clamp, I tie my flies with a very tight thread and have yet to find a pedestal with sufficient weight to counteract this completely, especially when I am being particularly enthusiastic with my fly tyings.

Fixing the hook in the vice could not be simpler, no matter what system the jaws use; just follow the instructions that come with it. One comment I would make here is about the position of the hook in the vice jaws. There appear to be two methods: the first hides the point of the hook within the jaws, thereby stopping the thread from catching the point and breaking. The second keeps as much of the hook free of the jaws as possible without compromising the grip. This second method allows the point of the hook to show. I have no doubt in my own mind that the second method is superior to

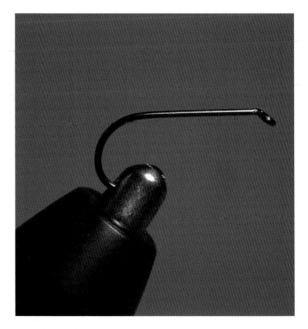

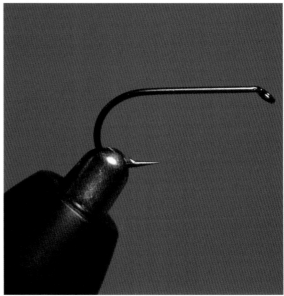

Top and above : two methods of fixing the hook in the vice.

the first, especially when using smaller hooks. With most of the hook free from the jaws, there is much greater freedom to manipulate the materials. The cutting of the thread by the hook point is only a short-term problem; practice will soon eliminate it. Fixing the hook this way also allows more play in the hook, minimising the chance of it breaking.

2. The Gallows Tool

If the vice is the fly tyer's third hand, then the gallows tool is the fourth. There is no need to explain why the tool is so named; when it is fixed to your vice it is obvious. The tool allows tension to be applied to materials already attached to the hook shank, freeing both hands. Originally designed for tying parachute flies, it allows the post around which the hackle is wound to be held taut. Most parachute flies can be tied successfully without a gallows tool. However, due to the technique used in tying Paraloop flies, not to use a gallows tool can severely impair the tying of a fly and in all but a few cases one is vital. The tool is cheap to purchase. Many a tyer has built one using a metal coat hanger, but I have found that the effort required to build your own hardly justifies the saving on what is normally an inexpensive product.

The gallows tool is usually attached to the vice by removing the latter from its clamp or pedestal, then sliding on the attachment. The vice is then returned to its clamp or pedestal. The

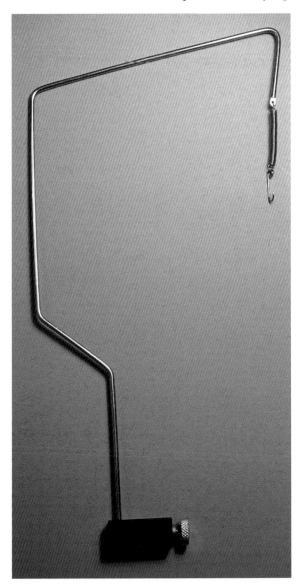

A typical gallows tool.

The attachment of the gallows tool to the vice post. The screw allows the fitting to be moved up and down, so adjusting the height of the gallows tool.

height of the gallows tool is adjusted and locked in place with a screw fixing. The spring hook should be directly over the position of a hook set in the vice jaws. This can sometimes require some adjustment including (depending upon your vice) bending the gallows tool itself. The photographs show clearly the setting up of the gallows tool and the position of the hook above the jaws. I like to leave around 4 in (10 cm) between the hook in the vice jaws and the hook on the gallows tool to allow room to manipulate materials easily. Each set-up is a little different and usually requires a little experimenting with before it is comfortable to use.

When using a gallows tool it is necessary to tie a loop of some suitable material to the hook shank. In the tying chapters this is explained clearly, indicating where the loop of material should be tied on the hook shank and how, for each different pattern of fly. The gallows tool hook is then pulled down into the loop of material. When the gallows hook is released, it will apply tension to the loop. This should be very tight. If it is not, then adjust the position of the gallows tool on the vice post, moving it upwards until the loop is tight, then lock with the screw. You are now ready to use the tool. Mark your vice post with a pen, as a future reminder of the best position to set the screw lock. The main reason why a gallows tool is essential when tying Paraloop flies will become obvious after tying one or two. The length of what I refer to as the 'hackle brush' makes the tool indispensable, because it is impossible to create the hackle brush successfully without the post being held very taut.

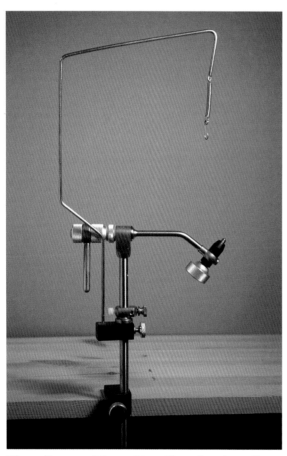

The gallows tool in position. Note that the gallows hook is placed slightly to the left of the vice jaws to allow the hook to be pulled into position when attached to a post loop.

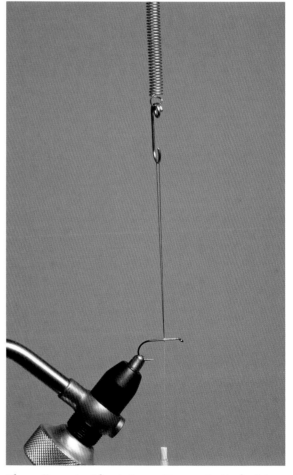

The gallows tool hook in position and attached to a post loop.

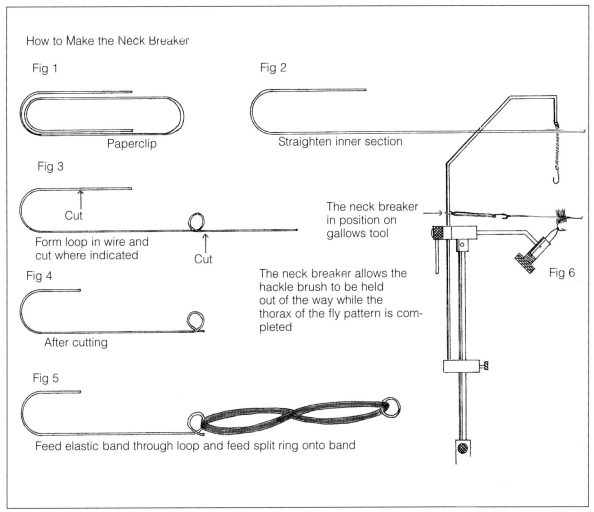

How to make a neck breaker and where to fix it on the gallows tool.

There is a little device that can be added to the gallows tool, which I call the 'neck breaker'. I developed it specifically for the tying of Paraloop flies and it has proved invaluable. It is easily made and fits on the upright of the gallows tool using a small split ring. When not in use it sits out of the way on the vice attachment of the gallows tool, but is ready to use within a moment. The purpose of the neck breaker is to keep the Paraloop hackle brush out of your way when completing the tying off of the hackle and tying the thorax. You will need a small split ring, big enough to fit on the upright of the gallows tool, a thin elastic band and a paperclip. Unbend the paperclip but leave the inner bend intact; this forms a long-shanked 'hook'. Form an eye by

bending the shank approximately ½ in (1.3 cm) from the point of the 'hook', and snip off the excess wire. Now take the elastic band and feed it onto the split ring and then onto the 'hook'. You should have something resembling the picture. The split ring can be fed over the gallows tool and the neck breaker left in place to be used when required. Effectively this device is an adjustable gallows tool on its side. The length of the elastic band will depend on the vice you are using. If it is too long you can tie a knot in it to shorten it or select another if it is too short. This tool, although it is not essential, does make the tying of Paraloop flies that much easier and more comfortable. I would encourage you to use one.

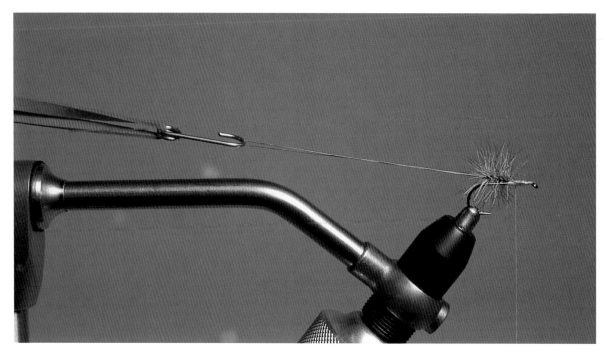

The neck breaker in action pulling the hackle brush away from the working area of the fly.

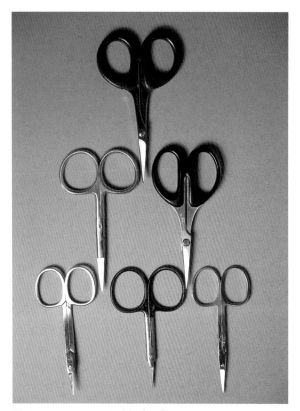

Various scissors suitable for fly tying.

3. Scissors

Good scissors are an absolute necessity in fly tying. A fine point and the ability to cut very light material cleanly are essential. Ideally at least two pairs of scissors are desirable, one for delicate work and a coarser pair for cutting harder materials, for example metal tinsels. If you only have one pair, when cutting coarse material do not use the point, but cut using the lower part of the scissor-blades; this will minimise any damage to the blades. When buying scissors make sure that there is no play or looseness between the two parts; if there is, fine materials will not cut easily. Scissors are one tool I would advocate spending a little extra money on. A good pair is a pleasure to use, a bad pair a nightmare. Finally make sure they are comfortable and easy to use, fitting the hand and fingers comfortably.

4. Hackle Pliers

Hackle pliers are generally used, as the name suggests, for helping to wind a hackle. There are various models and as long as the jaws grip firmly, it does not matter which you use. Personally I find them very useful, but not for the purpose they were intended for. In fact I seldom, if ever, use the hackle pliers for winding, preferring to use my fingers. By winding the hackle with the fingers, I feel I have more control over the tension and positioning of the hackle. I do, however, use them to hold loose materials and in the event of breaking the thread, for holding the loose end whilst I lock it with a couple of turns of thread. For these purposes alone hackle pliers are an essential tool in the fly tyer's armoury. That said some people find it difficult to hold the hackle feathers and wind using their fingers. If this is the case, do use the pliers as they were intended; they will serve you well.

5. The Bobbin Holder

The bobbin holder allows the tyer to hold the thread comfortably in the hand whilst tying. It gives control of the tension being applied when winding thread on the hook, or tying in materials. It also allows the release of additional thread as required. When the thread is not being used, the bobbin has sufficient weight to hold it in place without loosening what has already been wound, if the bobbin is left hanging from the hook. There are various models of bobbin holder and again most work well. The most important factor when choosing one, is that the edge of the tube out of which the thread runs is smooth and will not in any way restrict or damage the thread when in use. For this reason the tube or tube end is often made of ceramics. Although this makes the bobbin holder a little

more susceptible to damage and more expensive, it is worth it for trouble-free use. In some cases it can be advantageous to use a bobbin holder to dispense floss or other body material.

6. The Dubbing Needle

The dubbing needle is a multiple-use tool, which is used for many more tasks than that originally intended. It was originally intended to pick out individual fibres from dubbing which had been applied to a fly. Using it in this way allows for very precise placement of fibres, as opposed to the dubbing brush, which pulls out fibres over the whole of the area to which it is applied. The dubbing needle has evolved far more uses and is commonly used for applying cement or varnish to the head of a fly and to assist in keeping the thread tight when pulling tight a whip finish. It is an essential tool, and if we were to list all its uses a full page would be required.

7. The Dubbing Brush

The dubbing brush comes in a multitude of forms, mainly because most people make their own. Old lollipop sticks, bits of dowel or wooden pencils have all been used at one time or another. The common factor is that a small piece of Velcro is glued to the end. The Velcro used is the hook side and not the soft loops side. I was at a meeting of fly tyers a couple of years ago and one of them was complaining that my recommendation on

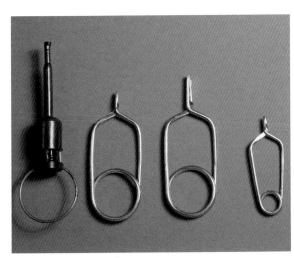

A few variations of hackle pliers.

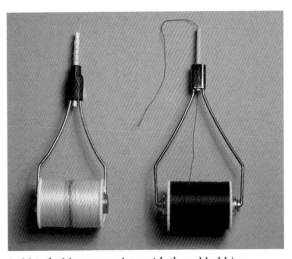

Bobbin holders, complete with thread bobbins.

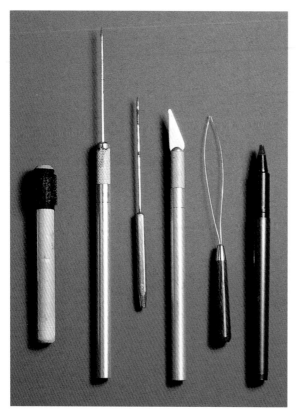

From left to right: a dubbing brush made from dowel and Velcro, a large dubbing needle, a small dubbing needle, a craft knife, a bobbin threader and a pen case used as a half-hitch tool.

how to make a dubbing brush did not work. Needless to say, he had used the soft-loops side of the Velcro. The dubbing brush shown in the picture is made from a small piece of dowel.

8. Whip-finishing Tool

The purpose of the whip-finishing tool is to lock the thread when completing the tying of a fly. Normally this is completed at the head, the whip-finish forming an integral part of the head. There are some flies which use the whip finish at parts other than the head, for example Devcaux-type funnel flies, which incorporate a whip finish behind the hackle. When completing a whip finish it is essential that it start away from the hook eye, with each turn of thread touching the previous turn and moving towards the eye. In many instances the completion of the whip finish is a random affair, the turns being placed haphazardly. This will seldom lock the thread and so destroys the whole point of using the whip finish. When pulling the thread to close up the whip finish, pull the thread directly backwards along the line of the hook shank. This will ensure that the whipping turns will sit tight at the rear of the whipping and creates a better conical-shaped head than when pulled from the side or forward.

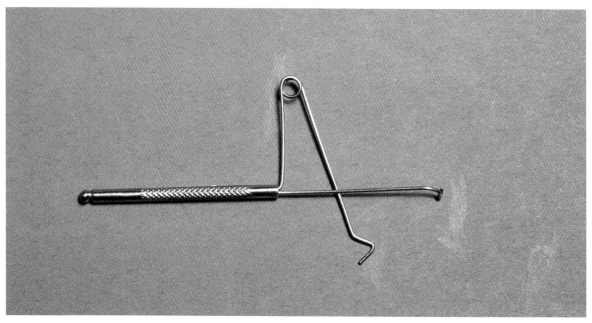

A whip-finishing tool.

It is many years since I last used a whip-finishing tool in my tying. I prefer to use my fingers to complete the whip finish. There are, however, many very accomplished tyers who prefer to use the tool. For anyone taking up fly tying for the first time, I would recommend the use of the whip-finishing tool to get them started. When teaching newcomers I always start them off using the tool and then teach them how to whip finish using the fingers. My problem is that one year I had completely forgotten how to use the tool and it took some time for me to remember – not the best position to be in when you have a new class full of pupils! These days I remind myself every now and again how to use one and, I am happy to say, I have not embarrassed myself again, at least not as far as the whip-finishing tool is concerned.

9. Hair Stacker

The hair stacker allows the tyer to level the tips of hair prior to tying in. There are various forms of hair stacker. At its simplest it is a simple tube, sealed at the base, into which the hair tip end is dropped. The tube is then tapped on a work surface, levelling the hair tips. In most cases this works extremely well. To make the extraction of the hair easier after levelling the tips, most manufactured models have the tube in two sections: the lower section with the sealed base and an upper section which fits into the lower, rather like a telescope. With the top section removed, this gives easy access to the hair. Some hair stackers channel the hair via an upper section funnel into a lower section shaper. In this case the hair tips are delivered slightly convex in shape. I personally find this more aesthetically pleasing than level tips, especially when tying tails and upwings. Tiemco, the Japanese fly-tying tool manufacturer, produce a model of this type which I find superb. It comprises a small detachable funnel used to channel the hair that fits on a weighted, bulbous lower section. When mixing different coloured hairs it is best to mix them before using the hair stacker. When a fly requires layers of different-coloured hair, use the hair stacker to level each colour separately, then tie in each separately. This greatly enhances the durability of the fly. A few words of caution: the sensible use of a hair stacker can usually enhance the look of a fly, but not always. In some cases it is best to leave well alone and tie in the hair without resorting to a stacker. For example, I seldom use a hair stacker when tying hair-winged salmon flies. I find that doing so produces a clinical-looking fly. In the case of Paraloop flies the hair stacker will be used to produce tails and split-hair wings on dry flies.

When using a hair stacker, first select the hair you wish to use on either the tail or the pelt. Use your fingers to separate the amount you require and cut as close to the base as possible. Holding the tips firmly in your fingers, use the thumb and first finger of your other hand to remove any soft downy hair or short hairs not required. Then use the hair stacker to level the ends.

Various hair stackers. The Tiemco tool is the one on the far left.

10. The View Board

Fly tying can often be very fine work and even when it is not, there is always an element of strain on the eyes. To minimise this and to allow the tyer to focus more easily on the construction of the actual fly, it is advisable to use some form of backboard set behind the fly. I call this backboard a view board and I believe it is essential

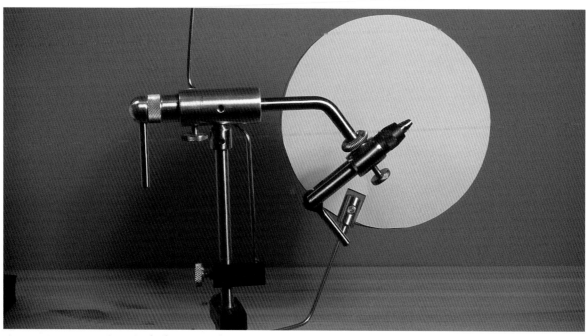

A proprietary view board which fixes to the vice post.

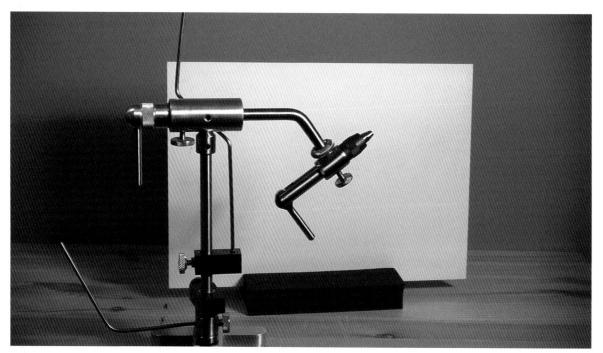

A home-made view board.

for tying flies in the long term. The difference when using one is significant. They can be purchased and are often an optional accessory to go with a vice. If you like to minimise the amount of gadgets fitted to the vice, a piece of white matt card fitted into a rectangular foam base via a slot is a useful alternative. The foam base is 6 in (15 cm) long by 4 in (10 cm) wide and 1 in (2.5 cm) deep. The slot is simply formed by cutting the foam in a straight line to a depth of ½ in (1.3 cm). The card is standard A4 size and is held very stable by the foam when slotted in. Although I tend to stick with just white card, some tyers like to use a dark card when tying light flies and light card when tying darker flies. No doubt there is some benefit in doing this.

11. Lighting

Good lighting is essential for tying flies. Not only does it allow you to see what you are doing; it also minimises eyestrain. I find that standard anglepoise lamps are ideal. They allow overhead light without adding more clutter to the actual tying space.

12. Miscellaneous

There are a few tools which are not essential but can be quite useful, and one which is essential but is not normally seen as a fly-tying tool.

The **bobbin threader** can be useful to guide the thread through the tube of the bobbin holder. Sometimes it can be useful when cleaning the bobbin holder tube of any stray wax. When using the tool to clean, instead of pulling thread through the tube, pull floss. The floss will pick up any stray wax, removing it from the tube.

The **half hitcher** pictured is simply an old pen case from which the ink cartridge has been removed. I find this tool useful when finishing off a fly prior to the whip finish. A loop of thread placed around the tip section of the pen case and then worked over the tip end whilst the pen is placed over the hook eye will place a locking half hitch into the thread. The tool can be used to push any wayward fibres out of the way prior to completing a whip finish. Many dubbing needles have a half-hitch tool at the top of the handle.

There are some patterns in this book which require material to be singed and melted. An ordinary **cigarette lighter** can be used for this. Do not let the flame touch the material; bring the blue section of the flame close to the material, close enough for it to melt. A little care is required when doing this. Always take great care that any combustible materials are well away from the working area before doing this.

A sharp **craft knife** can be a useful addition to any fly tyer's kit. Cutting of materials such as foam is often best done with a knife rather than a pair of scissors, although, if the foam is thin, then scissors are better. With some threads and flosses it is easier to cut them with a sharp blade when the material is under tension; GSP (Gel-spun polypropylene) and Kevlar often come into this category. So it is wise to have a good sharp knife available. I use a standard type, which has various-shaped blades available. The blades fit into the top of the handle section with a screw action. They are available from any craft shop or tool shop and are excellent value for money.

There are many more tools used by fly tyers; I have only highlighted those which are required to tie the flies within this book. If I have left out a particular tool which is a favourite of yours, it is not because I do not use it myself, but because it is not required to tie the specific patterns described here. That is not to say that Paraloop flies will never require the use of any tool omitted from this list – I am sure the ingenuity of tyers will soon find a requirement for using any tool when tying Paraloop flies!

A lighter for melting materials.

2 Materials

The materials used in fly tying are similar to the ingredients used in cooking food if they are good then the finished product should be good. This of course assumes that the chef knows how to prepare, blend and mix the ingredients properly. In fly tying, the right materials are essential for flies that not only look right but also do what is required of them. One of the skills of a good fly tyer is the ability to choose the appropriate quality of materials. The right choice of materials makes the difference between being able to tie a fly as intended, or ending up with some sad parody. As I become longer in the tooth as a fly tyer, the choice of materials becomes perhaps an increasingly important factor. A degree of skill is important, but good materials are essential to make tying flies easy and to achieve the desired result.

It is true that a fly that catches fish can be tied out of any old feather or fluff found lying around; indeed it can be an enjoyable exercise to do so. But if you have a goal to achieve in tying a fly, the use of fine materials will ensure that that goal is reached. Quality materials are predictable, you know what they are going to do when you tie them to your hook. It makes absolutely no difference whether you are tying size 28 midge patterns or 5/0 salmon irons for display work, choosing the right materials for the job will make tying flies easier and in some cases possible. As a fly-tying demonstrator, I often hear other tyers saying that they find it impossible to perform a particular technique, or tie a certain pattern to their satisfaction. They are often frustrated with their apparent inability, usually blaming it on their lack of skill. In a few cases lack of skill is without doubt the main culprit, but more often than not, I have found the

problem to lie in the materials being used; they are often completely unsuitable for the task to which they are being applied. This is the major contributor to their lack of success. When they are given a suitable material the task is performed easily and effectively. A high proportion of all frustrations experienced when tying flies, come from the use of inappropriate materials. Get the material right and the rest will follow.

When tying Paraloop flies choosing the right materials is no less important than with other flies; if anything, due to the low profile of the fly, it is more important. With so much of the fly actually in the surface of the water, or indeed under it, the right material tied in the correct place is essential. When purchasing materials for fly tying it is often a compromise between what you want and what you feel you can afford. But beware of false economy. Pound for pound a quality cape is more often than not far better value in the long run, than a cape at quarter of the price. The quality cape usually provides feathers for ten or even twenty times the number of flies the cheaper cape will provide. And normally the more expensive capes are far easier to use, the consistent shape of the stalks allowing for more controlled winding and the usable fibres on each individual feather being more abundant.

In the tying of trout flies, the choice of materials is no more important than when choosing feathers for hackles. The choice of the hackles used can make or break a particular fly.

1. Hackles

There can be no doubt about the importance of hackle choice when tying flies. The hackle is an

Various types of cock capes, from left to right: genetically bred saddle, genetically bred neck, Chinese and Indian.

A quality genetically bred cock neck cape, a Whiting Farms (Hoffman) dyed Medium Blue Dun.

Hackles from different sources. Outer, a genetically bred saddle, inner left, a genetically bred neck, inner middle, a Chinese cape hackle, and right, an Indian cape hackle. Note the differences. The saddle hackle is long enough to tie many flies.

A hackle colour chart.

important part of most flies, providing not only the look, but also a large percentage of the float-ability, and it is wise to use the best available.

Choosing a source of hackles can be confusing. There are so many different types on offer in the tackle shops and they are sold in so many different ways: Indian, Chinese, domestic, neck, saddle, rooster, hen, cock, henny cock, on the skin, loose or strung, natural and genetic, the list can appear endless. The first thing to establish is what colour hackles are required. For the flies illustrated or referred to in this book (including those pictured in the gallery), the following feathers are used.

1. Badger Cock
2. Badger Cock lightly dyed yellow
3. Grizzle Cock
4. Grizzle Cock dyed olive
5. Light Blue Dun Cock dyed
6. Medium Blue Dun Cock dyed
7. Honey Dun Cock
8. Light Ginger Cock
9. Olive Cock dyed
10. Golden Olive Cock dyed
11. Furnace Cock
12. Ginger Cock
13. Red Cock
14. White Cock
15. Black Cock dyed

The accompanying photograph will help identify the various colours. The number of each of the hackles listed corresponds to the numbers in the photograph.

The next question needing to be asked when choosing suitable hackles is what type of bird will provide the best feathers for tying Paraloop flies. To help answer this, it is necessary to look at the qualities required of a hackle.

Generally the feather fibres must be stiff, springy and fairly even in length. The feather itself must be relatively long. The central stalk must be reasonably thin, but not overly so, and it must be pliable and not brittle. Taking all these requirements into consideration, there is probably only one ideal option, and that is a genetic cape.

The next question is what types of genetic cape are best for providing the hackle on Paraloop flies, neck or saddle capes. In view of the long feather length, the even length of feather fibres and the thin, pliable central stalk, saddle capes would seem to be the obvious first choice. When you take into account that you can probably tie at least two or three flies from each hackle, this choice would seem to be confirmed. Indeed, some saddle capes provide excellent hackles for Paraloop flies, but not all. If the feather fibres are too dense, and curve excessively backwards as many do, this can cause problems when winding the hackle downward over the upward-wound hackle. Too many fibres may be caught under the stalk as it is wound down, producing an untidy and ineffective hackle. This problem can be remedied somewhat by releasing any fibres caught, using a dubbing needle, but this involves extra work and is a little clumsy. This problem is seldom experienced with a quality genetic neck hackle. Just make sure that the fibres do not curve excessively backwards; the straighter they are, the better. For most of my own tyings of Paraloop flies I use hackles from neck capes, as I find them easier to manipulate and complete a tidy finished hackle. This is not to say you cannot use other quality hackles. For the first two years of tying Paraloop flies I tended to use hackles from all sources and I still do. In fact many of the patterns described in this book are tied using hackles from various sources, but the neck cape is, in my experience, the easiest to use, being far more versatile and economical in the long run. But many of the other tyers who use the Paraloop Method choose saddle capes. Try what you have and if you find you have a problem when winding the hackle down through those that you previously wound, then try neck hackles.

A little digression here, about something that appears to confuse a few people. 'Genetically bred' does not mean genetically modified, which suggests that genes from an animal or plant are added to another different animal or plant. I have known fly tyers refuse to use these wonderful capes as they are against genetic modification. It simply means that the birds used to provide these exquisite capes have been selectively bred to produce the high-quality hackles available today. It does not mean that they have had a gene introduced from a cactus to make the hackles stiff and pointed!

Cutting a cape into two equal parts.

You may be thinking at this point that you need to spend a fortune on high-grade genetic neck or saddle capes to tie the patterns in this book. Please do not worry, use what you have or what is readily available. There is no question that good neck or saddle capes are ideal for tying

most of them but they are not essential. And a lot of dealers will sell half capes. Or why not share a cape, buy one with a friend and split it down the middle? If you do this, then, when you cut the cape in two, cut from the skin side using a very sharp blade, cutting from top to bottom most carefully. Doing it this way will not damage any of the hackles. And it gives each buyer an equal number of hackles of the same size. The picture shows where to cut the cape.

2. Wings

Materials used in this book to form wings are:

    hackle tips, either cock, hen or Chinese
    natural grey squirrel tail
    fine polypropylene fibres
    bronze mallard feather fibres
    cul de canard
    Z-wing

In addition to providing the hackles on flies, feathers are required for the wings. When tying Paraloop flies the feather wings illustrated in

From left to right: a hackle tip from a genetically bred cock neck cape, from a Chinese cape and from a genetically bred hen cape. Note the variation in width between the genetically bred cock hackle and the other two sources.

this book are usually of the **hackle-tip** variety, or feather fibres and not feather slips. This is not a matter of choice, but rather of suitability. The Paraloop Method is ideally suited to tying hackle point, hair and feather fibre wings. Tying slip wings, however, can be problematic, unless the 'open loop' method (4/3) is used and then the wings are set at angles useful for imitating spent-winged flies. I say 'usually of the hackle tip variety' because in the fly gallery at the end of the book there are examples of slip-winged flies including a slip-wing Paraloop fly I have named the Claw Wing. For the purposes of this book, when feather wings are included they are hackle-tip wings or feather fibres.

When forming hackle-tip wings the tyer has many choices of feathers. To simplify matters, I recommend three sources. If you prefer the hackle-tip wings to be thin in profile, then use cock hackles. The same capes that provide the hackles are ideal, the cock hackles providing tough, reasonably stiff and thin feather tips, but with enough give in them not to affect the fly in the air. If you prefer to have a wing with a wider profile then a good genetic hen hackle or Chinese cock cape will prove perfect for the job. My personal preference when tying hackle-tip wings is for a cock cape. Although the wing may be less accurate in its imitation of the real fly, being far thinner, this seems to make no difference when fishing. The wing is also less liable to spin the leader when casting; the hen and Chinese cock feathers often have a tendency to

act a little like a propeller and spin the leader, making it necessary to change not only the fly but also the leader. That said, when only slow, short lengths of casts are required this is not such a big problem. So I will leave the choice to you and merely illustrate the difference.

Ever since I was a young boy I have been fascinated by dry flies with wings; they still hold me equally in thrall today, there is just something very special about them. I am unsure what this attraction is, but they always give me a sense of satisfaction when tying them and confidence when fishing them. I am fairly certain, after many years of fishing, that in most circumstances – but definitely not all – the inclusion of an upright wing makes no difference to the fish taking the fly. I am equally certain that it seldom if ever detracts from the effectiveness of a fly. I have a certain idiosyncrasy, which was once described as an *idiot*syncrasy by one of my less than charitable friends. It is that I believe fly fishing starts at the tying bench and the time, care and effort taken in tying a fly should directly reflect the respect we have for the fish we pursue. If that means I take a little longer to add a wing, then add a wing I will, and a good wing at that! Making that little bit of extra effort adds to my overall enjoyment of fishing.

Squirrel-tail hair is one of my favourite materials and I use it for innumerable patterns, for all types of fish. It is extremely durable and can be used as natural or dyed, either unbleached, which allows the natural variations

A natural grey squirrel tail.

of colour to show through, or bleached, which gives a uniform colour throughout. Most fly-tying material suppliers can provide a reasonable selection. In this book the squirrel hair used is the natural grey. One of the problems when tying flies using squirrel hair is that the hair is very hard. This hardness allows very little, if any, give in the structure of the hair fibres when tying in. The hair can fairly easily be pulled out from the tying and once one hair fibre has come loose the rest are sure to follow. Chapter 4 gives advice on techniques of tying and includes a method for tying in squirrel hair successfully (4/8). Before you use this material make sure you are familiar with the technique described; it will enhance your tyings and make them last much longer, even with the abuse we fly fishers inflict upon our carefully tied flies.

Polypropylene is one of the wonders of the modern age for fly tyers and must be considered a blessing. Unromantic as the name sounds, it is vastly important to the modern fly tyer and fisher. It is available in many different forms, from GSP to proprietary specialised yarns, including hollow fibres. The common factor is that it floats, and floats very well, as it is lighter than water; its absorption of water is, for all practical purposes, nil. Polypropylene is included in many of the tyings in this book and is used for tying bodies, thoraxes and wings. For a wing it is used in a very fine fibre form. I have only been able to find a few sources of a suitable product and they are listed in the appendix. A product marketed by the Japanese company Tiemco under the name of Aero Dry Wing is excellent, as are the Siliconised Polypropylene Floss and Micro Wing marketed by Niche Products. Fly-Rite Inc. in the USA markets some excellent polypropylene products, including very high-quality yarns ideal for forming wings.

The problem often encountered when using polypropylene, is the lack of colour choice. I find, however, that if the available colours are mixed well together this problem can be resolved. Do not bother trying to dye polypropylene, it will not take a colour and any colouring will soon wash off. Permanent ink pens can help, but, even when these are used, the material very soon loses the colour; if you are lucky, it will last at the most for a single fishing session. The one

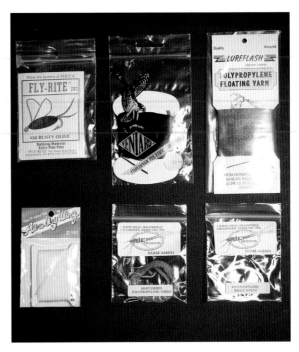

Various proprietary forms of polypropylene, dubbing and floss.

colour that does not appear to be available in polypropylene is red.

I would like to highlight two of the products mentioned above, for no other reason than that they are superb: Tiemco Aero Dry Wing and Fly-Rite Inc. dubbing. I use Aero Dry Wing throughout the book. I find it a pleasure to tie with and it fulfils all my expectations and more when actually fishing. It is very fine and has three hollow channels running through it, hence its ability to float even better than normal

Tiemco Aero Dry Wing colours

1	Fl.White	6	Medium Dun	11	Insect Green
2	Fl.Green	7	Dark Dun	12	Dark Brown
3	Fl.Orange	8	Tan	13	Cinnamon
4	Fl.Pink	9	Yellow	14	Camel
5	Fl.Yellow	10	Black	15	Golden Olive

Fine Aero Dry Wing colours

1	Fl.White	6	Medium Dun
2	Fl.Green	8	Tan
3	Fl.Orange	9	Yellow
4	Fl.Pink	10	Black
5	Fl.Yellow	16	Plain

polypropylene. Tiemco also produce a Fine Aero Dry Wing, which has the same hollow construction as the Aero Dry Wing but is finer in the fibre; however, there is not such a good selection of colours in the fine version. I have used many different forms of polypropylene floss and this product is my favourite, closely followed by the siliconised polypropylene from Niche Products. Aero Dry Wing comes in a fairly wide selection of colours. The photograph shows the colour choice available with both. Unfortunately even the company head office did not have all the colours available for the Fine Aero Dry Wing so numbers six (medium dun) and eight (tan) are missing. There does not appear to be a problem in the supply of the basic Aero Dry Wing. In the UK, Lureflash are the distributors and in the

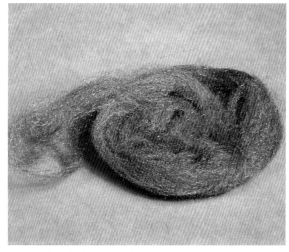

A sample of Fly-Rite dubbing.

The colour chart for Tiemco Aero Dry Wing. The eight colours on the right are all Lite Aero Dry Wing. This material is a very effective floating material made as it is from polypropylene and having three hollow channels running through each fibre.

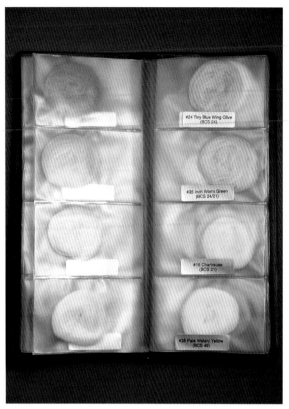

The Fly-Rite dubbing portfolio, containing forty-five different shades.

1	White	19	Light Tan	3	Dark Olive	33	Orange Sulphur
12	Cream	20	Dark Tan	15	Light Olive	11	Orange
25	Cream variant	39	Medium Brown/ Dun variant	41	Pale Olive	18	Rusty Orange
31	Pale Morning Dun	28	Dark Reddish Brown	23	Olive Sulphur	5	Rust
44	Ecru	6	Chocolate Brown	24	Tiny Blue Wing Olive	13	Claret
22	Cahill Tan	42	Dark Olive Brown	35	Inch Worm Green	21	Light Gray
30	March Brown	32	Rusty Olive	16	Chartreuse	26	Adams Gray
36	Ginger Cream	34	Quill Gordon/ Brown Drake Yellow	38	Pale Watery Yellow	7	Dark Gray
43	Camel	10	Blue Wing Olive	4	Bright Yellow	2	Black
17	Golden Brown	29	Western Olive	9	Golden Yellow		
37	Gray Drake/ Gray Fox	45	Mottled Caddis/ Pale Yellow Olive	14	Golden Amber		
27	Speckled Dun Light Hendrickson	40	Caddis Pupa Green	8	Golden Olive		

USA, Umpqua Feathers. Both addresses are available in the appendix.

The polypropylene dubbing mixes produced by Fly-Rite Inc. are the best I have used and I use them in most of the patterns described in this book. There are forty-five colours available and the dubbing is extremely fine and very easy to use. As I have said, it is not possible to colour the material using normal methods, and this can sometimes limit the usefulness of the material, but Fly-Rite has solved this problem for most situations. The colours available are designed specifically with fly tying in mind and include those more commonly used. Each colour is available separately or they can be purchased in a small portfolio, which includes all the available shades. The following chart details the colours available. The numbers are in order of shades as per the portfolio. The contact numbers and addresses for both Fly-Rite Inc. (USA) and Niche Products, the UK supplier, are listed in the appendix.

When mixing different colours of polypropylene floss, I use the following method:

1. Choose the colours of floss required to create the new shade.
2. Cut an equal length of floss of each colour then put the different colours together, ends together.
3. Tie a knot in one end of the hank of mixed colours.
4. Holding the knotted end tightly, use a dubbing needle to separate the fibres of the knotted flosses.
5. When the fibres have all been separated completely, use your fingers to mix them as much as possible.
6. When the fibres have been thoroughly mixed spin the separated fibres to re-form a yarn.

This method can be applied to other types of materials and the mixing of different materials, for example Antron and polypropylene yarns.

The only pattern using a feather-fibre wing described in the tying sections of this book incorporates the fibres from the breast feather of a mallard, commonly referred to as **bronze mallard feathers**. This material provides a light, mottled wing which, in the case of the Paraloop fly, is split. It is easy to use and readily available. When forming wings using these fibres it is unnecessary to use feathers of high quality; substandard feathers that cannot be used as slip wings can be used. So there is no necessity to use

Using a needle to separate and then mix the fibres of different colours of floss to achieve different shades.

the prized feathers you have been keeping for fully dressed salmon flies.

Commonly referred to as CDC, the use of **cul-de-canard** feathers has increased multifold in recent years, and quite rightly so. The feather is excellent for many purposes in fly tying. It is used for tails and bodies but its biggest impact is when it is used for wings. The feather was first used in Switzerland back in the 1920s, so it is not a recent innovation, but it is only in the last ten years or so that its use has become so widespread. The feathers come from two sources, ducks and geese. Goose CDC tends to provide a larger feather than duck. The feathers are available natural or dyed in many different colours. The qualities of CDC are many. The feathers are extremely light and very soft and they are semi-translucent. The floatability of CDC is astounding compared to other feathers. In this book the use of CDC is limited to tying loop wings.

Although there are many commercial sources of CDC, the quality is often dubious. The finest and most consistent quality I have found comes from two suppliers, Petitjean Fishing Equipment SA and Giorgio Benecchi. Marc Petitjean's product is first class and I suspect uses feathers from geese, as they are so large. The Benecchi product is again of the highest quality and is marketed under the name 'Giorgio Benecchi CDC

Bronze mallard feathers.

Cul-de-canard (CDC).

Deveaux' after the great fly tyer Aimé Deveaux. The consistency of quality in both these products is such that every single feather is usable.

Z-wing is a thin plastic semi-translucent material used to provide wings. It is used by Jim Cramer in chapter 10 for the tying of his Adult Damsel.

3. Tails

The materials used in this book to make tails are:

cock-feather fibres
micro fibbets
squirrel tail
polypropylene yarn
Antron floss

Tails of trout flies incorporate many different materials in varying amounts. In this book this ranges from the two or three feather-fibre tails used when tying some of the upwinged flies, including the tail of the Lunn's Particular to the generous bunch of squirrel-tail hair or bucktail used to tie the Grey Wulff.

Using the word 'tail' on artificial flies can often be misleading. The feature is often not a tail at all, but rather suggests the shuck (nymph exoskeleton) being left by an emerging fly, which is quite normal in the case of emerger patterns. In case you are unsure of what the word 'shuck' means, let me explain. When a nymph makes its way to the surface of the water ready to hatch, its outer skin – or more accurately the exoskeleton – starts to split, and the fly emerges from within it. It is this skin or exoskeleton of the nymph which is referred to as the shuck. Often when visiting the water early in the morning, many thousands of these discarded shucks can be seen left over after the previous night rise. Trout can sometimes be seen mopping them up from the water surface, although I wonder what real food value they may have.

Cock-feather fibres provide the tails on many fly patterns, especially dry flies. They are usually tied in as a bunch or as two or three fibres to imitate the two or three tails of the upwinged flies. Choosing a suitable feather to provide the tail can be problematic though, and genetic capes have in some ways added to the problem.

Long feathers with even fibres do not normally have fibres long enough to provide suitable tailing material, except for very small flies, and the large lower feathers are nearly always too soft, with a wide web. Spade hackles on a good neck cape are probably the best source. These are located around the shoulders of the cape – the spade feather is the short one with long, stiff fibres. Not all capes have them and if they do, there are sometimes only a few, so value them. I have also found that certain genetic neck capes provide excellent tail fibres from the larger lower feathers, but only when the web is small and the fibres extra stiff. If you look at a hackle you will see a change in colour or texture; this is where the web starts. It will run down the length of the feather either side of the stalk and normally gets wider the lower down it goes. The web section of a fibre is too soft to act as a tail and it absorbs

A spade hackle. Notice the long, springy fibres, lacking in web.

water easily, so the section of fibre beyond the web must be long enough to provide the length of the tail and a tying-in section.

Whether tied in as a bunch or as two or three fibres it is advisable to cut the fibres off the feather stalk together. Prior to doing this, it is helpful if the fibres are pulled downwards to sit at 90 degrees to the hackle stalk. Then level the fibre tips by bending the feather stalk if necessary and hold the tips between your thumb and first finger. Use scissors to cut the fibres away from the stalk with the tips level. I like to roll the fibres gently between my first finger and thumb if they are in a bunch, as this helps mix any set within the fibres, and makes the tail sit straighter. When choosing fibres for dry fly tails, it is essential that they are long, relatively straight (although rolling will help to set a bunch straight), stiff, springy and strong.

It is often worth checking Chinese capes for feathers with suitable fibres for tailing. As long as the correct colour is available these capes can often be the best and cheapest source of excellent tailing fibres. I use them much of the time.

The best techniques for tying single fibres,

Micro fibbets of different colours.

either as two or three tails, are described in chapter 4 (4/4).

Micro fibbets are a wonderful innovation. They were originally produced to provide fibres for artists' paint brushes but were soon highjacked by enterprising fly tyers. I have no idea what they are made of but suspect it is some form of nylon. They come in a variety of colours and actually look like a paintbrush. Each fibre is light, long and tapered, making it an almost ideal material to use when tying long tails of the two- or three-fibre variety. In chapter 4 I describe two techniques used for tying in perfect two or three tails, and although the methods explained could be applied to most other tailing materials, they are ideal for tying in micro fibbets. Due to the cost it is advisable to use micro fibbets only for tying in two- or three-fibre tails; used in bunches they would make very expensive tails indeed and add unneeded weight to the fly.

The **squirrel tail** used in this book to tie tails is natural grey. This material is thoroughly covered in section 2.

Polypropylene yarn is used in this book only for emerger patterns where the tail is effectively a shuck. Sometimes it is necessary to mix the polypropylene with another form of dubbing, for example Antron or SLF (Synthetic living fibre), but as neither of these materials floats there is a tendency for the tail to sit lower in the water than if only polypropylene yarn is used.

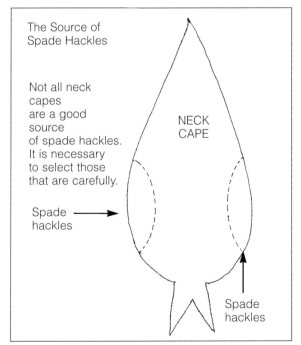

The Source of Spade Hackles

Not all neck capes are a good source of spade hackles. It is necessary to select those that are carefully.

Spade hackles →

NECK CAPE

Spade hackles

Spade hackles can be sourced from the shoulders of neck capes. The diagram indicates where. Not all capes are a good source of spade hackles, so it pays to check available capes for suitable hackles.

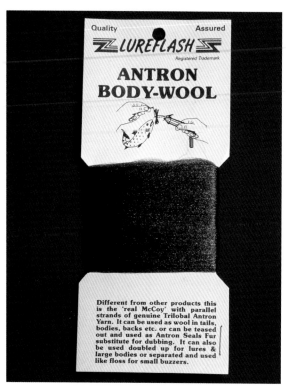

Antron floss, a very useful fly tying material.

Antron floss is another man-made fibre of tremendous benefit to the fly tyer. The material does not float, but if it is tied as a tail, air is normally trapped within the loose fibres, which allows it to float and gives a very attractive appearance. Antron is used in this book for other parts of a fly, beside the tail, but when tied as a tail it is usually to take advantage of its tendency to sink. For emerger tails it is sometimes used in conjunction with a floating body material. Then, if the tail is wet and the air squeezed out, the fly will sit with the tail under water and the upper body and thorax out of or within the surface skin. This position is highly imitative of the emerging fly and can be fished with tremendous effect. Antron comes in a kaleidoscope of colours and is readily available from fly fishing material suppliers either as a spun floss yarn or loose dubbing.

4. Bodies and Thoraxes

The materials used in this book to make bodies and thoraxes are:

polypropylene floss
polypropylene dubbing
Antron dubbing
feather stalk or quill
foam sheeting
Superfloss, Flexifloss, etc.
braided monofilament

Choosing the material for Paraloop fly bodies is no different from when tying any other fly. As I have said, however, the nature of the material used will affect how the fly will act when under, in or on the water. Not all dubbing materials are the same – far from it. The main difference is whether they float or not, or whether they absorb water or not, which often adds up to the same thing. Many tyers purchase lots of different types of dubbing, marketed under numerous proprietary names. More often than not in my experience, the tyer has little idea of the nature of the material being used to make the dubbing. If you are unsure of how your dubbing will act when on the water, then get a container of water and see what happens when it gets wet. Does it float or does it sink? How well does it float? What happens if you squeeze out any air bubbles? Make a note of the results and use them when tying. One note of caution; ensure that the container is clean of any detergent or residual washing-up liquid, as this can greatly affect the results.

Choosing the right material for a particular fly will allow that fly to do what you want it to do, far more readily than if a material is chosen at random. For instance, not all dry fly bodies must use floating materials, because the fly incorporates a hackle as the main source of buoyancy. The act of casting will dry the fly and the casting presentation allows it to drop gently upon the water. That said, personally I do like to use floating materials for the bodies of dry fly Paraloops whenever possible and in this book, with a couple of exceptions, all the bodies incorporate a floating material as a dubbing or floss. I believe this is important and it is part of what I refer to as the holistic approach to fly tying.

When tying the thorax of a Paraloop there is an additional area, which in conventional tyings is covered by the windings of the hackle. Normally most traditional hackled dry flies have no separate thorax area. In the Paraloop, however, the hackle brush bridges this area. This leaves a space which, if it is not treated separately, will result in a section of hook being covered only by thread. This makes it necessary, for both aesthetic and practical reasons, even when tying classic patterns, to include a thorax. When tying dry flies or emergers I always use a polypropylene dubbing for this section and on occasion foam or even sometimes both. Each of these materials greatly enhances the performance of the fly and its look. By using a different-coloured dubbing from the body, the fly can imitate the natural more closely than a traditional tying. The thorax and head are often darker than the rest of the fly. The dubbing can also be teased out slightly to imitate legs.

To avoid repetition only those materials not previously mentioned in other sections will be covered here.

It is sometimes difficult to obtain good **polypropylene dubbing**. It seems to be more readily available in yarn or floss form. I have outlined my favourite products in the section on wings, each of which, when cut up into small lengths, makes excellent dubbing. Fly-Rite Inc. produces a superb polypropylene dubbing and, with creative mixing in a whole range of colours, it is without doubt the best polypropylene dubbing I have come across. In the UK these products are available through Niche Products and in the USA through tackle dealers. Both Niche Products and Fly-Rite's addresses are in the appendix.

Feather stalk or quill is used in tying one of the classic dry flies Paraloop-style, as described in this chapter, the Lunn's Particular. Often referred to incorrectly as the quill, the central stalk provides a wonderful material for creating bodies. The quill, incidentally, is actually the

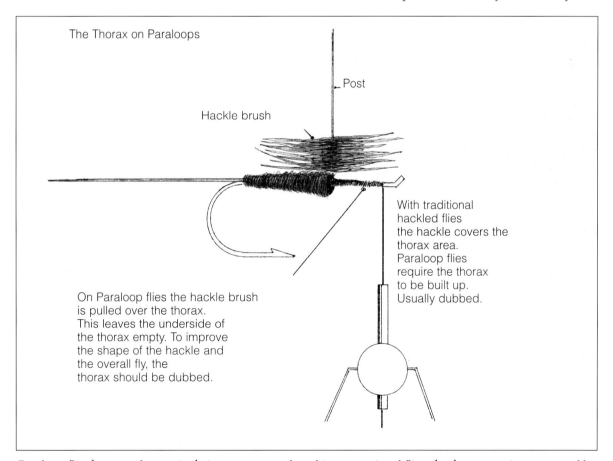

The Thorax on Paraloops

Post

Hackle brush

With traditional hackled flies the hackle covers the thorax area. Paraloop flies require the thorax to be built up. Usually dubbed.

On Paraloop flies the hackle brush is pulled over the thorax. This leaves the underside of the thorax empty. To improve the shape of the hackle and the overall fly, the thorax should be dubbed.

Paraloop flies have an element in their structure not found in conventional flies; the thorax area is not covered by the hackle. In most cases this thorax area is dubbed.

hollow section of a feather stalk. The feather stalk used to provide the body for the Lunn's Particular is obtained from a red cock hackle or a dark ginger hackle. When choosing which feather to use, pick one of the larger ones which is unsuitable for tying hackles. When on the bird these tend to be the lower feathers, the finer feathers being higher up the neck or saddle. Also, before picking out a particular feather to use as a body, make sure it is not suitable for tailing, as good tailing feathers are relatively rare and it is better to hold on to them and reserve them for providing tails. Prepare the stalk by removing the feather fibres. The easiest way to do this is by holding the feather firmly with the thumb and forefinger, with the top of the feather up, the root down. Then using the thumb and forefinger of the other hand, grip the fibres of one side and pull downwards. They will easily come away. Repeat this until all the feather fibres are removed from both sides of the stalk.

Before tying in and winding a feather stalk, it can help to moisten it in lukewarm water. Doing

Remove the feather fibres from the stalk by pulling them downward and off the stalk. Repeat for both sides of the stalk.

this will help prevent the stalk from breaking. When tying with a feather stalk the thin end is tied in at the tail position and it is wound in touching turns along the hook shank. I think the best results come from a stalk that is fairly well tapered over its length. This gives a very nice graduating finish to the body. The feathers which provide this taper most consistently are those from a cock neck cape. That said, any available natural red cape could provide a suitable stalk, just so long as the stalk is not too thick or too thin. If it is too thin, it will result in a disappointing body shape and if the stalk is too thick, it will be difficult to wind without breaking and will also look unsightly on the finished fly. A word of caution, the recommendation to dampen the stalk prior to tying in can be hazardous. Use warm water and not saliva. The chemicals used to preserve the capes can be hazardous to health and some are classed as possibly carcinogenic.

Foam sheeting is a wonderful material and it adds a floatability to a fly which few other materials can possibly aspire to. It is used, in the case of Paraloop files, as part of the thorax, either under or over the hackle. I like to use white sheeting, which is available from most fly-tying material dealers. White closed-cell foam can be coloured easily and effectively using permanent ink pens. Mixing the colours allows just about any shade or mix of shades to be achieved. I favour the foam marketed by Benecchi, which is extremely durable and is fairly inexpensive. Also see chapter 4, section 13.

Superfloss or Flexifloss is notable for the many different names under which it is marketed. In fact I can think of no other product that has so many names. Superfloss and Flexifloss are just two, there are many, many more. The product is made from Lycra and stretches at least six times its own length; it also has zero memory. The floss is available in many different colours and it can also be dyed. It is possible to produce a nicely segmented body using it, especially if the tension applied when it is being wound on the hook is varied. The material is also very light and just buoyant.

Braided monofilament is used in Jim Cramer's Adult Damsel pattern in chapter 10. Braided monofilament is readily available in

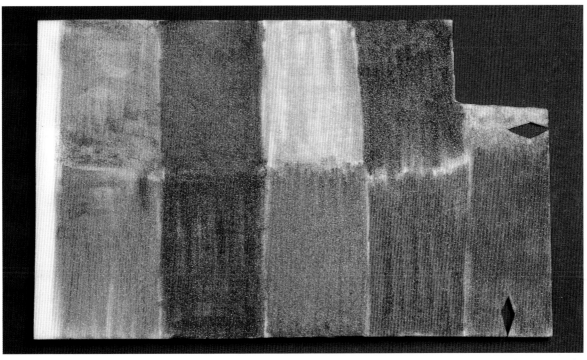

Closed-cell foam prepared for use by colouring in different shades. When foam is required it can be cut out of the sheet ready to use.

Superfloss comes in very many different proprietary names. They are all the same, in my experience.

tackle shops and is used as backing and to construct the loops at the end of the fly line. It makes a fine body, which is ideally suited to the thinness of the damsel fly body.

5. Ribs

The material used in this book for ribs are:

thread
silver oval tinsel
stainless steel wire
Globrite floss

As a general rule, unless the pattern absolutely specifies the inclusion of a rib, I prefer to leave it out of a tying. My own patterns of dry flies and emergers seldom include one. When one is included it is of treated **thread**. Thread used for ribbing is treated in the following way. It is placed in an airtight container – I use a Tupperware box. It is then generously treated with silicon spray. The box is sealed and left overnight. The thread is then left to dry completely in the open air. When dry it is lightly waxed and all of the excess wax wiped off. The thread I use is of a maximum size of 8/0.

The reason for only using thread instead of tinsel or wire is to minimise the weight of the fly.

The treatment may seem a little over the top but it does reduce water absorption. Another method is to treat the thread with Scotchguard. With traditionally hackled flies the hackle will normally hold the fly out of the water, rib and all. Paraloop dry flies or emergers sit low on the water, and adding any additional weight can make a lot of difference to how the fly performs over a period of time. I look on my treatment of thread for ribbing as a climber or hiker looks on their equipment: reducing the weight as much as possible. Tiny adjustments are made, which all add up. For a few casts it makes little or no difference, but it becomes obvious when fished over a longer period of time.

When tying wet flies, the problems associated with dry flies and emergers in regard to floating, to some degree or another are no longer applicable. Because of this the inclusion of a relatively heavy rib can be advantageous, helping to get the fly below the surface quickly and efficiently. To this end the few wet flies in chapter 9 and the gallery include a metal rib, using either **silver oval tinsel** or **stainless steel wire**. Both materials are readily available from fly-tying materials suppliers.

When adding a rib to a fly it is often desirable to use some form of material that is highly reflective or fluorescent. Globrite is a thin floss

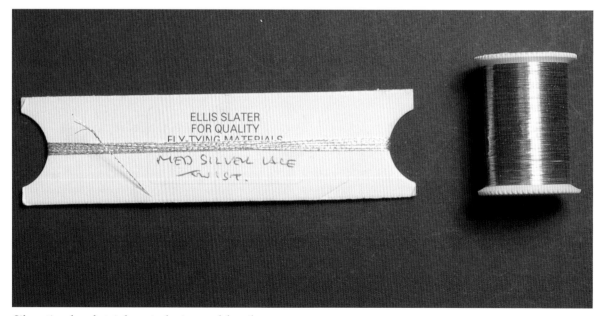

Silver tinsel and stainless steel wire used for ribs

material manufactured by Datam and it is fluorescent. It comes in many colours wound on bobbins. On imitative flies its use should normally be limited to small amounts, but, small amounts of such a material can have a dramatic effect on the overall usefulness of the fly. Globrite is readily available from most fly-tying material suppliers.

6. Posts

The materials used in the book for posts are:

GSP
Kevlar
Superfloss

As with parachute flies, the Paraloop Method requires a post for the winding of the hackle and forming what I refer to as the hackle brush. My personal choice of material for the post is **GSP** (Gel-spun polypropylene). I use it in a thin floss form. It is extremely strong, in fact I find it far stronger than Kevlar. It is relatively stiff, which makes it easy to control when on the hook. The one drawback is that it is difficult to cut, because the fibres are so fine. GSP must be cut under tension. When cutting off the excess GSP after tying in the hackle brush, I tend to use a craft knife. Place the blade at the point where it is to be cut and pull the GSP, holding the blade in place. This

GSP (Gel-spun polypropylene), ideal for use as posts; extremely controllable and very strong.

will normally cut the material easily. Take care when using this method to ensure that the thread is not cut at the same time.

I have never used **Kevlar** when tying Paraloop flies, but Brian Cornwall in chapter 10 swears by it. The material is very strong and, like GSP, fairly stiff, giving easy control when it is on the hook. It can also be difficult to cut and should be cut under tension. It is available from most fly-tying material suppliers.

Of the materials used for providing the post on Paraloop flies, **Superfloss** has to be the most ingenious, and I am grateful to Ned Long (chapter 11) for introducing me to it. The qualities of the material have already been covered in section 4, but, its use as a post is very interesting. Ned uses a single strand of Superfloss as the post, tying it on the hook shank and then pulling it over the top of the gallows tool, then tying it off with a knot, which applies the tension. After the hackle brush has been completed the Superfloss is released, which allows the material to contract back to its normal length. The result is automatic compacting of the hackle brush and an expanding of the Superfloss within the hackle brush, further securing the hackle.

7. Wax

I am never sure whether to include wax as a tool or a material, but after some consideration I have plumped for material.

The careful use of wax does, in my opinion, make the difference between a fly tied to last and one that will, like many of the flies we imitate in our tyings, have a brief lifespan. I suppose tying flies badly could be considered as part of the imitation process – the natural fly only lives for a few hours and so do the tied flies. Joking apart, judicious use of wax will improve a fly in many respects. Thread treated with wax will grip the materials being applied to a fly more efficiently. When well-waxed thread is applied around the hook shank it provides a solid and non-moving foundation. If the thread base of a fly is compromised then so will the whole fly. One of the first tests I have for a fly is to see if it twists around the shank. I am surprised at how often it does and even more surprised at how easy it is to do so. With a generously waxed thread

Left, beeswax; right, traditional cobbler's wax.

wound tightly around the hook shank, it is impossible to twist the fly around the shank without destroying the fly.

Many of the threads available for fly tying come already waxed, but they should be waxed again by carefully pulling them a few times through the edges of a block of wax. Two or three steady pulls will be more than sufficient and any excess wax should be wiped off. Enough thread should be pulled off the bobbin to tie a single fly, then waxed as above. After wiping off any excess the thread can be rewound onto the bobbin. The whole procedure takes around fifteen seconds.

At a demonstration in Edinburgh a few years ago I dubbed a thread with Antron. After the demonstration was finished, I was approached by one of the local fly dressers, a very competent tyer. He explained that during a previous fly-tying evening, to which a tyer well known for his writings had been invited, he had been asked by this tyer to dub a thread. He had been made to feel stupid and embarrassed by this guest because he used wax on the thread before applying the dubbing. Apparently the guest demonstrator went on about how it was unnecessary to use wax at all, implying that anyone who did so was stupid. My confidant was most upset by this

and asked for my opinion. My opinion was very clear: anyone can dub a thread without using wax, but why would they? The only time I could see it as beneficial was if a noodle of dubbing was required to be moved up the thread. Wax is the fly tyer's friend and unless there is a particular reason for it not to be used, it will always enhance the fly.

There are quite a few different types of wax available and it is a matter of personal preference which works best for each of us. My own choice is traditional dark cobbler's wax, followed by beeswax. It does all I can ask of a wax and it is unsurpassed in providing a solid base for the fly. This wax bonds materials so well that I seldom use varnish on my dry fly or emerger heads, tight thread and good wax being quite sufficient to secure and finish the fly.

8. Hooks

The hook is the one common factor with every artificial fly, every fly has one in some form or another. For the tyings in this book, I use a light wire hook for the dry flies, suspender buzzers and emergers and a substantially heavier one for the wet flies and some sinking buzzers.

For tying the Paraloop dry flies and spent

winged patterns I like to use Partridge Captain Hamilton dry fly hooks either up eyed, code no. L3B or down eyed, code no. L4A. My personal preference is the up-eyed hook, but I would have to admit that there is no particular reason for that, other than that I prefer the look of the finished fly when tied with the up eye. This preference is tempered by the L4A, which is a featherweight down-eyed hook and, due to its lack of weight, is ideal for tying many of the Paraloops. The size of the hooks used for the patterns in this book range from 10 to 18. The main reason I like to use the Captain Hamilton range of Partridge hooks is their lightness compared with most others I have used. However, there are other hooks which will serve equally as well, I have listed some of these in the comparison table below.

When tying the buzzer patterns, either the suspender type or the emerger, I like to use the Kamasan B100 Shrimp/Buzzer, which is a lightweight continuous-bend hook. When tying buzzer patterns and not attempting to make the fly float, I use the Kamasan B110 Grubber hook. This is a much heavier hook than the B100 and is perfect for getting the fly down under the surface of the water. The hook is used in sizes 12 and 14.

For the wet flies a much heavier hook is required and for this I rely on the Partridge YSH1 or the Kamasan B175. These add enough weight to sink the fly without too much trouble; if extra weight is required a few turns of lead will oblige.

When tying the emerger patterns there are three hooks I use. The first is the Partridge Oliver Edwards Nymph/Emerger (K14ST), an excellent shaped hook and one for which I have found it difficult to find a close substitute. The Partridge Klinkhamer hook (GRS15ST) is the second hook I use and the third is the Kamasan B100 Shrimp/Buzzer hook. All these hooks help to provide a suitable profile for the emerging fly and to present both the rear and the front of the fly in the correct position.

When choosing hooks, avoid any that are brittle or soft. A simple test for 'soundness' is to place a hook in the vice and 'ping' the hook with your finger. Pull the hook towards you by placing your forefinger behind the eye and suddenly

let go. The hook should return to its original position; if it does not it is too soft, and if it breaks it is too brittle. It is wise to check every hook as you use it by performing the above test. There is much frustration in finishing tying a fly only to have it snap or bend as you complete the whip finish. Also check for any faults in the hook itself. Badly formed or improperly finished eyes can all cause problems, including cutting your thread. Also check to see that the barb is not cut too deeply, as this can seriously weaken the hook.

With the increasing awareness of anglers of the need for sustainable fish stocks, more and more are opting for barbless or debarbed hooks. Some of the above come in a barbless version. But forming the barb is often part of the normal hook-making process, so barbless hooks require a different manufacturing method. This adds to the production costs and barbless hooks are thus usually more expensive than the equivalent barbed hook. If you prefer to use barbless hooks and either the hook required is not available in a barbless version, or you do not wish to pay the extra, then debarbing is quite acceptable. Use a pair of fine-nosed pliers to compress the barb back whence it came. The barb can also be filed down. It is best to debarb the hook prior to tying. This eliminates any chance of damage to the tied fly. It also removes any possibility of having to fumble around for your pliers, just as a hatch of the blue-winged olive starts to fill the air and the trout begin to rise in earnest. Discovering that the only fly pattern in your box which imitates the fly has a barb is not good for the nerves. At times like that it can be stressful enough just to tie the fly onto the leader, let alone debarb the hook.

The following diagram describes the anatomy of the hook, and the accompanying photograph gives examples of the hooks used in this book. If the precise hook described is not available to you, then it will provide a guide for finding something equivalent. The comparison chart gives fairly reasonable alternative hooks from different manufacturers. That is not to say they are exactly the same as the hook they are compared with, only that I consider them suitable for tying the flies concerned. The Partridge Oliver Edwards Nymph/Emerger hook is the most

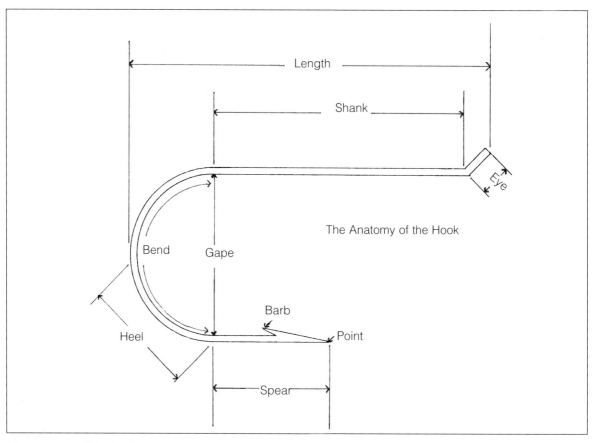

The Anatomy of the Hook

The anatomy of the hook.

	Partridge Captain Hamilton Dry Fly Up Eye **Size 12 Ref. L3B**		Partridge Captain Hamilton Featherweight Dry Fly Down Eye **Size 12 Ref. L4A**
	Partridge Oliver Edwards Nymph/Emerger **Size 12 Ref. K14ST**		Partridge Klinkhamar G/S Special Hook **Size 14 Ref. GRS15ST**
	Kamasan Shrimp/Buzzer (lightweight) **Size 12 Ref. B100**		Kamasan Grubber (Heavyweight) **Size 12 Ref. B110**

Examples of the hooks used in this book.

Comparison Chart – hooks by alternative manufacturers

Hooks specified in this book	Code No. of similar hook					
	Kamasan	Partridge	Tiemco	Daiichi	Orvis	VMC
Partridge Captain Hamilton Dry Fly Up Eye. Ref. L3B	B440		TMC501	1330		9289
Partridge Captain Hamilton Featherweight Dry Fly Down Eye. Ref. L4A	B400		TMC531	1480	1523/25	9288
Partridge Oliver Edwards Nymph Emerger. Ref. K14ST			TMC200R	1270	1510/25	
Partridge Wet Fly Heavy Wire. Ref. YSH1	B175		TMC3769	1530	1641/25	8526
Partridge Klinkhamar G/S Special Hook. Ref. GRS15ST			TMC200R	1270		
Kamasan Shrimp/Buzzer. Ref. B100		YK4A	TMC2487	1130	1639/25	
Kamasan Grubber. Ref. B110		YK2B	TMC2457	2170	8891/25	

difficult to find an alternative for and the hooks recommended are the nearest that I can find in shape, although they are still some way from being exactly the same. Where I can find no reasonable alternative from a manufacturer, I have made no recommendation at all.

9. Thread

There are very few flies that are tied without using thread. All the flies in this book require it. Thread is one of the most important materials used in fly tying. In fact it is more than a material, it is also a tool. It is important that the right thread is chosen. When asked about the thread they use, most of the tyers I talk to become pretty vague and indicate where they buy it rather than what it is. But choosing the best thread for the job will not only produce a better finished fly, but make tying it that much more enjoyable. Having said all that, it is a very personal choice; some tyers prefer a certain type, whilst others choose another. Some threads are beneficial when tying particular types of flies and are completely unsuitable for other types.

For the flies in this book a good-quality thread with a thickness of 8/0 is quite adequate. At a push a quality 6/0 thread is acceptable and you could use thinner than 8/0 if preferred, but certainly not thicker than 6/0 (the lower the number prefixing the slash, the thicker the thread). If you have a favourite then use it, but it should have the following qualities:

- It must be thin and strong. It should easily cope

with tight winding without breaking. If constant pressure on the thread is causing it to break then perhaps you need to change the brand – not all threads are the same. If the thread does break regularly, then it may be wise to check the lip of your bobbin holder to check that it is not cutting the thread.

- It must be possible to unwind the thread to allow it to be tied in flat and to wind it tight to give a more concentrated grip. This allows far more control when tying in materials and minimising the build up of materials (see chapter 4, section 12).

The thread is required to fulfil various functions when tying the patterns in this book. The following are the major ones:

- Forming a solid, sound foundation on the hook shank. This is vital in tying any fly. The thread

Microthread used by the Author.

foundation around the hook shank is the strength of the fly if wound well and its weakness if wound badly or loosely. When using some materials it is beneficial to space the windings on the shank, as this improves the grip on the material.

- Gripping and holding materials in place. When gripping and placing materials the thread is in effect another tool rather than just a material.
- Helping to form the shape of the fly body. This can either be as the body itself or as an underbody for some other material to cover.
- Forming the head of the fly and locking the materials in place with the whip finish.

Thread is made from many different types of materials: silk, cotton, polyester, rayon, Kevlar or polypropylene. My favourite for tying the flies in this book is polyester. It is very strong and unwinds flat or winds up tight like a dream. In fact it is little short of perfect. Its one drawback, which with a little care can usually be avoided, is that if it catches the hook point or any sharp edge it frays into tiny fibres. Although this does not normally break it, it can be a little irritating, so try not to catch the hook point. My own personal preference in thread, and the thread used for all the tyings in this book, is one that goes under the name of Microthread. It is marketed in Scotland by The Craftye Fisherman of Edinburgh. It is a multistrand 100 per cent polyester thread manufactured in the UK by Gutemann, code no. U151 SKALA. I tend to use only one shade and that is a natural-looking, slightly yellow colour. Unless a pattern specifies a particular colour and that colour is an important part of the fly, for example crimson thread when tying the Lunn's Particular, I always stick to my slightly yellow one. I am convinced this colour is stronger than the others in the same range. Maybe it has something to do with the dyeing process or perhaps it is just my imagination. When waxed, using cobbler's wax, the thread takes on an earthy olive shade, which is not out of place on most imitative flies. That being the case I seldom varnish the head, trusting to a well-tied whip finish and waxed thread to lock everything in place.

The threads I recommend include the following:

Benecchi: made in Italy, very strong and excellent for most work; very thin
Gudebrod: a little thick but excellent
Gutemann: the makers of the thread I use
Uni thread: very popular although it seems a little weak and does not flatten completely
Dynacord: very thin, strong and flattens well, excellent; spun in the opposite direction

Whether you choose pre-waxed or non-waxed thread is of little consequence when tying the patterns in this book. I recommend that both pre-waxed thread and non-waxed thread be generously waxed prior to tying (see section 7). The wax on pre-waxed thread appears to lose a lot of the qualities that make waxing so beneficial when tying flies. It is probably due to the wax drying out to some degree during storage or when on the shelf of the supplier.

For more information on the use of thread see chapter 4, section 12.

10. Varnish and Glue

On the whole I have a natural aversion to using glue when tying trout flies. Admittedly when tying large streamer or salt-water flies glue can be advantageous. I have, however, come across a few tyers who use glue on all their flies; I believe this is a mistake with relatively small imitative

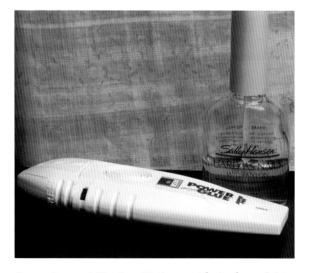

Superglue and Hard as Nails varnish, both useful in small doses.

flies and I look on such practitioners as 'fly gluers', not fly tyers or dressers. The glue is best left in the model-making cabinet; there is no necessity to use it on trout flies if proper and effective tying techniques are used. There may be some readers who disagree with this and who can give examples of a particular fly which requires the use of glue. That may be so, but the only ones I know of that come into this category are those highly representational patterns more akin to model making than fly tying. Glue is often recommended when tying in hard hair. Why? If proper techniques are used the hair can be tied in without compromising the integrity of the fly.

When tying the Paraloop flies in this book the only use of glue is when setting the two or three tails at the end of a detached body. In this case a very small drop of superglue can be used to fix the tails in position.

Varnish is also overrated and overused when tying imitative dry and emerger-type trout flies. Most of the tyers I know use varnish on most of their flies when finishing off the head. The logic behind this is that it locks the thread and forms an attractive head. If the head is finished off properly with a true whip finish, there is no way the thread will come loose; it will be completely locked. The addition of varnish for this purpose is like wearing braces and a belt – either is more than sufficient to do the job required of it. The problem arises when the head is not finished off correctly and especially when the whip finish is compromised. The whip finish must start at the material end of the head and progress in touching turns towards the eye. The thread is then pulled backward along the line of the hook shank. This produces a tight, neat conical head, which will not come apart. If the thread is waxed, so much the better.

In this book the use of varnish in my own tyings is limited to varnishing the body of midge pupa flies (buzzers) and the heads of the wet flies. I like to use Sally Hansen's Hard as Nails varnish, which is available from most places that sell nail varnishes and some enlightened fly-tying material suppliers. It is clear and contains nylon, it dries very quickly and it is easy to build up layers using it. The finished result is very hard and totally translucent.

3 Tying a Basic Paraloop Fly

The information in this chapter forms the basis for all the future tyings using the Paraloop Method. When I first started tying Paraloop flies, the basic pattern was the only type I was aware of, not having at the time developed the method beyond the simple concept, or being aware of any other patterns by fellow tyers. That said, the basic pattern is still proving itself. The technique is simple and, if the instructions are followed exactly, completing the fly should be no problem.

I was convinced from the very first day I tied a Paraloop fly, that it would fish in precisely the way intended. It just looked right, having that certain indescribable something that some flies have. Experience has shown that this initial impression was well founded. So often a newly designed fly can prove disappointing when it comes to actual fishing. I have made a few classic blunders myself, the newly created fly failing miserably to live up to expectations and forcing a discreet retreat back to the drawing board or the waste bin. My so-called 'upward swimming buzzer' was a case in point. It was the result of a brainwave and comprised two flies, the first of which was a heavy weighted buzzer. The second was a foam-based monstrosity. The leader was taken through the eye of the foam-based fly and allowed to run free, no knot being applied. The tippet was then connected to the

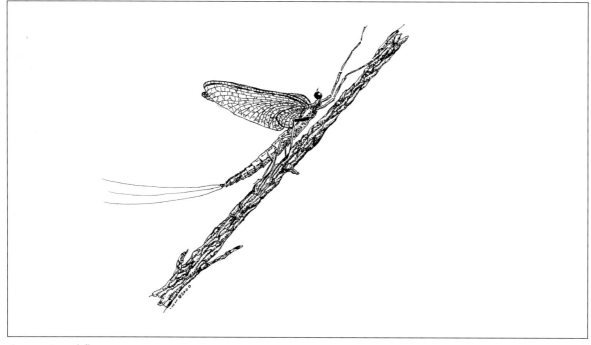

An upwinged fly.

heavy buzzer. The idea was to imitate the upward and downward motion of a natural buzzer. When slack line was offered the buzzer sank vertically from the floating fly and when the line was retrieved the buzzer rose vertically. It was great in theory, but in practice not quite what I had in mind. Not only did it fail to swim upward, it failed to hook any fish stupid or hungry enough to take a bite at it. The only good thing to come from it was the entertainment value to those watching its first demonstration.

Paraloops have never been a problem. The flies fished exactly as expected from day one. Even those flies tied in a fit of inspiration on that first day were successful. By successful I do not mean they just caught fish, although they certainly did, but that they performed in exactly the way intended, a far more satisfying way to make the rod bend. Over the last few years, the use of different materials has given more flexibility and choice in the tying of the flies. It has been this careful and judicious choice of the materials used that has extended the range of the basic Paraloop fly. Most experienced tyers will clearly see the possibilities offered by the technique and hopefully apply it to their own favourite fly patterns. I am sure any who do so will not be disappointed. For less experienced tyers, after completing the tying in this chapter, try out the basic Paraloop patterns in the gallery; they are all clearly labelled (see chapter 12). Then move on to the more advanced tyings. This will give a little extra experience and understanding of the method.

So let us get down to tying a basic Paraloop fly. Whenever you sit down to tie flies, it is a good idea to have the tools ready to hand and the materials prepared and waiting. The first example of a Paraloop fly will be the Olive Dun. The pattern is simple and relatively easy to tie, as well as being one of the most useful when on the water. The tools and materials required are as follows.

Tools

    vice
    gallows tool and neck breaker
    scissors
    hackle pliers
    bobbin holder
    dubbing needle and brush

Materials

    hook: size 12 Partridge Captain Hamilton dry fly
    thread: 8/0 olive or neutral colour
    body: olive floss – Tiemco Aero Dry Fly or similar fine-fibre polypropylene-based floss
    hackle: dyed olive cock
    tail: dyed olive cock hackle
    post: GSP very fine floss
    thorax: olive mixed with a little brown polypropylene fine-fibre dubbing (the body floss material can be used if cut into small lengths and mixed up well with a little brown dubbing material or Fly-Rite #34)

Tying

The Olive Dun imitates some of the most widely distributed of the upwinged flies (Ephemeroptera), commonly known as the Olives due to their greenish colouring. It is based on one of the great classic dry flies, G. E. M. Skues referring to it as the Medium Olive. For those who like their flies served Latin style *Baetis vernus* (Medium Olive), *Baetis fuscatus* (Pale Watery Olive), *Cloeon dipterum* (Pond Olive), *Cloeon simile* (Lake Olive) and many others can be imitated using this pattern. The hook size only needs to be adjusted to imitate the smaller flies. It has been well represented in fly boxes for well over a century in its many traditional forms and continues as one of the most important patterns to have readily available. Woe betide any angler who ventures out on the water without at least a couple tucked away somewhere safe. Purists will please forgive me for changing some of the materials normally associated with this fly. Each material, however, has been carefully selected for its appearance and performance.

Set up the vice with the gallows tool and neck breaker attached, as per the instructions in chapter 1. As this is the first example of tying a Paraloop fly, the instructions given for each stage of the fly will be in greater detail than in the tyings that follow. As explained in the introduction, when a reference is made to another chapter and section, this is written as two numbers placed in brackets, and separated by a slash. For example (5/3) refers to chapter 5, section 3.

Tying the Olive Dun Paraloop

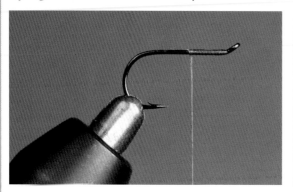

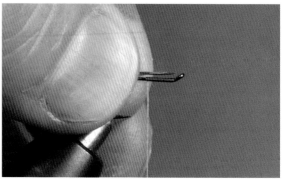

1. Insert the hook carefully into the vice jaws, testing it for soundness. Adjust the gallows tool (sometimes it is necessary to bend the gallows tool to fit), making sure the gallows tool hook is above the hook shank. Wax the thread by pulling it through a block of wax (2/6). Wind the thread approximately to the halfway point along the hook shank – just short of the halfway point is ideal – using flat thread. For information on winding flat thread, please see chapter 2, section 8.

2. The first item to attach is the post, which will form the foundation for the hackle. Take a 5 in piece of the fine GSP floss and fold it in two. Any very strong but thin polypropylene floss or thread will do, if GSP is not available. Offer it to the top of the hook shank with the loose ends facing the hook eye.

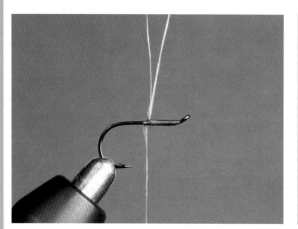

3. Using the loose-loop/pinch-and-loop method (4/5), tie in the floss on the top of the hook shank. Continue tying along the shank, using flat thread, towards the hook eye, and making sure you leave enough space for the head. Cut off any excess floss as you go. Return the thread to the post and make three turns of thread directly behind the post (on the hook bend side) to make the post stand upright. All the turns of thread must be tight and touching the previous turn. This completes the tying in of the post. This process is repeated in a few different ways throughout all the patterns in this book.

4. Pull the floss post over the hook eye to place it out of the way. Continue the thread down to the hook bend. When using GSP for the post it can easily be manoeuvred out of the way whilst tying the rear of the fly. Some materials are not so friendly and may need to be looped around the front of the hook to keep them out of the way. Note the flatness of the thread in the photograph.

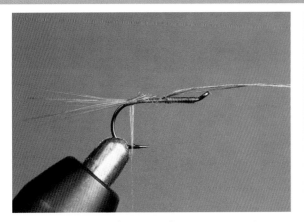

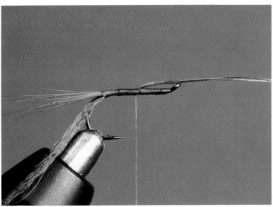

5. Take a small bunch of olive hackle fibres and using the loose loop/pinch-and-loop method (4/5), tie in with three turns on top of the hook shank. The length of the tail should be equal to the length of the hook (hook length = from end of eye to end of bend). Hackle fibres are removed from the feather by first selecting the fibres required; length and springiness are the main factors to take into consideration. See chapter 2, section 3, for the best way to remove fibres from the feather and maintain the tips on a level plane.

6. Tie in the olive polypropylene floss directly where the tail has been tied in. To give complete control when tying in floss, use the method described in chapter 4, section 11. Wind the thread back to the post, tying in the loose end of the floss body material under the hook shank as you do so. There should not be any excess floss, but if there is, cut it off before reaching the post with the thread. The thread should be wound flat throughout this procedure.

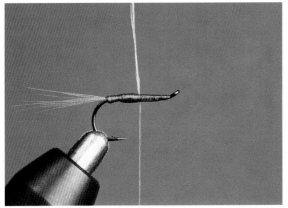

7. Take the floss and unwind any twists in it, allowing it to be wound flat. Wind it along the hook shank to the post using touching turns. Now, using the method described in chapter 4, section 10, create a body using the floss. When the body is completed, tie off the floss under the hook shank at the post and cut off any excess. Then return the thread to the post.

8. Attach the post to the gallows tool hook, adjusting the gallows if necessary to ensure that tension is applied to the floss post. Prepare the dyed olive hackle by removing all the soft fibres at the base of the feather, leaving only the springy fibres. Where the softer fibres end and the springy ones start is often referred to as the 'sweet point'. It is at this point that the hackle should be tied in. Offer the hackle to the hook at the base of the post and tie in as per the photograph. Please note that the good side of the hackle should mainly be facing you when tying in.

9. Cut off the excess hackle and return the thread to the post. Now comes an interesting bit. Take the hackle attached at the base of the post and wind it up the post for a distance equal to that from the post to the hook eye. The turns need not be touching and they can be fairly well separated. If you wish, use hackle pliers. Personally I do not, preferring the control given by using the thumb and first finger of both hands to wind the hackle.

10. Now wind the hackle back down the post over the top of the previous hackle turns, going all the way down to the hook shank. Then, maintaining tension on the hackle, pull the post in the direction of the hook bend. This will give space to tie the hackle in onto the hook shank, using two or three careful turns of thread. Try not to catch any hackle fibres when doing so. If any fibres are caught, take a dubbing needle and release them. The hackle now forms a hackle brush.

Please note: the turns of hackle up and down the post should not be touching turns. If a denser hackle is required, then wind the hackle higher up the post and use the technique for compacting the hackle (4/1) after initially tying the hackle in on the hook shank.

11. Remove the post from the gallows tool and attach it to the neck breaker. Doing so will place the hackle brush clear of the thorax and allows free access to this area of the fly. Brush back any hackle-fibres which stick out over the thorax area, using the thumb and first finger of the left hand (right hand if you are left handed). Complete the tying in of the hackle by winding the thread over the hackle feather, progressing towards the hook eye. Cut off the excess hackle and return the thread to the post. Make sure that enough space is left behind the hook eye to form a small head.

12. Now we must form the thorax. Add a little additional wax to the top 2 in (5 cm) of thread and dub the thread with the olive and brown mixed polypropylene dubbing (4/7). Wind on the dubbed thread to form a thorax. The thorax should be tapered at each end and be quite a bit wider than the body at its centre. Leave enough room behind the hook eye to form a head. The addition of a little brown dubbing to the olive is to imitate the slightly darker thorax of the Olive Dun when compared with the body.

13. Now it is time for another interesting bit. Remove the post from the neck breaker and take the hackle brush over the top of the thorax. This is a similar procedure to tying in a wing case on a nymph pattern. Ideally the hackle brush should end just at the head position. If the hackle brush is too long, then apply compact the hackle (4/1). Then tie in the floss post, immediately above the hackle brush at the head position, using three turns of thread.

14. Cut off the excess post and complete a small head. Complete the fly with a whip finish, either using a tool or by hand. Make sure that each turn of the whip finish progresses towards the hook eye; doing so will ensure that the whipping will lock the thread. Cut off the thread. Taking a dubbing brush or needle, tease out a few fibres of dubbing on the lower part of the thorax to imitate the legs of the fly. That completes the basic Paraloop, the Olive Dun.

The completed Olive Dun Paraloop.

If we take a look at the Paraloop Olive Dun we will see some important differences when compared to traditionally hackled flies.

- The most obvious difference is that there is no hackle attached to the side or base of the hook; all the hackle is attached on the top of the shank.
- The only hackle fibres extending below the level of the hook shank are the tips at the lowest part of the hackle brush.
- The result of this is that the fly will sit lower in the water than a traditionally hackled fly.
- The hackle is full, assisting in the floatability of the fly.

- On the water the fly has a very distinct profile.
- The hook point is clear of any materials.

All these points can make a real difference in how the fly appears to a fish and the way in which it acts when on the water. For many years I have pruned the hackle away from the lower part of a number of my flies using scissors, because I have found the 'pruned' fly often fishes more effectively than one with the complete hackle. The Paraloop Method gives the profile of a 'pruned' fly, indeed improves upon it. It does so in a far more elegant way than having to resort to cutting the lower part of the hackle away. Although some people might consider this unimportant, I personally consider elegance of method to be extremely important when tying flies.

By retaining a full and bushy hackle, the Paraloop Method greatly assists in keeping the fly afloat. One of the unfortunate qualities many of the dry flies I come across possess is the inability to float for very long. A few casts and they are half sunk, a couple more and they should be listed with the classic wet flies or spiders, insisting as they do to view the water from the perspective of a fish. There are usually a combination of factors involved when dry flies fail to maintain their floatability, not least of which is the quality and quantity of hackle they are inflicted with. When tying flies it is important to look at the whole fly, from hook to whip finish. What is required of it? And how can you, as a tyer, achieve this requirement? This is what I refer to as the holistic approach to fly tying. If a dry fly needs constant attention to remain afloat, regularly drying off and being treated with floatant, then maybe it is time to take another look at how it is tied and the materials used.

A typical Paraloop fly (on left) and a traditionally hackled fly (on right) of the same pattern on the water. The difference is clear, the Paraloop sits in the water whilst the other fly sits on top. This is not to say there is no place for traditionally hackled flies – far from it. The Paraloop is an alternative, in the same way as the parachute fly is an alternative to the traditionally hackled fly.

Let's face it, many traditional wet flies, if treated similarly, would float just as well, for just as long. If you tie the Olive Dun as instructed, it should behave itself and not seek adventure below the surface of the water, being content with its position as a dry fly!

The profile of a fly is unquestionably of major importance. The success of parachute flies and others has proved this beyond any reasonable doubt. Fish are extremely partial to flies sitting in the surface of the water, as much as when they are floating high on the surface, if not more so. The Olive Dun tied using the Paraloop Method clearly shows that the method allows the fly to sit in the water, supported by a well-formed hackle. The use of the other materials and the choice of hook all contribute to this.

If we take a view of the same flies from underneath the water, it is clear that the profiles are completely different. It is my belief that it is this difference that often makes the Paraloop fly so successful when compared to other methods of presenting the artificial fly.

4 Techniques Used When Tying Paraloop Flies

It might appear at first that this chapter would be better placed before the previous one. However, as some of the techniques described here require a basic knowledge of the Paraloop Method, it is, I believe, better for it to follow it.

As I explained in the introduction, this book has been designed not only for experienced tyers but also for those who are less experienced. Many of the techniques explained here will be familiar to the more experienced fly tyer, but some of them may not be. In order not to repeat the explanation of each technique when describing the tying of each of the flies, this chapter will cover each one in detail.

Even experienced tyers can often learn from the methods employed by others. Some of the best and most useful techniques of fly tying that I use have been explained and demonstrated to me by other tyers and I am most grateful to them for doing so. Similarly, I hope that a number of the following techniques will prove useful to the more experienced readers. I am confident that some of them will.

The first techniques explained are those that are directly applicable to the tying of Paraloop flies, having been developed from the tying of these flies. It is essential to use these techniques when indicated. They often make the difference between a fly that fishes poorly and one that does exactly what you want it to.

1. Compacting the Hackle

As I have explained, the hackle on a Paraloop fly is wound up a post fixed to the fly and then returns back down again to be tied in on the hook shank. This forms the hackle brush. The length of this hackle brush will depend on the distance between the hook eye and the hackle post, as well as the type of Paraloop fly being tied. The technique of 'compacting the hackle' is extremely useful in more ways than one. It allows any hackle which is wound too far up the post to be reduced in length without having to untie the hackle brush. If a denser hackle brush is required, perhaps to allow a fly to float better, then compacting will also achieve this. If you are tying standard, basic Paraloop flies, when winding the hackle it is unnecessary to have each turn close to its predecessor, because compacting will achieve this after the hackle brush is completed. When tying Paraloop flies regularly, this technique will prove invaluable. It is very easy to use and the only word of caution is not to overstress the hackle brush when performing it.

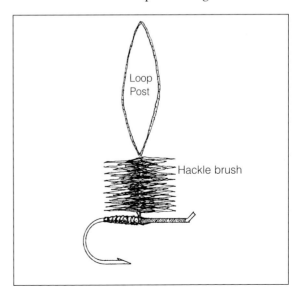

1. Remove the hackle brush loop from the gallows tool; it is important that there is no twist from the top of the loop and the top of the hackle brush.

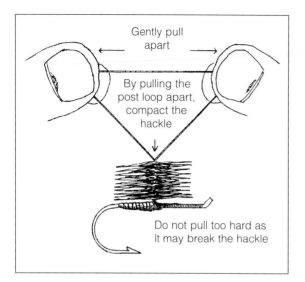

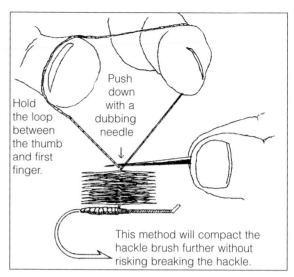

2. Hold one side of the loop between the thumb and first finger of your left hand. Hold the other side of the loop with the thumb and forefinger of your right hand. Gently pull your hands apart. This will open up the loop above the hackle brush and force the brush downwards. Using the two sides of the loop, carefully ease the hackle brush down. Do not pull the loop too hard as this will break the top of the hackle brush and render it useless.

4. If you need to reduce the length of the hackle brush further, either to fit the fly or to make it denser, *do not* just pull the loops harder. Place the thumb and forefinger on either side of the loop as in the photograph. Place a dubbing needle into the 'V' formed at the top of the hackle brush and gently push downwards with the dubbing needle, whilst maintaining pressure from the loop. This will maximise the compacting.

3. The position of the fingers after compaction of the hackle brush.

It is not always necessary to remove the post from the gallows tool when compacting the hackle; it is often easier with the post attached to the gallows tool. Leaving the post attached is sometimes necessary when using a dubbing needle to complete the procedure.

2. Doubling the Hackle Paraloop-Style

Most experienced tyers will be aware of how to double a hackle. However, I come across very few tyers who regularly double hackles for any fly. This is unfortunate as it gives a far better look to a fly when done correctly than when it is not done. I would go as far as to say that the difference between an average, run-of-the-mill fly and one that is exceptional is the doubled hackle. Not all hackles should be doubled, but when they can and should, it makes all the difference.

Doubling the hackle Paraloop-style is very useful in most tyings, but it must be used with caution and care. Overuse of the technique will ruin what would otherwise have been a well-tied fly. It should be used much more sparingly than compressing the hackle. The word is 'little and often'. It is better not to double at all than to over-double.

The purpose of the technique is to reset the hackle fibres so that they are not crushed against the thorax when the loop is pulled into place. It will give you control over how the hackle will look and act on the water. Overuse will produce a fly with a hackle that resembles a Mohican hairstyle. There are some Paraloop techniques which do not require any doubling of the hackle brush, such as open loops (see below), where doubling the hackle brush will actually spoil the overall look and effectiveness of the fly.

When tying spent winged flies Paraloop-style,

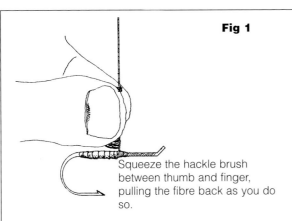

Fig 1

Squeeze the hackle brush between thumb and finger, pulling the fibre back as you do so.

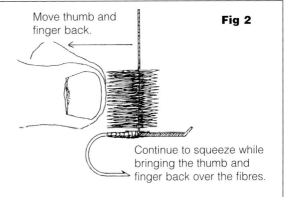

Move thumb and finger back.

Fig 2

Continue to squeeze while bringing the thumb and finger back over the fibres.

Fig. 1 and 2. Having completed the fly up to the point just prior to pulling the hackle brush over the thorax, take the hackle brush between the thumb and forefinger and gently pull it back over the fly, using a gentle brushing motion. This will move the hackle fibres from the hook eye end of the hackle brush and place them more to the hook bend side. The diagram clearly shows the position of the fingers and the movement required. The hackle brush is best left in the gallows tool while the doubling procedure takes place; the technique is far easier to perform when the post is taut.

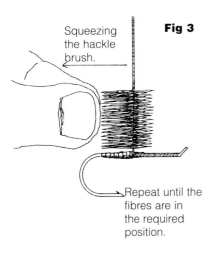

Squeezing the hackle brush.

Fig 3

Repeat until the fibres are in the required position.

The result of doubling the hackle brush is the resetting of the hackle fibres so that they are moved from the front of the hackle brush and moved towards its rear

Fig 4

Resetting the fibres reduces the number of fibres caught between the hackle brush post and the hook shank, when the hackle brush is pulled over into position.

Fig. 3 and 4. The ideal result is as in the diagram. The hackle fibres on the hook eye side of the hackle brush have been repositioned, the fibres forming a 'V' shape ready to be pulled over the thorax. When set in place over the thorax there should be no fibres trapped between the hackle brush and the thorax. This maximises the useful hackle fibres.

The consequence of over-doubling.

The open loop.

it can be useful to apply the technique as described and then to do it the opposite way. By brushing the fibres one way and then the other, the hackle is better balanced and the fibres set to receive the thorax cover.

3. Open Loops

The open loop technique was originally developed for tying emerger patterns. It provides control over how the fly sits in or on the water and is, I believe, one of the most important developments in the Paraloop Method of tying. The technique gives the tyer control over the action of the fly in the water to a degree found in few, if any, other methods. I am certain that experienced tyers will recognise the potential for their own tyings. I initially only applied it to emerger patterns. I now apply it sparingly to some dry flies and rigorously to wet flies. The profile of the fly created using this method is unique and, although the flies do not resemble any traditional form of fly pattern this in no way affects their success. I have just three words to describe my attitude to open loop flies: they are great.

Open loops are formed when a hackle brush is tied which is far longer than is required to tie a normal Paraloop fly. The hackle is seldom compacted, and if it is, minimal compaction is applied and there is no doubling of the hackle. The hackle brush is pulled over, forming a hump on the fly. This is the open loop. I originally called this technique the 'Loose Loop' and flies tied in such a way were called 'loose loop emergers' or 'loose loop dries'. However, this confused the technique with the loose-loop/pinch-and-loop method of tying in materials.

The position on the hook shank used for tying in the post can be varied using this technique. This has resulted in a simple system to identify where the post should be tied. As the changing of the position of the post mainly applies to emergers, the system refers to the various stages of the emerging fly. This is admittedly not an exact science, but it is a system that helps to identify where the post should be tied in on the hook shank, which is the start position of the open loop. There are three positions: early, medium and late. Early refers to the fly just starting to emerge and the position of the post is set just short of the halfway point along the hook shank. Medium refers to the fly halfway through the procedure of emerging. The post is tied just beyond the halfway point along the hook shank.

The three positions used when tying open loops. From left to right: late, medium and early.

Late refers to the fly in the final stages of emerging, when most of the fly has emerged from the nymphal sack. The post is positioned at least two-thirds of the way along the hook shank, and occasionally all the way to the bend. I must stress again that this system is not an exact science, only a method by which the post position can be identified easily.

> early: just before the halfway point along the hook shank from the eye
> medium: just beyond the halfway point along the hook shank
> late: two-thirds or more of the way along the hook shank

This method allows a variable depth of presentation for the fly, with the hook almost fully submerged or only the bend submerged. All flies will, however, sit in the surface of the water with the hackle acting as buoyancy.

I love open loop Paraloop flies and find them extremely useful in many fishing situations. My own fly boxes are packed with them and in any hatch of flies, I feel completely confident when using them. The chapters which follow include various flies tied using this method. The instructions will specify the position at which to set the post. A lot of anglers will be put off using these flies by their different shape and unfamiliarity. This would be a mistake, as they are extremely effective on still waters, rivers and streams. I cannot recommend their use too highly.

4. Tying Tails

Tying in tails for the flies illustrated in this book requires more than one technique. Some tails can be applied using the loose-loop/pinch-and-loop method. Others, however, require a different approach. The method required is specified with each tying. When tying imitations of the upwinged flies it is often necessary to tie in two or three single-fibre tails, depending on which fly is being imitated. This is mostly appropriate when tying some of the dry fly patterns and the spent spinner patterns. The following, in my opinion, explains how best to do this. Also see chapter 2, section 3.

Tying Two Tails
When tying imitations of upwinged flies, mayflies, olives etc., it is often necessary to tie in two or three single-fibre tails, depending upon which fly is being imitated. The problem when tying two tails is that they should ideally form a distinct 'V' shape. This shape should be maintained throughout the life of the fly and it should be very apparent when the fly is on the water, as it is one of the trigger shapes for trout. It is possible to bend tail fibres after they have been tied in to give the desired shape, but this is most unsatisfactory. Once the fly is wet and has suffered the indignity of a few casts the distinctive shape is lost. The idea is to set the tails so that they are fixed in position no matter what happens. To achieve this I know of no better method than the following:

Tying Two Tails

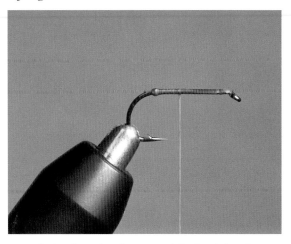

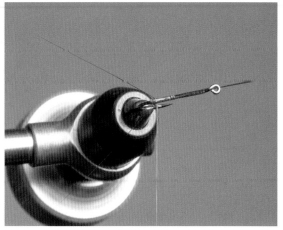

1. With the thread at the start of the hook bend, form a small ball of thread. It is not necessary to make this ball large; a small bulge will suffice. With the thread ball formed, make half a dozen turns of thread winding flat along the hook shank towards the hook eye (4/12).

2. Using the loose-loop/pinch-and-loop technique (4/5), tie the micro fibbets onto the top of the hook shank, making three turns towards the thread ball to hold the tail fibres in place. Take the ends of the tails between the thumb and first finger of the left hand (right if you are a left-handed tyer) and hold the fibres in the 'V' position on either side of the thread ball. Then wind the thread right up to the thread ball, which will force the fibres into the correct position.

Tying Three Tails
When tying in three tails I find it best to use either of the two following methods:

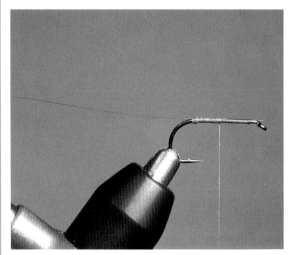

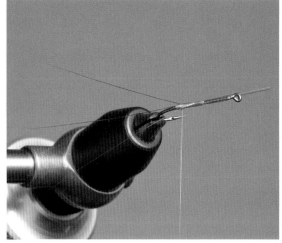

1. With the thread at the bend of the hook, tie in one of the tail fibres, using the loose-loop/pinch-and-loop technique (4/5). This tail fibre must be tied directly on top of the hook shank and stick out directly, following the same line as the hook shank.

2. Then complete the instructions for tying in two tails. This will result in three tails, all sitting in the correct position.

The following alternative method for tying two or three tails is excellent and simple. It does not require any ball of thread and so reduces the bulk of material at the tail position. I highly recommend it and these days it is my preference:

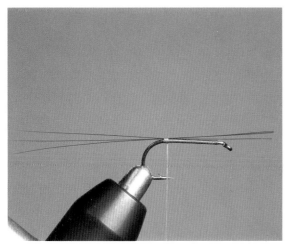

1. With the thread at the start of the bend, using the loose-loop/pinch-and-loop method (4/5), tie in three tail fibres, making sure they are positioned next to each other. In the photograph I have used three tails, but the technique is exactly the same for two tails, except that you omit the central tail.

2. Take a piece of thin, light thread (I use as light as 17/0), and loop underneath the hook bend. For the purposes of clarity I have used a thick red thread in the photographs; this is solely to allow the process to be seen easily.

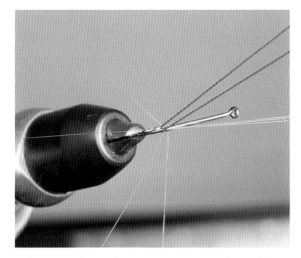

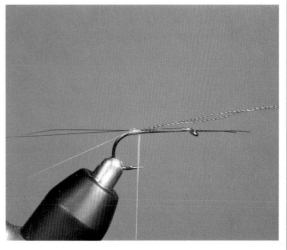

3. Bring the thread loop up and around the middle fibre of the tail; the left and right fibre will be on either side of the thread loop. If you are tying in two tails, just bring both sides of the thread up between the tails.

4. Without pulling the loop over tightly, tie it in on top of the hook shank. It will force the left and right tail fibres out from the centre tail. The more the loop is pulled, the more pronounced the 'V' of the outer tails will be.

5. The Loose-Loop/Pinch-and-Loop Technique

This technique is commonly referred to as the 'loose loop' or the 'pinch and loop'. To save confusion I shall use both names throughout the book. Most experienced fly tyers will be very familiar with it, using it in most of their tyings at some time or another, so the explanation is primarily directed toward newcomers. That said, I find it is one of those common techniques which is often used incorrectly, resulting in poorly finished flies. So if any experienced tyers require reminding, here is a basic description of how to do it.

This technique is one of the most important used for adding materials when tying flies. In some cases, it is essential if the material is to be applied correctly. It is used when control is required to set the material being applied directly on top of the hook shank, and is normally required when tying in tails and wings. There is a problem when tying the materials onto a hook shank; the thread will have a tendency to pull the material round the hook shank when tightened. Sometimes this tendency is a distinct advantage, when spinning deer hair, for example, and with some materials it is not all that important, as they can be realigned after being initially tied in. There are some materials, however, that cannot, under any circumstances, be realigned and even with those that can, it is better to tie them on in one procedure rather than mess around later. The loose-loop/pinch-and-loop technique allows you to do this.

When tying feather slip wings the technique not only allows the tyer to set the wings on the top of the hook shank but it also directly lays the feather fibres on top of each other, allowing the wing to sit correctly. Without acquiring the skill of using the loose-loop/pinch-and-loop technique a tyer will be severely handicapped in the choice of flies available to tie. When tying the Paraloop flies covered in this book the technique is used to tie in posts, tails and wings.

To illustrate the use of the technique, the tying in of a post is used; as every Paraloop fly includes a post it would seem to be a suitable example.

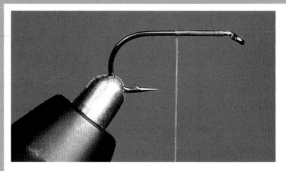

1. Set a hook in the vice, offer the thread and wind it on to about the halfway position along the hook shank, cutting off the excess thread as you are winding, so as not to leave an untidy end.

2. Take a piece of floss approximately 6 in (15 cm) long and form a loop by bending the floss back on itself; both loose ends should be together. Offer the loop of floss to the hook; the loose ends should be lying over the hook bend.

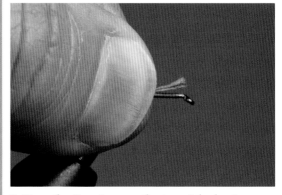

3. Place the floss loop on the top of the hook shank, holding it there between the thumb and first finger. Bring the thread up between the thumb and the floss, bending the thumb tip backward a little to open a space to allow the thread to sit between the thumb and floss.

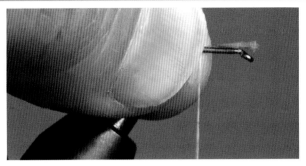

4. Close the thumb onto the thread. Bring a loop of thread over the top of the hook shank, extending the loop just beyond the top of the thumb and finger. Bend the finger holding the floss backwards slightly, manipulating the thread into the space between the floss and the finger. Close the finger back to hold the thread against the floss and hook shank. There should be a small loop of thread sticking up and held between the thumb and finger.

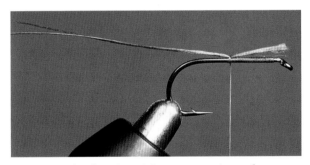

5. Keeping the thumb and finger pressed together tightly, gently but firmly pull the thread down onto the floss. This is where most errors are made – if the thumb and finger are not pressed tight the tying is compromised. If this is completed correctly the floss will be tied down firmly on the top of the hook shank and it will not have pulled round the far side. Repeat as required.

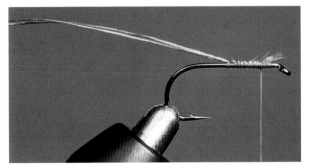

6. The end result is that the floss loop is tied only on the top of the hook shank.

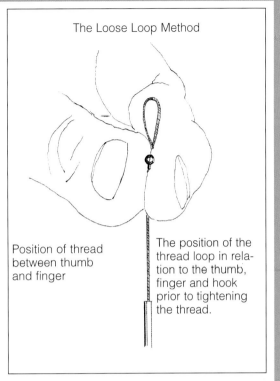

The Loose Loop Method

Position of thread between thumb and finger

The position of the thread loop in relation to the thumb, finger and hook prior to tightening the thread.

It is often advisable to bring the thread up between the thumb and hook shank again before pulling the thread tight. When pulling tight the thread is pulled upwards. This prevents any side pull on the material being applied to the hook. The diagram shows the position of the thread loop in relation to the thumb, finger and hook eye.

After a little practice, this technique could not be easier and beginners who follow the instructions will find themselves fairly proficient after a short period of time. There can be little doubt that this technique is one of the most important in fly tying and should be mastered.

Tying in Hackle-Tip Wings

1. First it is necessary to choose the feathers. I often use the excess feathers cut off when tying in a hackle. As the tips only are used it is fairly easy to find two that match. I prefer to take the feathers from a cock cape, the same as I use to provide the hackle (see chapter ?) The feathers should be well shaped and matching. It is necessary initially to measure the length required for the wing. This is normally the total length of the hook unless otherwise specified. Hold the feathers together, with the insides touching and the good sides facing outwards. Measure them up against the hook length. With the two feathers firmly held with the thumb and first finger of the right hand (left hand if left-handed), align the tips with the hook eye. The hook bend indicates the length of the wing. Follow a line up from the outside of the hook bend to the feather, and using the thumb and first finger of the left hand (right hand if left-handed), pull the fibres down the stalk from that point. The feather tips are now ready for the next stage of preparation.

2. Take each feather separately and snip the fibres as in the photograph. It is important not to remove all the fibres as these assist in locking the wing in place and help prevent it from pulling out. Leaving the cropped fibres on the stalk of the feather tip will also assist in tying the wings in the correct position, as well as strengthening the hold. The wings are also less liable to twist when being set in place.

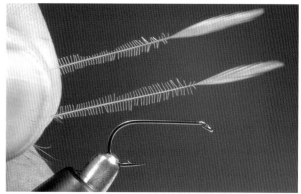

3. Place both feathers together again, good side out, and hold them between the thumb and first finger of the left hand (right hand if left-handed). The point to tie in on the wing is just below the start of the untrimmed feather fibres. It is necessary to leave a small section of stalk between the tying-in point and the untrimmed fibres when tying the winged emergers in this book. Do not leave this trimmed stalk showing when tying traditional flies. Leaving the small section of stalk showing when tying emerger patterns helps to keep the feather fibres of the wing in place when setting them in position. The position on the hook to tie in is normally just behind the hook eye when tying emergers. When tying traditional paraloop patterns you must leave a generous space for the head and the tying in of the hackle brush.

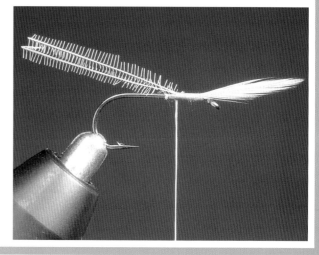

6. Tying Hackle-Tip Wings

With the exception of hair wings and an experimental feather slip wing illustrated in the gallery, all the wings used in this book are formed from hackle tips. The method for preparing the feather and tying on the hook is described opposite. Over the years there have been many methods used to tie in hackle-tip wings. Some involve bending the hackle stalk to stop the feather from pulling out from the fly. My experience is that if a bed of well-waxed thread is laid prior to tying and similar thread is used to tie in the correctly prepared feather tips, there is no chance of them becoming loose. The wings will break long before they part company with the fly by slipping.

After following steps 1 to 3, remove the excess stalk and continue to tie the fly. When tying dry and emerger Paraloop flies the wing can be forgotten about until after the hackle brush has been tied in. It is unnecessary to 'figure of eight' the thread around the wings to set them in place. In the case of dry flies the wings are set into position during the tying of the thorax. In emergers the formation of the head will take care of the positioning of the wings. This is why there is a small section of trimmed hackle stalk left clear of the hook shank and the wings are tied in immediately behind the hook eye, when initially tied in on the hook. When tying traditional-style winged dry flies and spent spinners with hackle-tip wings, there should be the minimum of stalk showing below the fly and the tying-in point.

7. Dubbing the Thread

Dubbing a thread is one of the techniques that most newcomers to fly tying soon learn. There is, however, a lot more to dubbing a thread than simply rolling a dubbing material between the thumb and forefinger.

What sort of effect is required? If a body is being formed with the dubbed thread, does it need to be shaped or undefined? It is questions like these that may lead to adjustments to the way in which we apply dubbing to a thread.

If a defined body is required there is no point in heavily dubbing the thread, as doing so will add too much dubbing to the hook with each turn of thread. This greatly reduces the ability to form a shaped body. When forming a shaped, defined body it is necessary to apply very little dubbing to the thread at any one point but to spread it over a greater length. This allows more turns of thread to help form and build up a specific shape. When forming an undefined

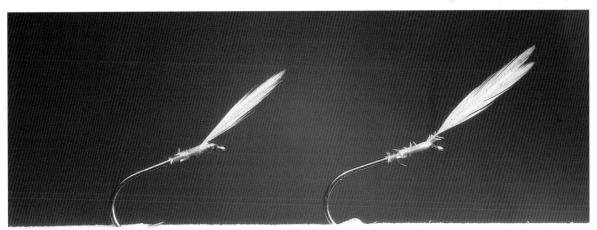

This photograph shows two hooks with wings tied in. The one on the left shows the wing as used on a normal Paraloop dry fly. Notice that the feather fibres start at the point where the wing has been tied in. The hook to the right has the wings tied in as they would be when tying most of the emerger patterns described in this book. Notice that a small amount of stalk is showing below where the feather fibres start and the hook shank. This is most important when tying the emergers where the wings are finally set to run either side of the hackle brush. When tying high-winged emergers less trimmed stalk is left showing than on those with sloping wings; half the amount will suffice.

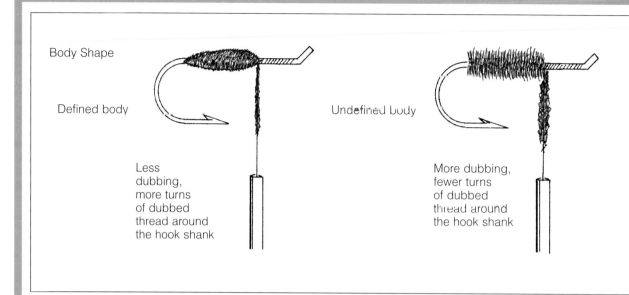

Body Shape

Defined body

Less
dubbing,
more turns
of dubbed
thread around
the hook shank

Undefined body

More dubbing,
fewer turns
of dubbed
thread around
the hook shank

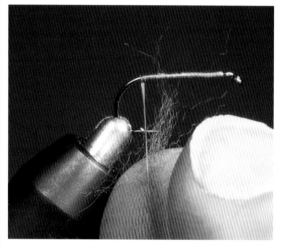

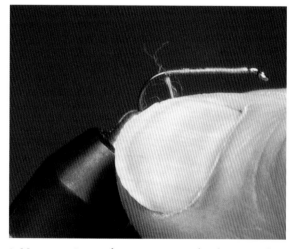

1. Start with the hook already inserted in the jaws of the vice and the thread wound to the start of the hook bend. Take a small block of wax and rub it gently over the area to receive the dubbing material. Take a pinch of dubbing material and open it out using your fingers, forming a loose rope out of the material. Take a small piece of dubbing between the thumb and first finger of your right hand (left hand for a left-hander) and offer it up to the thread closest to the hook. It is important to keep the thread tight whilst applying dubbing material, so hold the bobbin holder with your other hand, maintaining tension at all times. If the thread is well waxed, it is possible to dab the material onto it and it will be held.

2. Now, starting at the top, squeeze the thread with the dubbing material attached between your thumb and first finger. When squeezing, pull your first finger over your thumb; this will roll the dubbing around the thread. Do not push your first finger back over your thumb, as this will unravel the dubbing material from the thread. Release the pressure between thumb and first finger before returning to the first position to repeat the roll. Keep the thread held taut at all times.

The difference between what I refer to as a defined body and an undefined body.

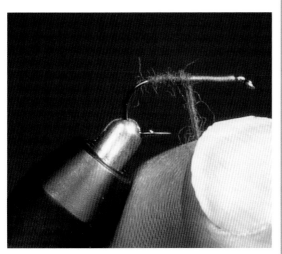

3. Move down the thread adding more dubbing material as required. Do not extend the length of the dubbed thread beyond that which it is easy to control. Wind onto the hook and add more dubbing to the thread if and when required. Little and often is far better than a lot all at once.

Management of dubbing materials will always add to the effectiveness of a fly in addition to improving its appearance. The use of different types of dubbing material radically affects the way a fly behaves when on the water. The way in which we apply dubbing materials has a similar effect. It is possible, after some practice, to feed the dubbing onto the thread in a continuous action, controlling the amount applied at any one point.

body more dubbing can be applied to the thread and less turns made around the hook shank. Both methods will allow the dubbing needle or dubbing brush to be used to pick out fibres.

8. Tying In and Locking Hard Hair

There are many types of hair and fur fibres used by the fly tyer, and each one has its benefits and its drawbacks. Tying in hard hair fibres can be problematic because there is no give in the fibre when it is tied in with the thread. The fibres can thus easily become detached, and once one fibre becomes detached, the others are obliged to follow. Some tyers get around this problem by applying glue. Whilst there is no doubt that this holds the fibres firmly, and from a commercial tyer's point of view, can often be the best solution, I prefer not to use it.

I am a great fan of squirrel-tail fur fibres, using them in many of my own patterns for trout, salmon and other fish. The problem is that it is a hard hair. When working with this material, I like to use what is known as locking turns to fix the fibres firmly to the hook and prevent them from coming astray. There are a few fly patterns in this book which use squirrel fur fibres either as a wing, a tail or both, so the following shows how to lock hard fur fibres. Most tyers who are aware of the effects of hard hair tighten up the thread when tying in squirrel hair, because it increases the tension or force that can be applied to lock the hair in place. There is a down side in doing this and that is that the tightened thread does not adhere to the hair fibres very efficiently. Also the area of thread which actually makes contact with the hair is vastly reduced. The method described below is, I believe, very much more effective and involves initially using flat turns of thread, thereby maximising the amount of thread actually gripping the hair. This is then over-wound with very tight spun thread. This combination of thread techniques locks the hair in place better than any single method. I have not seen this technique described before and I hope it is of interest to those tyers who regularly use hard hairs. I use a wing similar to those used when tying a Wulff-style fly as an example:

Tying In and Locking Hard Hair

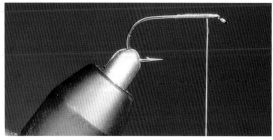

1. Fix the hook in the jaws of the vice. As this is just an example, almost any hook will do, but a size 10 or 12 is ideal. Wax the thread thoroughly by running it through a block of cobbler's wax or a wax with the same qualities. Attach it to the hook and wind it flat (see section 12) to the halfway point of the hook shank and then back again to the normal position used to tie in the wing. It is most important that this base of waxed thread is in place.

2. Take a generous bunch of squirrel-tail fibres and, using scissors, cut them from the tail. Hold them between the thumb and first finger of the right hand (left hand if left-handed). Remove any loose fur or short fibres by pinching out, using the thumb and first fingers of the other hand. Place the fibres into a hair stacker and level the ends. Offer them to the hook, the tips of the fibres facing over the hook eye. The wing should be approximately the length of the hook; I prefer it to be a little shorter.

3. It is now important to make the next turns of thread using flat turns (see section 12). Using the loose-loop/pinch-and-loop method (see section 5), make five or six tight touching turns of thread around the shank and fur fibres (remember these turns are flat), towards the rear of the hook. Then make five or six turns going back over the previous ones, again wound flat. Lift the hair wing with the non-winding hand and bring the thread up over the hair fibres, remembering to use flat thread, and then under the hair, without going under the hook shank. Effectively the thread is now being wound around the wing, without going around the hook shank. Repeat three times. It is important to keep the thread very tight and tied flat.

4. Now wind the thread tight and make a few turns directly in front of the base of the wing (hook eye side) to set it at the correct angle required by the fly. Continuing with the tight thread, wind over the previous turns of thread used to hold the wing. The tight thread will enhance the grip of the flat wound thread, preventing the fibres from working loose. Cut off the excess wing fibres at an angle and finish tying in. Those of little faith can apply a small drop of varnish to the fibres prior to finishing tying in.

This method will hold the fibres very effectively and once mastered it takes no more time to do than any other less effective method. I use this technique to tie most of my squirrel-hair patterns, including large salmon flies and saltwater flies. There is never any problem with fibres coming loose if it is done correctly, but I must emphasise the need for waxed thread to maximise the grip.

9. Forming Detached Bodies and Emerger Shucks

It may seem strange to include detached bodies with emerger shucks but I have found the method used to make one is perfect for forming the other; the main difference tends to be in the materials used. When a dry fly detached body is tied, the material used in the Paraloop patterns in this book is floating. When used as a shuck it is non-floating. A shuck also tends to be wider than a detached body, although not always.

Forming a detached body could not be simpler, yet it is one of those techniques that, when seen for the first time, really impresses. The body formed is durable, easy to form into a precise shape and it takes just a few seconds. The bodies formed using the method are sometimes referred to as furled bodies.

The diagram describes the steps taken to form a detached body or shuck.

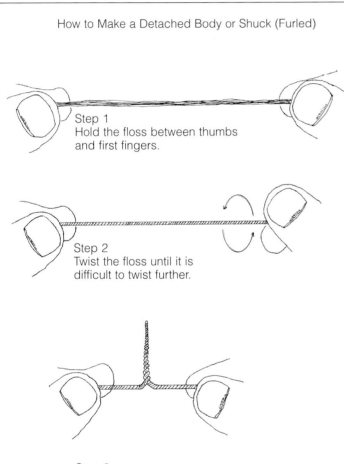

How to Make a Detached Body or Shuck (Furled)

Step 1
Hold the floss between thumbs and first fingers.

Step 2
Twist the floss until it is difficult to twist further.

Step 3
Gently bring the thumbs and fingers together. This will allow the floss to twist upon itself forming the body.

Option
After Step 3 has been completed the process can be repeated using the already furled floss.

1. Take a piece of polypropylene floss about 4 in (10 cm) long. In the example I am using Tiemco Aero Dry Fly, but any fine fibre polypropylene will do. Hold one end tightly between the thumb and first finger of the left hand. Keeping the floss taut, take the other end between the thumb and first finger of the right hand.

2. Roll the floss between the thumb and finger, tightening the twist of the floss with repeated rolls, until it becomes difficult to apply further twists.

3. Relax the tension on the floss between your hands by moving them closer together. Do not release the ends. The floss will now twist upon itself, forced to do so by the tension of the twisting applied along its length. Ideally this twist should be centred in the middle. If it is too far off to one side, pull your hands apart, remembering to maintain your grip on the ends of the floss and before bringing the hands together again, touch the centre of the floss with the second finger of either hand. This touch is a catalyst for the floss to twist at the point touched. The floss should now twist upon itself, centred where you placed your second finger.

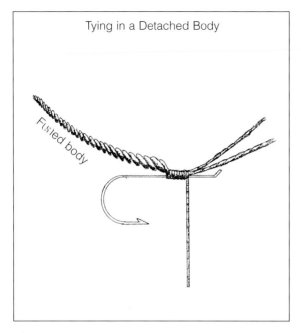

Tying in a Detached Body

The twisted (furled) floss forms a lovely, segmented body shape that can be tied to the hook as shown.

As an extension to this method I often double up the process. Taking a longer piece of floss than I normally use, I follow the procedure described above. This will produce a length of furled floss long enough to be able to repeat the process, following the existing twist. Now allow the already furled floss to twist back on itself again. Effectively the procedure has been doubled. The result of this is, in my opinion, a better-looking body and one that is more durable. An example of such a body can be seen in the Sherry Spinner in chapter 8. The first photograph of the tying sequence clearly shows the double furled body. It is sometimes wise to reduce the thickness of the floss used initially.

When using fine polypropylene floss the body formed is highly buoyant and is ideal for dry flies such as Mayflies. Sometimes, where the body being imitated is mottled, I include a strand of coloured thread with the floss, which automatically produces a mottled effect. An example of this is when imitating the mayfly; some bodies of the natural fly are cream with brown mottling. Cream floss with a dark brown thread, double furled as explained above, produces a remarkably fine mottled body.

10. Forming a Simple Body Shape

When forming a body shape using floss, lightly dubbed thread or a similar material, it is easy to create a tapered body by using the following method. One important factor always worth bearing in mind when forming bodies, is that the less material added to the hook with each turn, the more scope there is in the choice of body shape. When using floss it is a distinct advantage to unwind the floss and to apply it to the hook shank flat. Using touching turns means fewer turns to cover the hook shank and less build-up of material at any one point.

In the illustration opposite, floss is used for the body, but the principle can be applied to any number of materials with small adjustments.

It will be apparent that if very thick material, for example heavy floss, is used, the build-up of the material on the hook shank will restrict the number of times the thread can be returned. So stick to lightweight, thin materials when building up a body shape on relatively small flies. It is all a matter of control, and doing so will give the greater control necessary to achieve the result required.

Another method which can be used to build up a fly body is to tie the body material in at the hook bend. Take the thread back to the other end of the body. Now wind the material, initially using touching turns, then using overlapping turns. The further you get towards the other end of the body, the more the material should overlap. This method is very effective when using floss and produces a finely shaped body.

11. Applying Floss, Wire, Tinsel, etc.

Over the years I have seen many methods used to apply floss, tinsel, wire and other similar material to the hook. Often the techniques appear haphazard, to say the least. Control over the application of material is one of the skills of a good fly tyer, but unfortunately when it comes to applying floss and tinsels etc. most of this control is often lost. I have lost count of the times I have seen highly skilled fly tyers adding materials by catching in loose ends. For years this was my way, until I saw the light – and what a simple light it was. I will always be grateful to Poul

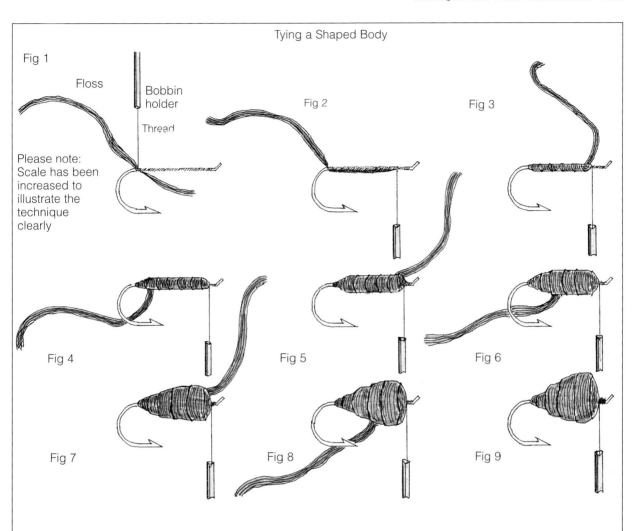

Tying a Shaped Body

Fig 1

Floss

Bobbin holder

Thread

Please note:
Scale has been
increased to
illustrate the
technique
clearly

Fig 2

Fig 3

Fig 4

Fig 5

Fig 6

Fig 7

Fig 8

Fig 9

1. Start with the floss tied in at the tail position.
2. Wind the thread to the other end of where the body will start.
3. Unwind any twist in the floss and wind the floss flat in touching turns along the hook shank to the thread.
4. Keeping the floss unwound and tying flat, reverse back along the hook shank going approximately three-quarters of the way back over the first layer of floss.
5. Return the floss, keeping it flat, back to the front of the body.
6. Return the flat wound floss to the halfway position on the hook shank.
7. and 8. Repeat the above, each time reducing the distance taken back along the hook shank.
9. This will result in a suitably shaped body. Note that the build up of material illustrated in the drawing has been exaggerated to emphasise the results of using the technique.

Jorgensen who, through one of his videos, introduced me to this technique. When demonstrating, I always include it, and of all the complex matters covered during a demonstration, this technique is the one that other tyers seem happiest to be shown. I count it amongst the top five of all fly tying techniques. Simple and effective, it gives complete control when offering these materials to the hook, allowing the material to be tied in exactly where and how you want.

Applying Floss, Wire, Tinsel, etc.

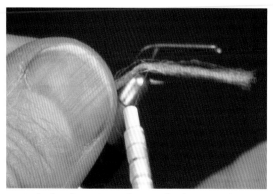

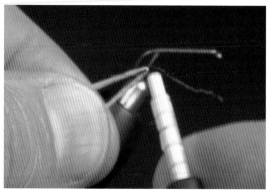

1. With the thread attached to the hook at the position the material requires to be tied in, take a piece of floss between the thumb and first finger of the left hand (right hand if left-handed). Pull the bobbin holder out towards yourself and maintain a tension on the thread. Place the floss on the top of the thread with approximately 1 in (2.5 cm) of floss extending over the thread.

2. Bring the thumb and first finger up to where the floss crosses the thread and with the finger to the far side of the thread and the thumb on the near side, pull the floss down over each side of the thread. This forms a loop of floss over the thread.

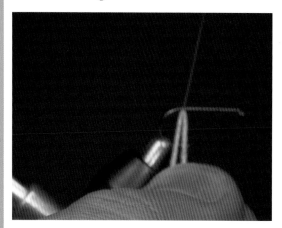

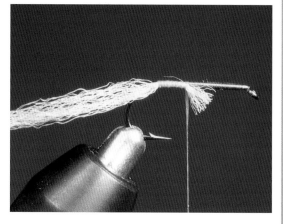

3. Maintaining the tension on the thread, lift the bobbin holder up, drawing the floss loop along the thread to the hook as you do so. This will set the floss in the position for tying in (usually underneath the hook shank). The bobbin holder should be held well above the level of the hook at this stage. The floss will have been brought under the thread on the hook shank if the bobbin holder is being held at the right position.

4. Bring the thread up around the floss; this will hold it in position. Release the short end and wind thread to hold. By maintaining tension on the thread, the floss can be pulled back to eliminate any need to cut off any excess. (Note that it is not possible to pull the material back when using tinsels, and any excess material must be cut off.) The tying-in position of the applied material can, using this method, be controlled precisely.

When using tinsels and wire (stiff materials) a loop can be formed prior to placing the material on the top of the hook. Use the loop to hook the thread and continue the process from photograph 3.

Once mastered it is difficult to imagine that any other method could or should be used when applying floss, tinsels and wires etc. I thoroughly recommend it to anyone who is not already using it.

12. Thread Management

Threads are a little like flies: we often keep many, different types and colours, but if we look at the ones we actually use, they are very few. In my case, in any year I might use only half a dozen different threads, but I keep many hundreds. It is exactly the same with flies – I have thousands stored away, but if I look at the number I use over a season, it is sometimes less than twenty.

Thread management does not mean keeping many different threads in some semblance of order, although that can be a good thing. It refers to the way in which we apply the thread when tying flies.

Thread can be applied in three ways: flat, tight and normal.

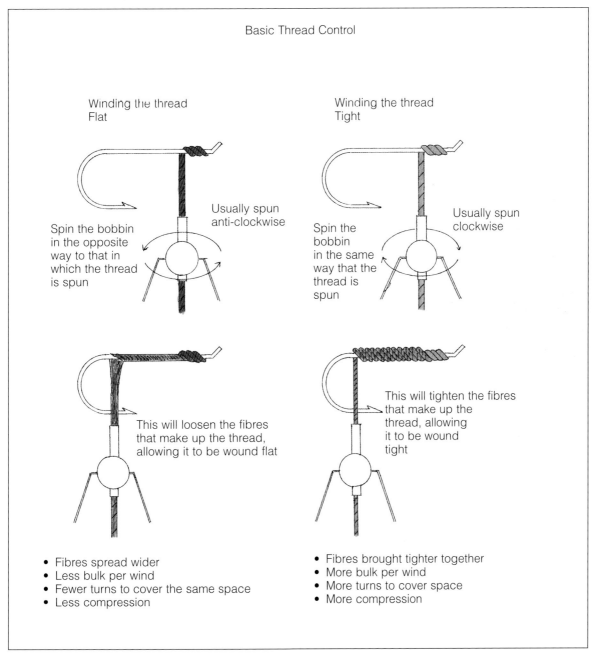

Basic Thread Control

Winding the thread
Flat

Spin the bobbin in the opposite way to that in which the thread is spun

Usually spun anti-clockwise

Winding the thread
Tight

Spin the bobbin in the same way that the thread is spun

Usually spun clockwise

This will loosen the fibres that make up the thread, allowing it to be wound flat

This will tighten the fibres that make up the thread, allowing it to be wound tight

- Fibres spread wider
- Less bulk per wind
- Fewer turns to cover the same space
- Less compression

- Fibres brought tighter together
- More bulk per wind
- More turns to cover space
- More compression

Tying Flat

When applying thread to the hook shank or forming a body or an underbody, it is advisable to add as little bulk of thread as possible. This is done by unwinding the manufacturer's twist in the thread. The threads recommended for tying the flies in this book are made up of very fine fibres twisted together. Removing this twist allows the thread to be wound on the hook flat. Effectively the fibres are spread out further. One benefit of doing this is that fewer touching turns are required to cover the hook shank. There is also less bulk of thread. Some materials are best tied onto the hook using flat thread, either to prevent damage to the material or to adjust the grip of the thread. An example of this is described in section 8.

Tying flat should be the normal procedure when applying thread to the hook shank in the tyings illustrated in this book, or when forming a body shape. When flat thread is required the instructions will say so.

To untwist the thread, first attach it to the hook, letting the bobbin hang free after it is secured. Most manufacturers apply a clockwise twist to produce the thread, but not all. At least one major manufacturer applies a counter-clockwise twist. Spin the bobbin for a few seconds in the direction opposite to the inherent twist. If you are unsure in which direction to spin the bobbin, try counter-clockwise, as most threads are wound clockwise. Now wind the thread along the hook shank. If it is even tighter than normal, then you have spun the bobbin the wrong way, or over-spun it. Try spinning it the other way. Initially a little trial and error will be required until you are familiar with the twist of the thread you are using. Eventually it will be second nature.

Tying Tight

This is the opposite to tying flat. The bobbin is spun the same way as the inherent twist, tightening up the thread. This is most useful when tying in certain materials which are not easily damaged and require a deep, cutting hold. Most thread will require a clockwise spin to tighten the thread.

Normal

The thread is used as supplied from the manufacturer normal, and no spinning is required. Unless specified differently, when tying the flies in this book use the thread as it is.

The very act of fly tying will wind or unwind the thread, depending on which way the thread is spun. Thread management can control this and allow more efficient and effective tying.

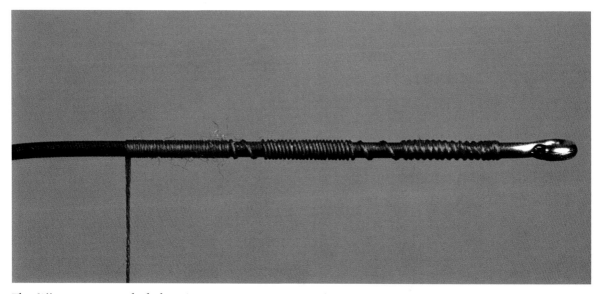

The different ways in which thread is applied. From left to right: flat, normal, tight. A heavy thread has been used to enhance the difference between the three methods.

13. Using Foam in a Thorax

The recognition of foam as a useful material in fly tying has been growing over a number of years. It is flexible, easily shaped and some types will float for ever. With these properties it is surprising that we do not use it more. Personally, I believe we will see more and more patterns incorporating foam, in its many forms, over the next few years. There are two types which you should be aware of. The first is known as 'closed cell' and it is this type which is used in this book. The closed cell structure stops the material from absorbing water and it will float indefinitely. The second, 'open cell' foam will soak up water and is therefore unsuitable for the flies described here.

In this book foam is used principally in the thorax area of a fly, either under, or in the case of spent winged flies, over the hackle. I normally use white foam sheeting and colour it, using permanent ink pens, prior to incorporating it into a fly. A piece of thin foam sheet is split up into a number of squares, a little like a section of a chessboard. Each square is then coloured a different colour or mix of colours and is then available when needed, as shown below.

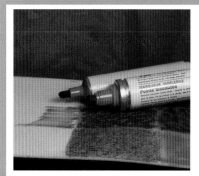

1. Prepare a sheet of foam by colouring it in squares.

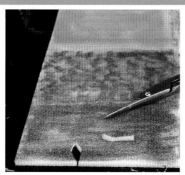

2. Cut out a diamond shape as required.

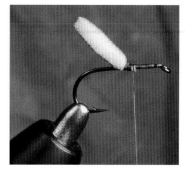

3. Apply this to the fly with the colour side down.

4. Pull and stretch it over the thorax area and tie it in behind the hook eye, leaving enough space for a small head to be formed. Cut off excess foam.

Another method I use for applying foam to flies uses a foam cylinder. I use this technique regularly these days, often in preference to the last one. The foam can be coloured as required.

When using foam for the thorax I have found it best to cut a small diamond shape from the sheet of the colour required. Scissors are the best tool to use, as they give more immediate control than a craft knife. The reason for using a diamond shape is that the narrow ends can be used to tie in on the fly, so reducing the bulk added to the fly. The size of the piece cut out depends on the area being covered by the foam. It is necessary to stretch the foam when finally tying in to get the best results, so do not make it too long. If the foam appears too long once it has been initially tied in, just trim it before finally tying in.

The cut edges of the foam can be coloured in after tying in if the white foam shows, but I often find that stretching the foam eliminates any need for doing this and any small sections of white foam showing can enhance the overall look of the fly. It is a matter of personal choice.

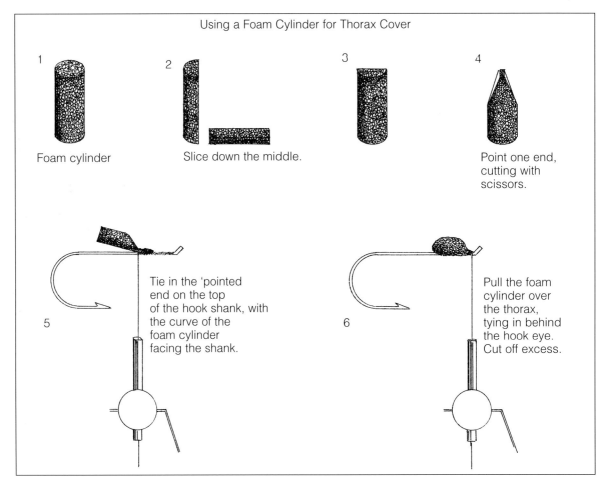

Using a Foam Cylinder for Thorax Cover

1 Foam cylinder

2 Slice down the middle.

3

4 Point one end, cutting with scissors.

5 Tie in the 'pointed end on the top of the hook shank, with the curve of the foam cylinder facing the shank.

6 Pull the foam cylinder over the thorax, tying in behind the hook eye. Cut off excess.

1. Take a cylinder of closed cell foam. Those supplied for use in boobies are ideal, but make sure the diameter of the cylinder is not too large; for most of my flies a diameter of about ³⁄₁₆ in (00.5 cm) is perfect.
2. Cut the cylinder in half along the length, Scissors are fine for doing this.
3. Take one half.
4. Slightly taper one end.
5. Tie it in on the hook shank at the appropriate position, making sure the curved side is facing downward and that the foam is lying opposite to where it will be pulled over. Finish tying any section of the fly which needs to be completed before the foam is pulled into position.
6. Pull the foam over into position and tie it onto the hook shank. Remove any excess foam.

5 Traditional Dry Flies Paraloop-Style

One of the many benefits of using the Paraloop Method is that it can be applied to a whole range of different types of artificial flies, but seems especially useful when used to tie imitative patterns. It is ideally suited for traditional dry flies – the flies that we all know and are familiar with, the classic patterns which have contributed so much to the world of fly fishing. Normally tied using the conventional hackle, these flies provide the angler with additional opportunities when they are tied using the Paraloop Method.

The method is well suited to the tying of simple hackled flies, as we saw in chapter 3, with the tying of the Olive Dun. What might not be so obvious is how perfect it is when tying hackle-tip, feather-fibre and hair-winged dry flies. Feather-slip wings are problematic when using the Paraloop Method, but even these can be tied with certain adjustments, and an example can be seen in the gallery (chapter 12) under the heading of 'Claw wing'.

When I first started tying Paraloop flies my repertoire was limited to non-winged, simple hackled dry flies and I found no end of patterns to which I could turn my hand. Any traditional pattern which incorporated a hackle but no wing was fair game for the Paraloop Method. My fly boxes were full of them, and they still are: Ginger Quill, Black Gnat, Olive Dun, Grey Duster, Iron Blue Dun, Cherry Spinner, Green Drakes, Beacon Beige and many others. They have provided many happy hours of successful fishing. It did not matter if still waters or rivers provided the sport, fish would seldom fail to be seduced by these flies, finding themselves attached to a well-sprung rod. Samples of these flies were sent around the country and then the world and the feedback was always more than encouraging. Stoic Scottish ghillies and antipodean fishing guides, well set in their ways and the flies they used, agreed that these flies took fish, sometimes when all others failed.

To single out one particular event of note from my own experience is difficult, because of the number of times the flies proved themselves to me. There is one notable occasion, however, which occurred soon after I first started using the Paraloop flies.

It was fairly early in the trout season, which for us begins in mid-March, but on some river systems does not start until April. I was invited to spend a little time in Northumberland. This is one of the most beautiful and diverse areas in the whole of the UK. From a fishing point of view it is many times blessed. It is the county of the south bank of the lower River Tweed, and also boasts many other legendary rivers, including the Tyne (which is considered by many to be the premier salmon river in England), the Till, the Aln, the Coquet and many others. I have seen streams in Northumberland which are so small it is difficult to find their name, but which are filled with sea trout at certain times of the year, to the extent that the whole river bed seems to move. It was when fishing one of these lesser-known streams that the following incident occurred.

The day and the water appeared perfect, the river running clear and at a good height, and the only life around seemed to be a few scraggy sheep. They barely lifted their heads in acknowledgement of my arrival. The cry of a heron from a distant pool reached my ears, as its slow lazy wings lifted it clear of the bushes and trees. The few hours I had to fish promised to be exciting.

There was little evidence of any fly life, but sitting quietly taking in the surroundings, I became aware of the occasional large upwinged fly making its way upstream. There were also a few large black midges that appeared very keen to make my acquaintance as they buzzed around my head. The water came fast from above into a large deep pool where, every so often, the surface was broken by a growing ring, the result of a rising fish. Running out of the pool was a long stretch of fairly fast water which, at its deepest, was no more than 2 ft (60 cm) from the gravel bed to the surface. At the end of this run the water took a right bend out of sight, but holding a pledge of much to come. With the surface of the water broken by the occasional rise of a fish, the pool seemed to offer real possibilities. Although the pool itself was deep and sluggish, the flow into it was anything but. Fast and

rough, it came tumbling down the rocks steeply, to lose its energy gradually in the dark depths. A generously hackled fly dropped inches to the left or right of the fastest water, and then allowed to drift into the pool, seemed to be worth a try. The runs into deep pools are often the spots to cast the fly, especially if there is little surface activity to indicate where the fish may be. Trout have a tendency to lie just out of or under the main current, waiting for food to be brought to them. This can be the magic spot to pick up the bigger fish in the swim, especially if they have not been disturbed. But these fish are not only the biggest, but usually the most wary, which is why they have become large in the first place.

The choice of fly seemed to be between a large Black Gnat or a Large Olive and, after some thought, I opted for the Black Gnat. I extended the fly line so that it did not spook any fish, away

The upper River Tweed flowing through the wonderful Borders landscape.

from the pool; I turned and tapped the line out over the water. Down the fly dropped and was instantly captured and made prisoner by the current. My line-hand worked overtime to keep the rod tip in touch with it. As it was carried into the slower water it disappeared, almost imperceptibly. If my eyes had been anywhere else, even for a split second, I would have missed the take. The bend of the rod as I lifted into the fish confirmed it was hooked. The ensuing struggle was magnificent. Four and a half pounds (2 kg) of wild brown trout, my largest to date, was soon returned, ready and able to pick off flies for another day.

That glorious morning saw me catch four trout in excess of 2 lb (1 kg) and many more up to 1 lb (500 g). All these fish were taken on the Black Gnat Paraloop-style. I did miss one rise to the fly; all the trout hooked were landed. This was a far better average than I had been used to

and it added further weight to my confidence when using Paraloop flies.

Appropriately the next tying is the Black Gnat Paraloop-style. Due to similarities in the tying to the Olive Dun, only those procedures that differ will be described.

The Black Gnat Paraloop

Materials

hook: size 14 Partridge Captain Hamilton dry fly
thread: 8/0 thread of your choice
body: black polypropylene floss (Tiemco Aero Dry Wing)
hackle: black cock
rib: I do not include one, but if you wish to, use dark grey thread
post: black GSP fine floss
thorax: black polypropylene fine dubbing (Fly-Rite #2 Black)

A typical small border stream. It is always surprising what can be found in these small waters.

Tying the Black Gnat Paraloop

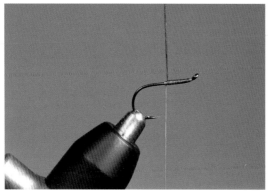

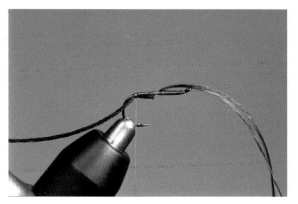

1. Fix the hook in the vice and check it for soundness. Wind the thread flat (4/12) to just before the halfway point along the hook shank. Form a loop from the GSP floss, and with the loose ends of the loop towards the hook eye, tie it in as a post, using the loose-loop/pinch-and-loop method (4/5) and winding the thread flat towards the eye. Cut off any excess GSP and return the thread to the post. Make three turns of thread directly behind the post to set it vertical.

2. Place the post out of the way. (If required a small piece of wire can be spun around it and just behind the hook eye to assist in keeping it clear whilst tying the body. When using thin GSP floss this is normally not necessary, as the material is stiff enough to stay out of the way without the assistance of a wire loop). Wind the thread flat to the hook bend and tie in first the rib, if required, followed by the body floss.

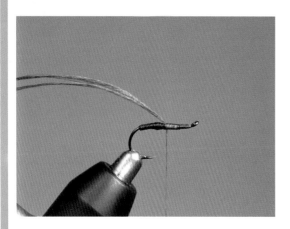

3. Wind the thread, using flat turns, to the post and then also wind the floss flat to the post. The floss can be wound onto the hook flat, in exactly the same way as thread can. Then build up a body (4/10). When the body is complete tie in the floss under the post and thorax, cutting off excess floss. Return the thread to the post and, if included, wind on the rib, securing as per the floss.

4. Attach the post to the gallows tool. Prepare the hackle and tie it in at the base of the post. Complete the hackle brush, tying in on the hook shank with two or three turns of thread. To assist when tying the hackle to the hook shank, pull the post over towards the hook bend. This will give enough space to manoeuvre the thread under the hackle brush to allow the hackle to be tied in. The hackle brush should be equal in height to the distance from the hook eye to the post.

5. Unhook the gallows tool and attach the neck breaker. Finish tying in the hackle and cut off the excess. Return the thread to the post. Wax the thread, about 1½ in (4 cm) will be enough, and dub with the black polypropylene fine dubbing. Build up a thorax, which should be wider than the widest part of the body.

6. Now unhook the post from the neck breaker. Reattach the gallows tool. Slightly double the hackle (4/2), but only slightly, and compact the hackle if the hackle brush is too long (4/1).

7. Unhook the post from the gallows tool and pull the hackle brush over the top of the thorax. Tie it in behind the eye, form a small head and complete with a whip finish.

That concludes the tying of the Black Gnat Paraloop. It is a fly that I have enjoyed much success with. It is a Basic Paraloop, as it does not include any special techniques other than a simple Paraloop hackle. It can be fished successfully whenever there are very dark or black flies on the water, and this includes terrestrial flies blown on by the wind. If there was ever a fly fishing version of *Desert Island Discs* and I was allowed only one fly to take to my fly fishing paradise, it would, more than likely, be this one or a version of it. Black flies have always given me success and I find them extremely useful when I am unsure of which fly to use owing to the lack of fly life on the water.

Tying the Lunn's Particular

The next tying is a hackle-tip winged fly, examples of which include the Adams and the Lunns Particular. I have chosen the wonderful pattern devised by William Lunn, the renowned water keeper on the exclusive Houghton beat of the River Test, to illustrate how to tie a hackle-tip winged Paraloop. This fly has been one of my favourites since I was a young boy. I was first introduced to it just before I was allowed to go fishing on my own. The family were on holiday in Devon and a licence for a day's fishing on a local river had been bought for me as a special holiday treat. I was to be left alone to wander this river. This was particularly thrilling for me, as the previous year we had spent some time on holiday by the wonderful River Nith in south-west Scotland and I had not been allowed to fish. But this year I was to be free to do so. My knowledge of fly fishing was minimal – and even that is generous. Until then the only fish I had caught on the fly were carp, dace and roach. I had in fact

never been trout fishing. I am not sure if I slept at all the night before, I was so excited.

The day before my father took me to a local tackle shop to choose a few flies. I still remember the place well, it was on the first floor of an old traditional property and was entered from the street by going up steep wooden stairs. The entrance was all wooden panels and smelt of wax. Entering the shop was for me like entering into a treasure cave, although unfortunately my natural shyness stopped me from investigating everything I saw. My father explained that I was going to be fishing a particular river, and the shopkeeper kindly asked me what flies I intended to use. Now for a young boy this was a terrible question; I knew the names of absolutely no flies, but did not wish to appear anything other than an expert. My answer was along the lines of, I was not sure but could I see what he had. This bought me a little time. The trays were brought out for me to see. Amongst the many flies on view one stood out for me – the fly which I now know as the Lunn's Particular. The wings,

1. Place the hook in the jaws of the vice and test it for soundness. Wax the thread well and wind it flat to halfway along the hook shank and then back towards the hook eye to a point about a quarter of the way along. Take the prepared hackle tips and, with the good sides of the feather tips facing outwards, tie them in (4/6). The hackle tips should be facing over the hook eye. The length of the wings should be the length of the hook. Cut off the excess hackle stalks.

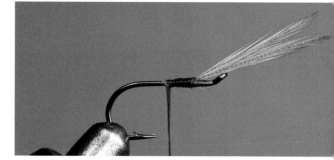

2. Wind the thread to just before the halfway point along the hook shank. Take the post floss, form a loop and using the loose-loop/pinch-and-loop method (4/5), tie in the post on the top of the hook shank. The patterns described so far have had the post tied in with the loose ends towards the hook eye. Due to the wing being in place, it is not always possible to do this on hackle-winged patterns. As an alternative in the case of winged flies the loose ends of the post should extend towards the hook bend. Wind the thread flat

(4/12) along the top of the hook shank towards the hook bend, tying in the post as you do so. Before the bend is reached cut off any excess post floss and continue the thread to the start of the hook bend. Using the loose-loop/pinch-and-loop method (4/5), tie in the tail fibres. These can be either tied in straight or, if you prefer, use the thread loop method (4/4), making sure a very fine thread loop is used. The length of the tail should be at least the length of the hook shank and no more than the hook length (2/3).

the colour, the delicacy of structure had me well and truly hooked and needless to say I chose this one first, followed by a few others just for show. The shopkeeper commended me on my selection, which proved nothing other than his generosity of heart in dealing with young boys. The Lunn's Particular was the first fly I tried on that following day when I was dropped off by the riverbank – which was unfortunate because it was also the first fly I lost up a tree on my first cast.

The hackle-tip wings in the Lunn's Particular are ideal when tying Paraloop flies, in fact I would go as far as to say that the technique could almost have been designed for it. When the hackle brush is pulled over the thorax it separates the two wings and allows them to be placed at any angle. From spent winged (horizontal) to upright, the wings can be set as desired. My personal preference when tying the Lunn's Particular is to have them set at an angle just above the horizontal. One of the other advantages the Paraloop offers over other methods of

tying when using hackle-tip wings is that when spent winged patterns are tied, the wings can actually sit on the water and are less inhibited by the hackle. This position is a far closer imitation than that used traditionally. Traditional methods of forming the hackle have a tendency to obscure the overall effect of the wings.

Materials

hook: size 14 Partridge Captain Hamilton dry fly
thread: crimson 8/0 thread
body: red cock hackle stalk stripped of feather fibres
hackle: red cock
tail: three fibres red cock
wing: blue dun hackle tips (4/6)
rib: none
post: white or brown GSP fine floss (approximately 6 in – 15 cm)
thorax: crimson floating dubbing, or if that is difficult to find, Fly-Rite #13 which, although a claret colour, can have a little crimson dubbing added

3. We are now going to add the stripped feather stalk/quill as a body. If you are unsure how to strip a feather, here is a simple method. Use one of the larger feathers from a neck cape. This will provide a strong pliable stalk which tapers nicely. Sometimes the feather which provides the fibres for the tail is suitable, although good tailing fibres are valuable, so unless you have a good supply use a feather of lesser quality. Holding the feather at its tip end, pull

the fibres on one side of the stalk downwards using the thumb and first finger of the hand not holding the tip. This will pull them away from the stalk. Continue down the stalk until the side is clear of fibres. Then repeat on the other side. This leaves a feather stalk complete with a few feather fibres at the tip end, where it has been held. Cut off the tip section; it is usually too thin for tying.

Now take the stripped feather stalk and dampen it with warm water. Some tyers use saliva, but considering some of the preserving techniques and chemicals used on capes, this is probably not a good idea. Tie in the narrow end of the stalk exactly where the tail starts. It should be tied in on the underside of the hook shank. Continue to tie the stalk in along the underside of the hook shank by winding the thread flat (4/12) towards the post. Cut off any excess stalk just before you reach the post with the thread windings and then continue the thread to the post.

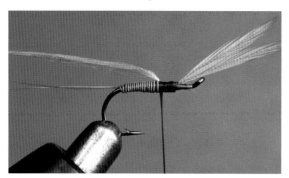

4. Wind the hackle stalk in touching turns to the post. The stalk has a tendency to become wider the further down it goes, which gives a very nice segmented body shape. Tie it in underneath the hook shank in the thorax region of the fly, taking care not to extend as far as the wings. Cut off excess stalk and return the thread to the post.

5. Attach the post to the gallows tool. Prepare and tie in the red cock hackle. Wind it up and down the post up to a height equal to that of the distance from the post to the hook eye. Do not be too concerned if it exceeds this height, as it can be beneficial to compact it. This forms the hackle brush. Pulling the post back towards the hook bend, manoeuvre the thread under the hackle brush and tie the loose hackle end onto the hook shank with two or three turns of thread.

6. Unhook the gallows tool and attach the neck breaker. Complete tying in the hackle and cut off the excess. Return the thread to the post and wax 1½ in (4 cm) of thread, dubbing it with the crimson dubbing. Wind the dubbing to form the thorax, taking the dubbing in front of the wings. Winding the dubbed thread directly in front of the wings whilst holding the wings out from the hook shank will bring them into the upright position. Make sure enough space is clear behind the hook eye to form a small head.

7. Pull the wings apart and then, unhooking it from the neck breaker, pull the hackle brush over the thorax in between them. Check to see if the hackle brush is the right length; compact it if it is too long. Tie in the hackle brush behind the hook eye. Cut off the excess post floss, form a small head and complete with a whip finish. The well-waxed thread will hold it all in place, but if you are the sort who wears braces and a belt, add a little varnish to the head.

8. The position of the wings and the positioning of the tail fibres.

That completes the tying of the Lunn's Particular Paraloop-style. The wings will be held in the split position by the hackle. To adjust the angle of the wings, just pull them into position. The hackle fibres are normally sufficient to hold them when set in place.

The Grey Wulff

The Quill Gordon, the Merry Widow, the Polymaydun, the Rat-Faced MacDougal and the Wulff patterns all incorporate a split hair or bunched feather-fibre wing. They are just a few examples of the vast array of flies that do so. The superb Wulff patterns, originally designed by the renowned and innovative American fly fisher, Lee Wulff, seem on their own to be endless in the variations available; I seem to come across new varieties or variants every few weeks. I still have absolutely no idea why they should be so successful; let's face it, the Royal Wulff resembles nothing that hatches on our waters and yet it is a highly effective pattern. I have always found it most useful when fishing for difficult wild brown trout, often tying it on my leader as a last resort and getting immediate results. This has not been an isolated odd event, but one experienced regularly on the lochs of Scotland, the loughs of Ireland and rivers, both spring chalk streams, and freestone spate rivers. Tying the Wulff patterns using the Paraloop has not reduced this effectiveness.

Some tyers choose to tie these flies with a single upright wing, I prefer to tie them with a split wing. As such they are, just like the hackle-tip winged flies, eminently suitable for tying Paraloop style. It is possible to tie the single, upright wing Paraloop-style. The hackle brush is pulled over the thorax, the thorax being slightly wider than normal. The floss loop is opened above the hackle brush and the wing is fed through the loop prior to completing the head.

As with all traditional flies, when a Paraloop hackle is applied in place of the normal hackle, it allows the fly to sit lower in the water. It is my belief that the addition of an upright wing on a dry fly becomes more important the lower the fly sits in the water. Classically the hackled fly is supposed to be supported on the water by the tips of the hackle and the tail fibres. We all know that this is seldom the case; the flies have a tendency to sink lower in the water. Any upright wing on such a fly will be well clear of the water. Although it is often angled over the hook eye, the angle of the fly will find the wing at least in the vertical and probably leaning backwards. This reduces the chance of the trout seeing it clearly through the hackle at such an angle. If the trout cannot see it clearly, what is its purpose? With a fly sitting with a low profile in the water the wing becomes an integral part of what the fish can perceive. This is even more relevant when one takes into account that the trout sees a mirrored image of the wings and not just the underside of the fly.

The following example is the Grey Wulff, which was first introduced into the UK from America in the 1950s by the well-known tyer Peter Deane, and it has proved popular since that time. In this tying I have attempted to keep as close to the original dressing as possible, but it can be advantageous to use a floating dubbing for the body and thorax area if you prefer. If natural materials are used for the body and the thorax, pretreatment of the material with water repellent is advisable. Scotchguard or some silicon sprays will help sustain the fly on the water. Treat it well in advance and give it plenty of time to absorb the treatment before using.

Tying the Grey Wulff Paraloop-Style

Materials

    hook: size 10 Partridge Captain Hamilton dry fly
    thread: own choice 8/0
    body: grey squirrel body fur
    hackle: blue dun cock and red cock
    tail: grey squirrel tail
    post: white GSP fine floss (6 in – 15 cm)
    wing: grey squirrel tail
    rib: none
    thorax: fine fibre grey polypropylene dubbing (Fly-Rite #37 Grey Drake/Grey Fox)

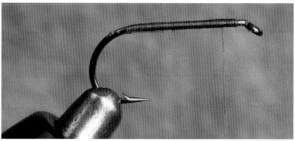

1. Fix the hook in the vice and test it for soundness. Wax the thread thoroughly, offer it to the hook and wind flat (4/12) touching turns to the start of the bend on the hook shank. Then wind it back to approximately six turns from the hook eye. The reason for doing this is that the well-waxed thread forms a foundation for the squirrel-tail fibre wing to be tied upon. Squirrel hair is very hard and one of the most difficult hairs to tie in successfully. The waxed thread is a vital constituent of the process and greatly assists in binding the hair to the hook.

2. Separate a generous portion of squirrel tail fibres from the rest of the tail and using scissors cut them from the tail close to the roots. Remove any loose hair or underfur. Place them in a hair stacker (1/9) to level the tips (4/8). I prefer the funnel-type stacker, as this gives a rounded end to the levelled tips which is, I think, more pleasing to the eye, although I am sure the trout have no opinion on the matter. Remove the hair carefully from the stacker, ensuring that all the loose and short hairs have been removed and offer it to the top of the hook shank, held by the thumb and first finger of the left hand (right hand if left-handed). The hair tips will be facing out over the hook eye. The wing should be generous, the same length as the hook. The thread is currently at the tying-in point, so using a flat thread make four turns around the hair and hook shank, using the loose-loop/pinch-and-loop method (4.4). These turns should be towards the eye and touching. Make sure the wing stays on the top of the hook shank and is not pulled too far around the shank by the turns of thread.

3. Now lift up the hair wing at the tip and make three turns of thread around the wing base only, not around the hook shank. Again these turns should be made using flat, well-waxed thread. This will control the shape of the wing and assist in holding the hair fibres together. Now tighten the thread by spinning the bobbin in the opposite direction. It should be far tighter than normal. (4/8)

5. Tie in a generous tail using the loose-loop/pinch-and-loop method (4/5) and the same locking turns as used when tying in the wing. Make the tail relatively short, certainly no longer than the hook shank and much shorter than the wing length. Use the tail fibres to make the body smooth up to the wing fibres and cut off any excess. Take the thread back to the hook bend.

4. Wind the tightened thread over the top of the flat thread, in tight touching turns. Leave the wing in the low-angled position for the time being. Cut off any excess hair at an angle and continue the thread over the hair, forming a smooth body. It can be useful to go back to using flat wound thread at this stage. Return the thread to the centre of the hook shank and with the loop facing over the wing, tie in the post by winding the thread flat towards the tail position. Cut off any excess post floss before you reach the start of the hook bend.

6. Wax the thread and dub it with the grey squirrel body fur (4/7). Wind the dubbed thread to form a body, taking it as far as the floss post. The body should taper to be slightly wider at the post than at the tail position – more dubbed thread rather than less thread with more dubbing. Trim the dubbed body to remove any excess dubbing material and any wayward guard hairs.

7. Fix the post to the gallows tool. Prepare the two hackles and tie both in at the same time, bringing the thread back to the post. Cut off the excess hackle stalks. Wind up and down the post to form the hackle brush. When winding the hackles down over those previously wound up, they should be worked and wiggled through the up windings to minimise the number of fibres caught. Tie in on the hook shank by pulling the post towards the hook bend and making two turns of thread around the hackles and hook shank. The height of the hackle brush should be the distance from the post to the outside of the hook eye. The additional height of hackle brush allows for a larger thorax. If you are not careful – and sometimes even if you are – winding the two hackles will catch quite a few fibres around the post. If this is the case take a dubbing needle and release them, whilst the hackle brush is attached to the gallows tool and the hackle has been initially tied in. Carefully double the hackle, but only very slightly (4/2)!

9. Wax the thread and dub it using the grey polypropylene dubbing. Build up a generous thorax, bringing the dubbed thread in front of the hair wing. By winding the dubbed thread directly in front of it, the wing can be set at the desired angle.

8. Unhook the gallows tool and attach the neck breaker to the post. Complete the tying in of the hackles, cutting off any excess and taking the thread back to the post.

10. Unhook the hackle brush from the neck breaker. Take the dubbing needle or tweezers and split the wing into two equal parts. Hold the wing fibres closest to you between the thumb and first finger of the left hand (right hand if left-handed) and gently pull them away from the remaining hair fibres. At the same time, using your right hand (left if left-handed), pull the hackle brush over the thorax and between the near and far sections of wing. The hackle brush will effectively split the wings and hold them in position. I prefer the hackle brush to be tied in slightly in the open loop style (4/3), which means that the hackle brush must be slightly longer than the distance from the post to the hook eye. In the case of the Wulff patterns, this adds a little extra something.

11. Tie in the end of the floss post behind the hook eye. If the hackle brush is too long, then compact it before tying in. Cut off the excess floss and build up a small head. Complete with a whip finish.

There we have the Grey Wulff Paraloop-style. It does not matter which Wulff pattern you tie, the above tying sequence can be applied to them all, with the obvious variations.

It is possible to tie non-split wings when using the Paraloop Method. This procedure shows how.

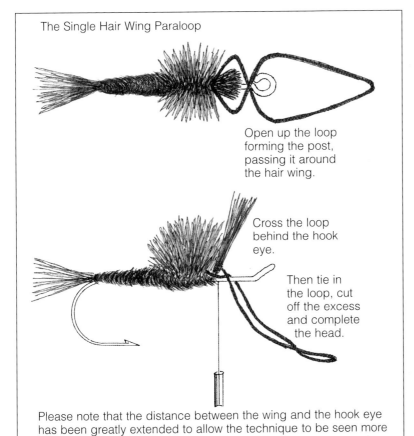

The Single Hair Wing Paraloop

Open up the loop forming the post, passing it around the hair wing.

Cross the loop behind the hook eye.

Then tie in the loop, cut off the excess and complete the head.

Please note that the distance between the wing and the hook eye has been greatly extended to allow the technique to be seen more clearly. In the actual fly the proportions of the fly are as normal.

If a single wing is preferred to a split wing, then the wing should be tied in slightly closer to the eye. When pulling over the hackle brush do not split the wing, but open up the floss post loop above the hackle brush and pull it down around the wing. A touch of dubbing on the thread to tie in can be an advantage for the first couple of turns, as this hides any floss post which may show. Crossing the floss post in front of the wing can make it easier and more controlled when tying in. Then complete with a small head and whip finish.

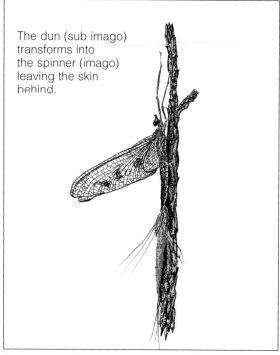

The dun (sub imago) transforms into the spinner (imago) leaving the skin behind.

The spinner (imago) emerges as a fully developed adult fly from the exoskeleton of the dun.

There are two occasions when I find fishing the Grey Wulff extremely useful. The first is when large duns are emerging from the water. When fished at this time, the artificial fly would appear to imitate the emerged fly, before it takes to the air, a case of the fly that hesitates is lost. The second situation where I would be tempted to use it is when all else is lost. After trying what would appear to be the logical and sensible patterns indicated by the circumstances and failing to inspire the trout to follow this line of logic, the Grey Wulff can save the day. It has often done so for me.

The Detached Body Green Drake

This fly is excellent, and one of my own favourites. When the large mayflies are on the menu, this pattern can be extremely deadly. If there ever was a fly that looks right this is it, on or off the water. I tied it once at a demonstration, where one of the audience suggested that it was a fly for fly tyers and not for fishing. I had no hesitation in contradicting this opinion, asking the question: what is it we look for in a dry fly?

The answer was unequivocal: the fly must float and it in some way must resemble the natural insect. When a glass of water was found and the fly dropped into it from a height, it floated. Not only that, it floated when thrown; in fact it was almost unsinkable. The image of the fly from above the water and below settled the case, this was not a fly for fly tyers but a serious fishing fly. The natural fly is a mouthful for the trout and so is the artificial. Tied with detached body it appears to be bigger than the size 12 hook would indicate, but this size is no disadvantage when it is on the water. At first look, the pattern may seem to be a little complicated, but it is quite straightforward.

The techniques used here can be applied to any number of flies. In the pattern described I sometimes include a secondary thorax cover of foam. It not only provides a very alluring shape, but also adds that important ability to float under all circumstances. Its inclusion is wholly optional, however. The fly is excellent tied as described, with just the dubbed polypropylene as a thorax. I tend to use the flies that include foam when fishing fast flowing and rough water, and those without foam in more placid waters. The fly floats well whether the foam is included or not, giving a wonderful impression of an emerged dun which has failed to take to the wing and is stuck in the surface of the water. The time to fish this fly is when the Green Drake dun is emerging from the water, the fly cast to covering rising fish. The other situation when the fly can be extremely effective is when the spinners have returned to lay the eggs and the water starts to collect the dying flies. Although not deliberately designed as a spent winged fly, the pattern is a good imitation of many spinners when they first fall upon the water.

This pattern can be used to tie imitations of all the mayflies, with colour of materials and hook sizes changing according to the size and colour of the fly being imitated. I have a preference for mayflies with detached bodies. A detached body allows the fly to be tied big, which is what the flies are, without having to resort to a large hook. This assists in two ways: first the fly pattern is not dominated by the hook itself, and second the weight of the hook is minimised, increasing the fly's ability to float.

1. Mix the body floss colours together thoroughly. Then form a detached body (4/6). Take three separate micro fibbets of approximately the same colour as the body and thread the cut ends onto a thin needle. Take the fibbets through the eye of the needle about ¼ in (0.5 cm) and then fold them back. Now, starting at the end feed the needle through the body. Do not worry if this squeezes it out of shape, because when the needle is removed the body will resume its correct shape. When the required length of tail is extending from the end of the body, remove the fibbets from the needle. Place the detached body to the side ready to be tied onto the hook when required.

2. Insert the hook into the jaws of the vice and test it for soundness. Wax the thread, attach it to the hook and wind it, using flat turns, to the halfway position on the hook shank. Take the detached body and tie it in on the top of the hook shank using the loose-loop/pinch-and-loop method (4/5). Make sure the ends of the fibbets are tied in at the same time.

3. Cut off any excess body material and wind the thread back to where the body was first tied in. Take the GSP floss and form a post. Tie the post in at this position, immediately where the body starts. The loop end should be over the hook bend and the loose ends towards the hook eye. Tie in the post on the top of the hook shank. Cut off any excess post well before you reach the hook eye. Take the two prepared blue dun hackle tips for the wings and tie them in on top of the hook shank facing over the hook eye. Leave the wings in place and return the thread to the post.

4. Attach the floss post to the gallows tool and tie in the hackle at the base of the post. Wind the hackle up the post for a distance slightly in excess of the distance from the post to the hook eye, and then wind the hackle back down. Tie in the hackle onto the hook shank with two or three turns. Remember to pull the post back to give access to the hook shank.

5. Unhook the post from the gallows tool and attach the neck breaker. Complete tying in the hackle, cut off the excess and return the thread to the post.

6. Wax the thread and dub it using the thorax dubbing. Wind on the dubbed thread, first behind the wings. Then pull the wings into position, fixing them by winding the dubbed thread in front. Continue forming a shaped thorax. Leave sufficient space behind the hook eye to tie in the remaining materials and form a small head.

7. Unhook the hackle brush from the neck breaker and reattach it to the gallows tool. Slightly double the hackle (4/2) and compact (4/1) if necessary. Then pull the hackle brush over the thorax and tie it in behind the hook eye, making sure the wings are on either side of the hackle brush. Cut off the excess floss.

8. Form a small head and complete a whip finish. Now go to the tails and with your fingers set them in the correct position; one middle tail and two forking out either side. Put a touch of superglue at the point where the tails enter the body and hold them in place for a few seconds. This is normally sufficient to keep the tails in the correct position.

The fly incorporates a detached body with three tails. The body is very easy to form by twisting polypropylene floss and allowing it to twist upon itself (4/9). This method is also used when tying shucks. Bodies formed using this simple, but highly effective, method are automatically segmented. Either the single- or double-furled method described can be used. Three tails are included after the body has been formed and prior to its attachment to the hook shank. A needle is used to feed the micro fibbets through the tail. The technique looks fiddly and complicated, but I can assure you it is not and it takes just seconds to complete. There are many different ways in which a detached body can be formed and all of them can be adapted to suit the Green Drake Paraloop. I have a fondness for the furled twisted floss method, owing to its simplicity and effectiveness. To produce a more substantial body the technique can be repeated on the same piece of floss, which produces a body which resembles a woven body but without the effort involved in tying one.

Materials

hook: Partridge Captain Hamilton dry fly size 12
thread: 8/0 of choice
body: fine polypropylene floss, green and yellow mixed (Tiemco Aero Dry Wing)
hackle: light ginger cock
tail: 3 micro fibbets
post: GSP
wing: blue dun
thorax: olive polypropylene dubbing (Fly-Rite #32 Rusty Olive)

There you have the Green Drake Paraloop style. On the water the fly floats extremely well, with the tail, thorax and hackle all combining to add to the floatability.

The flies in this chapter give a little taster of how the Paraloop Method can be applied to the tying of many of the flies with which we are familiar. The difference is, however, in how the flies perform when on the water and it is this difference that, I believe, makes the Paraloop Method, when applied to traditional-style flies so successful. Take any fly, better still take your favourite all-round fly and apply a Paraloop hackle to it. The first thing to note is that the fly looks good. Secondly, it sits low in the water. As for tempting fish, you can enjoy the pleasure of finding that out for yourself.

The flies described in this chapter.

6 Tying Emerger Patterns Using the Paraloop Method

Before tying the patterns covered in this chapter, it is important that you understand what is actually meant by the term 'emerger'. In recent years many flies have appeared under this label. The differences in these flies can sometimes make one wonder what exactly is being referred to when the term 'emerger' is added to a fly pattern. Moreover, many patterns that are not normally considered emergers could, because of the way they sit in the water, be fished as such effectively.

One might say that any fly that starts its life cycle in the water and at some stage leaves it is a candidate for the name 'emerger'. In fly fishing terms, however, it is unfortunately not quite as straightforward as that. To be considered an emerger, a transforming insect must complete the transition from pupa or nymph to fly in or on the surface of the water, emerging from the water into the air – hence the name. The effectiveness of emerger patterns is due to this transformation taking place in the meniscus, where the fly is effectively held by the water's surface tension, albeit sometimes for just a moment, before entering the fly stage of its life cycle. This moment is long enough for the trout to take it.

The requirement that it must emerge in or on the water surface means many different flies are excluded. Not all flies which start their life cycle in the water complete the transition to the actual fly in such a manner. Many crawl out over rocks, up branches and roots, through marginal shingle or up weeds and reeds, or any other suitable exit. The transition takes place either out of the water or in the surface of the extreme shallows; in either case they do not provide much of an opportunity for the fly fisher to take advantage of. A delicately presented emerging fly pattern placed on an overhanging branch or riverside rock is unlikely to excite any interest with the resident trout, no matter how well the fly was tied! Some stone-flies, upwinged flies, dragon-flies and damsel-flies live the earlier part of their life cycle in the water as nymphs, but they could not be considered as emergers from a fly fishing point of view, emerging as they do up reeds and rocks.

Amongst the fly types which can be considered as possible emergers, are upwinged flies (Ephemeroptera), caddis or sedge flies (Trichoptera) and flat-winged flies (Diptera). Not all the flies within these groups can be regarded as emergers in a fly fishing sense, but plenty of them can, and more than enough to satisfy any fly fisherman or fly tyer. Identifying those that do is one of the many enjoyable aspects of fly fishing.

If we look at the life cycle of the upwinged flies it is clear how important the emerger pattern is for the fly fisher. All upwinged flies start their lives as eggs in the water, deposited either loosely via the surface or by attaching them to underwater objects, the female adult fly enveloped in an air sack, crawling under the water to do so. This egg hatches into a nymph, and it is in the nymphal stage that the insect lives the greater part of its life. After some time, which appears to depend on various factors including temperature, the nymph heads out from the relative safety of the silt, rocks or weeds to the surface of the water. The skin, or more correctly the exoskeleton, of the nymph cracks open at the surface of the water and the fly, at this stage known as the dun, or sub-imago, emerges. As I have said, the outer skin of the nymph is often referred to as the shuck. There can be little doubt that the emerging stage of the fly provides a relatively easy meal for the fish.

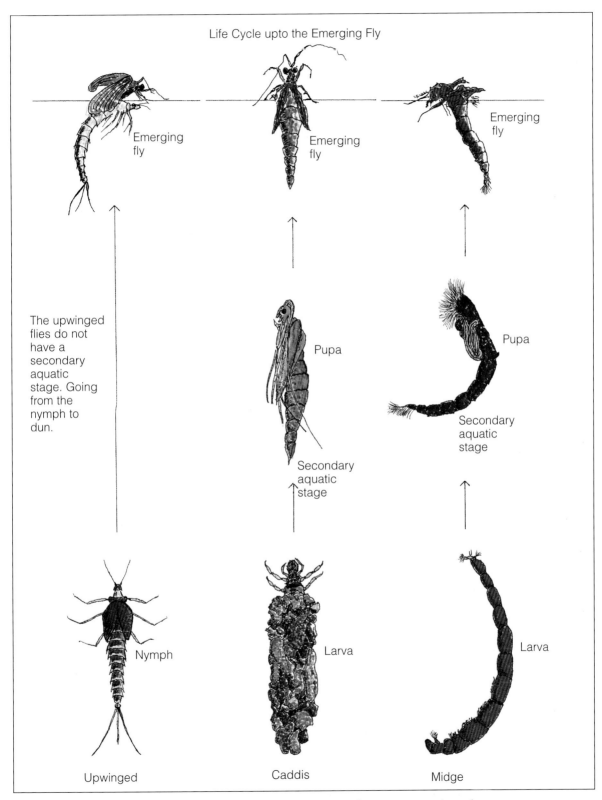

Life Cycle upto the Emerging Fly

Emerging fly

Emerging fly

Emerging fly

The upwinged flies do not have a secondary aquatic stage. Going from the nymph to dun.

Pupa

Pupa

Secondary aquatic stage

Secondary aquatic stage

Nymph

Larva

Larva

Upwinged

Caddis

Midge

The life cycle of the upwinged, caddis or sedge and midge, up to their emergence from the water.

During what are often regarded as the golden days of dry fly fishing, around the end of the nineteenth and beginning of the twentieth centuries, there was in England a very strong movement dedicated to fishing solely the dry fly. This group of fly fishermen was generally centred on the chalk streams of southern England, and at its head stood Frederick Halford, whose mentor, George Selwyn Marryat had been so influential in the development of what we recognise today as dry fly fishing and the dry fly. It was at this time that many of the classic dry flies we still recognise and use today were developed. An attitude of what can only be described as blinkered superiority grew within this movement, and all methods of angling other than the dry fly were looked upon as a lesser sport. This was surprising considering that Frederick Halford started out as a coarse fisherman and he had a wide range of fishing experience.

It took intelligence, strength of character and the ability to see things as they are to expose this narrow attitude for what it was. Such qualities were to be found in G. E. M. Skues. Skues well deserves our gratitude, for he more than anyone else opened up the way for anglers to understand and fish using patterns at all stages of the fly's life cycle, especially the nymph He gave it the kick-start it needed, and what a fine and mighty kick-start it was. This is not to say that Halford's contribution to fly fishing was not substantial. One only has to read his book *Dry Fly Entomology* (1897), to see that he had a deep understanding of the craft and made a pivotal contribution to the development of dry fly fishing. Skues, however, extended the fly fisher's outlook, understanding and opportunities. The legacies of both these anglers reverberates around us even today and there is not a single part of the world where fly fishing is practised, where their influence cannot be seen and felt.

There is, however, a mountain of irony in this

Frederick Halford's *Dry Fly Entomology*, a wonderful book, even today, which clearly shows Halford's understanding of his subject.

ancient controversy, as anyone who regularly fishes rivers and streams using classic-style flies will know. When fishing these flies, how often do they sit on the water as intended? Not very often, I would say. The theory behind the dry fly at the time was that it sat on the top of the water, supported by the hackle and the tail fibres. In fact the proportions of the fly were intended to accommodate this, with a straight line being able to be taken from the tip of the tail through to the tip of the hackle, touching the hook bend on the way. In practice a good part of the fly is usually in the surface of the water and more often than not a good part is under the water when taken by a rising fish. Fishing the flies used at the time – flies tied with the materials then available, often quill, wool or seal's-fur bodies – I have no doubt whatsoever that they were fished and taken as emergers. In some cases they sit so low in the water that fish will take them as the nymph. Frederick Halford may well be turning in his grave at such heretical ideas but anyone who fishes with their eyes open and with a willingness to see things as they are, will know it is true. So when the evenings are warm and the spinners move to their age-old dance, and the sedge fly cuts the water as the twilight deepens into dark, maybe, just maybe, the ghost of Frederick Halford, wandering the banks of his beloved rivers, will appreciate that imitative fly fishing is skilful and sportsmanlike, no matter whether the adult, emerging or nymph fly is used.

The caddis or sedge flies and the flat-winged flies both include excellent emergers. The life cycles of these groups of flies differ from those of the upwinged flies. Whilst the upwinged flies have another stage after becoming an actual fly, with the dun (sub-imago) changing into the spinner (imago), the caddis and the flat-winged flies have this additional stage *before* developing into the fly. The larva becomes the pupa, and it is from the pupa that the developed adult fly emerges.

The flat-winged flies (Diptera) cover a vast range and are, in many areas, the major source of food for trout throughout the year, especially in still or slow-moving waters. Those flies in this group which are important to the angler start their life in the water as eggs and develop into larvae, then pupae, eventually emerging at the water surface as flies. Other flat-winged flies useful to the fly fisherman are land based but are blown onto the water by the wind; these are known as terrestrials. The flat-winged flies are of such importance to the fly fisher that chapter 7 concentrates solely on these flies.

Trout love caddis flies and especially emerging caddis flies, and many a warm summer's evening is spent gorging them. When they are on the water it is a time of plenty for the trout. At times I have seen hatches of caddis flies to more than rival those of the upwinged fly. A couple of years ago, fishing in Ireland on the Cong Canal, I experienced probably the largest rise of caddis flies I have ever seen. The Cong Canal is not like any other canal, it is the outlet from Lough Mask, the great trout lough of County Mayo. It is the result of an attempt by an English engineer to connect Lough Mask with Lough Corrib. After

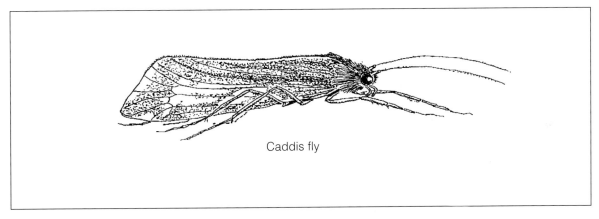

Caddis fly

The adult caddis fly.

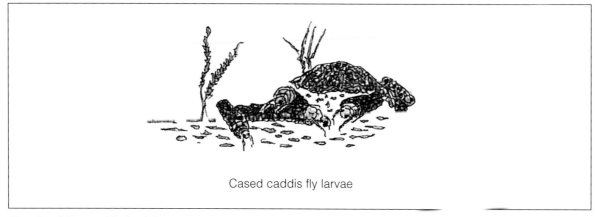

Cased caddis fly larvae

Cased caddis provide food for trout.

many years of work, the canal had finally been completed, and the water was released from Lough Mask. However, it subsequently disappeared well before arriving at Lough Corrib. The unfortunate engineer had not taken into consideration the effect of the canal being built on limestone. The water had just disappeared into the ground, never more to be seen. What is left is the Cong Canal, a fast-running river of about ½ mile (1 km) running into a small lough. The area is strange and uncanny in a wonderful sort of way. The canal is fast flowing and is more like a river than many rivers. The fishing on this small piece of water can at times be awesome; the fish are very large and appear in some numbers. The

evening in question started off with a few small dark caddis flies flying around. By the time I had caught my first fish, the air was full of these small flies, hundreds and thousands of them, in fact probably millions of them. If I opened my mouth they flew or crawled in. When I took a breath they went up both nostrils. Every inch of clothing was covered and as for the trout, they never stopped rising. The problem was keeping my eyes, mouth and nose free of the insects. In the end I had to watch from the car as the trout continued to gorge; being suffocated by flies seemed a distinct possibility. Watching those trout rise through the haze of flies was a frustrating but fascinating experience and I shall buy

Caddis pupa leaving the larva case

The caddis pupa is especially vulnerable after leaving the larva case and heading to the water's surface to emerge as the adult fly.

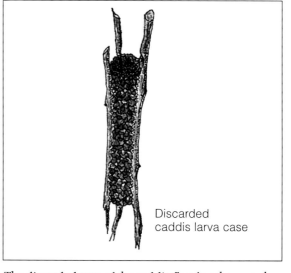

Discarded caddis larva case

The discarded case of the caddis fly after the pupa has left.

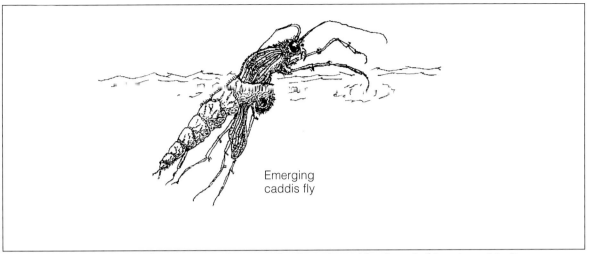

Emerging
caddis fly

The emerging caddis fly at the water's surface can often be indicated by the splashing rises of feeding trout.

suitable headgear for when I arrive again on those banks.

Trout eat caddis flies as larvae, pupae, emerging flies and adults, but in this chapter I am concentrating on the emerging fly. When the time comes for the pupa to head for the surface of the water, it is particularly likely to become food. When it reaches the surface and the adult fly starts to emerge it is especially open to attack from feeding fish. The slashing rise of a trout feeding on emerging caddis is often the first indication the angler has that a hatch has started. Fish will often leave the water to catch the flying insect and I have seen them jumping nearly 1 ft (30 cm) out of the water in an attempt to grab emerged flies. When trout start to feed on caddis there can be no stopping them; nothing else will do and imitating the fly is the only way to maximise your sport. I have even had trout grab the fly at my feet as I try to undo a tangle of line. I initially had to play it by hand until the tangle was removed. This seemed to provide more fun for my fishing companions than myself; they compared my antics to a Keystone Cop with rod in hand.

The emerging upwinged fly and caddis, or sedge, are two of the most effective flies available to the fisher. Trout are attracted to them, seldom taking without real enthusiasm. Recognising when to use them is easy; if there is a rise of flies then there must be emergers – find out which type of fly and then use an emerger pattern. It is

my opinion that the emerging fly provides a far greater proportion of the trout's food than the adult fly.

When tying emerger patterns using the Paraloop Method, I like to use the open loop technique (4/3). The technique is a development of the basic method of tying Paraloop flies and uses three different positions for tying the loop post. As I explained in chapter 4 these positions imitate the stages of emerging from early to medium and finally late. This technique allows the fly to be tied so that when it is on the water a varying amount is submerged.

Tying the Brown Sedge Emerger

The first Paraloop emerger pattern I describe is a medium emerging sedge. It can be tied in various sizes, but in the example it is tied quite large on a size 12 hook, and is an imitation of the Brown Sedge. The fly is tied 'early-style'.

Materials

hook: size 10 Kamasan B100 shrimp/buzzer hook
thread: 8/0 thread of your choice
body: fine brown polypropylene dubbing (Fly-Rite #32 Rusty Olive or #34 Quill Gordon/Brown Drake)
hackle: furnace cock
shuck: mix of cream and brown Antron floss
post: GSP fine floss

Tying the Brown Sedge Emerger

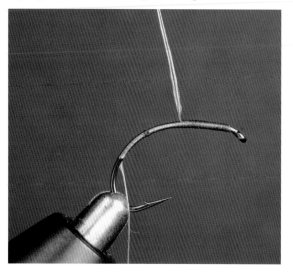 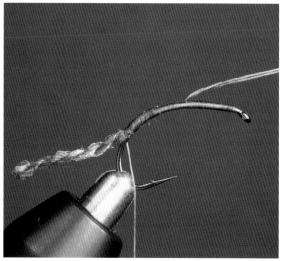

1. Set the hook in the vice and test it for soundness. Apply the well-waxed thread and wind it flat to just before the halfway position on the hook shank. Tie in the GSP floss loop onto the top of the hook shank, with the loop end over the hook bend, using the loose-loop/pinch-and-loop method. Wind the thread over the floss towards the hook eye and back, cutting off the excess floss as you go along. Remember to leave enough room behind the hook eye to tie in the required materials and form a small head. Take the thread to the other side of the post and make two or three turns directly against the post to make it stand upright. Now wind the thread to just around the hook bend.

2. Now for the rear end of the fly; what would appear to be the tail is in fact the nymph shuck, out of which the fly is emerging. The tail should be of a light colour and given the impression of translucence, imitating the emptying shuck. Because this should be under water I use Antron, a sinking material. Take the mixed cream and brown Antron floss and form a detached tail/shuck (4/9). Tie it in at the position the thread has been wound on top of the hook bend, using the loose-loop/pinch-and-loop method (4/4). This shuck should be approximately ½ in (1 cm) long. Wind the thread towards the hook eye, tying the floss on the upside of the hook shank as you go. Cut off the excess Antron winding the thread over the cut ends.

3. Bring the thread back to where the shuck was first tied in on the hook bend. Make sure it is well waxed and dub, using dubbing made by cutting up the excess Antron from the shuck into small pieces of around ¼ in (0.5 cm) long (vary the length). Mix the fibres well before using them as dubbing, so that they lose all semblance of floss. If there is not enough dubbing, prepare some more, but only a little is required so the excess should suffice. Wind the dubbed thread to the post. Place the floss post onto the gallows tool and tie in the prepared furnace cock hackle at the base of the post. Wind the hackle up and down the post for a distance well in excess of the distance from the post to the hook eye; just less than double the distance will form the ideal hackle brush. Pull the post back towards the hook bend and make two turns to tie in the hackle end.

4. Unhook the post from the gallows tool and attach the neck breaker. Finish tying in the hackle end by winding the thread towards the hook eye and then back to the post, cutting off the excess hackle as you go. Wax the thread and dub it with the fine brown polypropylene dubbing. Wind the dubbed thread towards the hook eye, leaving plenty of space to tie in the hackle and form a small head.

5. Unhook the post from the neck breaker and attach it to the gallows tool again. Compact the hackle slightly (4/1), but no more than would make the hackle brush less than one and a half times the length from the post to the hook eye. Slightly double the hackle brush (4/2), but only very slightly!

6. Unhook the gallows tool and pull the hackle brush over the dubbed body. Form an open loop with the hackle brush (4/3) and tie in the end behind the hook eye.

7. Cut off the excess floss post, form a small head and complete with a whip finish. Remove the fly from the jaws of the vice and take a cigarette lighter or match and carefully, without actually touching the fibres with the flame, melt the end of the tail, but only the end. Immediately after melting it, wet your thumb and first finger with saliva and press the melted end between them. This will hold the tail together and more importantly assist in sinking the shuck. Take the dubbing brush and use it to release some of the fibres from the underside of the thorax. There you have the Brown Sedge Medium Emerger Paraloop.

This fly will sit with the tail/shuck under the water and the hackle will sit high on the water, imitating a sedge fly well into the process of emerging from the nymph shuck.

I have found the fly fishes best just as the sun starts to go down on a summer's evening, although it can be effective at other times. When fishing still waters, I find it best to cast the fly out and just leave it, only casting again when the wind or slight current has brought it too far around. I have sometimes given this fly to others, who seem to find it impossible just to leave it static in the surface; the temptation to retrieve it appears to be irresistible. Although retrieving it will sometimes produce dramatic results, it is far better left static with only the occasional twitch to add a little extra life and inducement. That is what the fly has been designed for.

Sedges are often big flies, and trout in still waters will cruise around searching for them and they are all the more likely to find your imitation if it is static. Although casting to rising trout is to be recommended, when doing so allow the fly to land on the water and immediately give it a little twitch, then again just leave it static.

When fishing a river, I also find it best in the evening, but, if sedges are rising, use it anytime. If fished over rising trout it will normally invite a take. These takes are often quite violent – there is little subtlety involved when trout are feeding on the sedge fly. One mistake I have often made is to fish with too light a leader; the take on the sedge fly being quite violent can often result in a break. I now seldom fish with anything less than 5 lb breaking strain and often a greater strength if the current is fast and the fish run big.

Tying the Yellow Dun Emerger

Applying a wing to a Paraloop emerger can at times make a big difference. I have absolutely no idea why, but having tried non-winged and winged emergers at the same time, there are times when adding a wing definitely does make a difference. That is not to say that all of the flies should have wings; I tend only to add a wing to those emergers tied 'late' (longer open loop). Two forms of wings are used when tying Paraloop flies and both are formed from hackle tips. The first has the wings sloping backwards from the eye and along each side of the hackle brush. The second sticks straight upwards in the style which has become known as high-winged. In both cases I use two hackle tips for the wings, although the high-winged style has the two wings acting as one. I prefer to use two hackle tips so that if one breaks off, the other is still there. The pattern used to illustrate the tying of a winged emerger is the Yellow May Dun (*Heptagenia sulphurea*).

The yellow may dun starts its life like all upwinged flies, as an egg deposited in the water. It is not a fly I see hatching in large numbers, but due to its distinctive yellow colouring it stands out very clearly from all the other flies. On most of the rivers I fish, I see this fly hatching in ones, twos and threes throughout the early summer months and into high summer, hatching and

then flying upstream. It is often confused with the yellow sally, which hatches around the same time and is also a distinctive yellow colour. The yellow sally is not an upwinged fly but a member of the stone-fly family. The fish do not care what we call them, but it is wise to make sure you use the right imitation to catch them. It is a fine sight seeing the yellow may dun make its way upstream on a summer afternoon, standing out like a beacon against the green foliage of the bankside vegetation, a star amongst all the other flies.

In some rivers it is not seen as a fly that trout are particularly fond of, but I suspect this has more to do with the fact that the rising fly is more sporadic and accordingly the fish are less accustomed to them. I have no doubt in my mind that familiarity with a food source encourages fish to take. There are many anglers who value the fly highly and swear to its success. I have therefore chosen it as an example of a winged emerger. My friend Richard Hunter, who had the patience to proofread this book and who fishes the Rivers Tummel and Tay in Scotland, chooses this fly above most others when fishing in summer. He finds that it is one of the most effective flies he has ever used and his most successful days have been when the yellow may dun has been tied on his leader. For myself, I normally fish it from early afternoon into the evening but only if a few such flies can be seen on the water. The great River Tweed, famous for its salmon fishing, is not so well recognised as a trout river, but I have had some success with the Yellow May Dun on it and its tributaries. In this pattern the fly is tied open loop style 'late'.

Materials

hook: size 10 Partridge Oliver Edwards nymph/emerger hook
thread: 8/0 thread of your choice
body: yellow polypropylene dubbing (yellow Aero Dry Wing Floss fibres split and cut up or Fly-Rite #9 Golden Yellow)
hackle: badger coloured light yellow
wing: blue dun cock
shuck: mix of white and yellow Antron floss with a touch of yellow SLF
post: white GSP fine floss

Tying the Yellow Dun Emerger

1. Place the hook in the vice and check it for sound-ness. Take care to ensure that the shank is horizontal, as this will assist in the correct placement of materials. Prepare and tie in the hackle-tip wings (4/6), making sure that there is approximately ⅛ in (3 mm) of prepared stalk free at the base of the wings. The wing must be tied in directly behind the eye, with no space left for head etc. Let the wings sit pointing out over the hook eye; do not attempt to position or separate them at this time. Wind the thread flat to the point on the hook where, if the thread is allowed to hang loose, it touches the hook point (hence the reason for setting the hook horizontal), and tie in the GSP floss post, loose ends towards the hook eye. This sets the post at the 'medium' position. Use the loose-loop/pinch-and-loop method (4/5) to tie the post onto the top of the hook shank. Cut off the excess floss and return the thread to the post. Make a few turns onto the hook bend side of the post to allow it to sit upright.

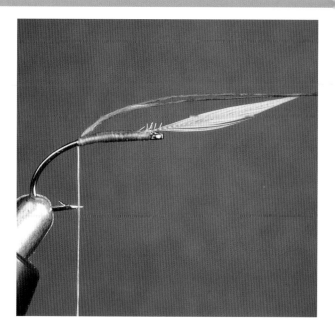

2. Pull the floss post over the hook eye to keep it out of the way. Wind the thread flat to the point where, if the thread is allowed to hang loose, it is just behind the hook barb. Mix the Antron floss and yellow SLF together thoroughly and form into a rope. Using the furling method for preparing a shuck or detached body (4/9), twist the material, allowing it to twist upon itself to form a suitable shuck. Using the loose-loop/pinch-and-loop method (4/5) tie it on so that it is pointing slightly downwards from the hook bend. Cut off the excess Antron/SLF mix. Cut up this excess mix to form a dubbing, wax the thread for about 1 in (2.5 cm) and use the prepared dubbing to dub the thread. Wind this dubbed thread to the base of the post to form the rear part of the fly body. Remove any excess dubbing from the thread.

3. Attach the gallows tool to the floss post. Tie in the prepared hackle at the base, cutting off the excess hackle stalk. Wind the hackle up the post for a distance of approximately twice the distance from the post to the hook eye and then wind back down again. Pull the post backward towards the hook bend and make two or three turns of thread around the hook shank and the hackle to secure it, taking great care not to tie in any fibres from the hackle brush. Unhook the gallows tool and attach the neck breaker.

4. Wax the thread and dub it using the fine yellow polypropylene dubbing. Wind the dubbed thread towards the hook eye to form a shaped body. Remember to leave enough room to tie in the additional materials and form a small head. Remove the neck breaker from the floss post and reattach the gallows tool. Compress the hackle brush (4/1) gently, reducing it to approximately one and a half times the distance from the post to the hook eye. Do not double the hackle brush (4/2). Pull it over the dubbed body using the open loop method (4/3) and tie it in, leaving enough space to form a small head between it and the wings. Cut off the excess floss, taking care not to cut off a wing. Bring the thread in front of the wings by lifting them up and placing the thread behind the hook eye.

5. The next move is to position the wing, and it will now become clear why a small amount of prepared stalk was left showing when the wing was originally tied in. As you will probably have noticed, the tying-in position of the wing is closer to the hook eye than normal. The reason for this is that the wings are now reversed in position by being pulled back over the hackle brush, one wing on either side. The thread is now wound over the trimmed sections of the wings to set them in place and to start forming the head. Now form a small head and complete with a whip finish. Remove the fly from the jaws of the vice and singe the end of the shuck using a lighter, and using wet fingers, immediately press the melted end between the fingers.

That is the Yellow May Dun Emerger completed. Give the fly a try whenever you see the natural upon the water or making its way upstream. It is one of those flies, like the Grey Wulff, which can bring fish up from deeper water when they are not seen rising.

6. The fly on the water sits very much more horizontal than the sedge fly. This imitates the fly almost at the point of fully emerging, wings out and the hackle brush imitating the struggling body.

Tying the Blue-Winged Olive High-Winged Emerger

I first came across the term 'high-winged emerger' a few years ago and it appears to originate, as with so many innovative fly tying ideas, in the USA. The fly is often tied using a single wing, but personally I prefer to use a pair of wings placed back to back. There are two reasons for doing this, both of them eminently practical. The first is the look of the fly; two wings produces a more solid-looking wing. Secondly, if one of the wings breaks off, the other will continue to deceive the fish.

Tying the high-winged emergers Paraloop-style is very similar to tying the Yellow May Dun. So as not to repeat the same instructions, therefore, the description of the Blue-Winged Olive High-Winged emerger will only highlight the differences in technique. It should be noted that the high-winged style differs from the more back-sloping wing of the actual insect, but this does not seem to make any difference whatsoever.

Fished whenever the blue-winged olive is on the water and the trout are rising to the emerging flies, it will usually bring success. This pattern is tied open loop medium-style.

Materials

hook: size 14 or 16 Oliver Edwards emerger hook
thread: 8/0 thread of your choice
body: fine olive brown polypropylene dubbing (Fly-Rite #32 Rusty Olive)
hackle: light ginger
wing: blue dun cock
shuck: red and olive Antron floss with a touch of cream SLF
post: white GSP fine floss

Fishing emergers, whether they are upwinged, flat-winged or sedge flies, is always a treat. The enthusiasm shown by trout for the emerging fly can make for highly exciting fishing. Even when there is no obvious rise, emerging flies, fished carefully with a gentle presentation, will encourage

1. Place the hook in the vice jaws and test it for soundness. Prepare two wings as described previously. The wing should be *longer than normal*, the length of the hook and a little bit more. Apply the wing as per the Yellow May Dun, but leave very little trimmed stalk showing where it is tied in and tie it in at a position which allows for a very small head.

2. Complete the fly as per the yellow may dun, using the materials above. Tie in the hackle brush behind the wing and cut off the excess floss. Pull the wings upright together and bring the thread in front of the wings. Wind the thread tight against the base of the wings to set them upright. Build a small head and complete with a whip finish. Remove the fly from the jaws of the vice and melt the tail end, pressing the melted end together immediately, as previously explained. You now have a completed Blue-Winged Olive Emerger with a high-winged Paraloop style. Note that the wings are not split, but should sit, back to back, as near as is possible like a single wing.

trout to make the effort to sample your well-tied wares, especially when using the larger flies. I am often asked which fly is my favourite and my stock answer is the one I present the best. More often than not lack of success has more to do with bad approach and clumsy presentation than with the chosen fly. Making the correct choice of fly and presenting it correctly is the real skill of fly fishing. Choosing the right fly and presenting it badly will not bring success. It would be better to choose the wrong fly and present it well. That said, when fishing a still water using the emerger, all that is required is patience and the will power not to retrieve the fly. Just leaving it sitting in the water for as long as possible will produce more takes than casting and retrieving. Covering rising fish will also prove successful, but again without retrieving; just the occasional nudge will add all the movement needed, often inducing the fish to take. On the rivers and streams we do not have that luxury and the presentation and positioning of the fly is vital. Allowing the fly and line to land gently upon the water, preventing the current from dragging the fly and covering fish will always be important when fishing the rivers and streams,

and thankfully these are skills that can also be learned.

A few years ago I wrote a couple of articles on small-stream fishing, a type of fishing I have always enjoyed immensely. As a result I was labelled a small-stream expert, a title for which I was wholly unqualified, and which I was certainly not looking for. The result was that I had a spell of time where many of the casting and fishing lessons I gave were, at the request of the clients, on small streams. The common factor with all the participants was their inability to cast a fly so that it landed gently upon the water without it or the line frightening the fish. I think the plethora of stocked fisheries had thrown the art of casting out of the window. Up to the time of their lesson their only concern when casting was to chuck the fly out as far as they could. The ability to land the fly where you wished it to land, without frightening the fish is essential, especially when fishing for wild fish. It is this ability, which can be learned, that makes all the difference in the world. In many ways books like this are irrelevant if they result in the flies being presented in such a way that, rather than inviting a rise, they frighten the fish away.

The flies described in this chapter.

7 Tying Buzzer Patterns Using the Paraloop Method

Of all the insect life which provides food for trout, the flat-winged flies (Diptera) are by far the most numerous. They are important to the fly fisher because some spend the earlier parts of their life cycle in the water and are thus available as food. Some land-based flies are blown onto the water by the wind in such numbers that they also become an important food source. Flies in this category, commonly known as terrestrials, include the daddy-long-legs (crane fly), heather fly, dung fly and hawthorn fly. In this chapter we will be looking at those flies which spend the earlier part of their life in the water and emerge as adults. There are quite a few different flies within this category, including the mosquito and midges, and it is midges (Chironomidea) in particular that this chapter will be concentrating upon.

The life cycle of the midge is extremely interesting, following more closely that of the sedge, or caddis, than upwinged flies. Both have three stages in the water – egg, larva and pupa – and a final stage where the complete adult fly emerges from the surface of the water and takes to the wing. Unlike upwinged flies, there is no secondary stage of development after the fly has left the water. The midge in its larval stage is a worm living mainly in the mud of still or slow-moving water; one example is the bloodworm. It is in the next stage, the pupa, that they are commonly known as buzzers. Fishing the buzzer has become of major importance to fly fishers, particularly as the value of the midge as a major food source has become better understood and appreciated. It is fished in various ways – as a sunk fly, an example of which is the simple epoxy buzzer, as a suspended fly (CDC buzzer or polystyrene ball buzzer), or as the emerging

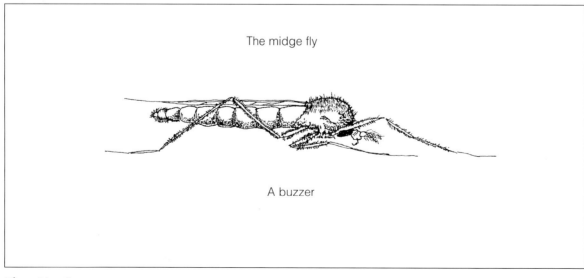

The midge fly

A buzzer

The midge fly.

fly. All are effective. The insect is also imitated in its larva form and a good example of this would be Arthur Cove's phenomenally successful Rubber Band Fly.

It has long been recognised that the midge is of great importance to the fly fisher on still waters. What is often underestimated is their importance on rivers and streams. Admittedly medium to fast-flowing water provides very little suitable habitat to support midges, but there are few river systems that do not have slower-moving water or backwaters where muddy bottoms can support the larvae. Wherever you find suitable water, no matter how little, you will find the midge. It is one of the greater opportunists, which is why it is so numerous; any amount of water seems to do. It has never been the glamorous fly of fly fishing; the beauty of the mayflies, olives and sedges often made it the wallflower of the bug ball. And the great strides in the development of fly fishing over the last 120 years, to a great extent initially ignored the humble midge. This was probably more to do with the fact that the greatest influences tended to be based around the southern English chalk streams. But times change and these days the

necessity of being able to imitate and fish the buzzer is well recognised. What the buzzer lacks in panache, it more than makes up for in its effectiveness when fished.

The earliest reference that I can find to what we today refer to as a buzzer, is in a book first published in 1913. It was written by a remarkable angler Dr J. C. Mottram, and bears the title *Fly Fishing: Some New Arts and Mysteries*. It is one of the most fascinating books I have ever read on fishing. It contains many items of note, some of which, in hindsight, are a little dubious in their accuracy. There is, however, much in it to interest the fly fisherman of today. Dr Mottram was well acquainted with what he refers to as the 'pupa of the Diptera' and he was well able to turn this familiarity, gained through observation of the insect, into a practical approach for fly fishing. His ability to design an artificial fly to imitate the buzzer is quite clear in line drawings. There is no doubt that his pattern would not be out of place in a modern fly box; it is well thought out and constructed, the result of a very careful approach. Mottram's ability is even more apparent when you consider he anticipated the modern buzzer by nearly sixty years. The use of

A sinking epoxy buzzer.

Arthur Cove's successful Rubber Band Fly.

Type	Hook	Body Colour	Rib	Thorax	Hackle
Red Midge	12	Dark Red	Brown	Orange/Red	Ginger
Green Midge	10–12	Dark Green	Brown	Light Brown/Green	Light Blue Dun
Grey Midge	12	Silver	Red	Dark Brown	Medium Blue Dun
Olive Midge	12	Olive	Cream	Olive	Light Blue Dun
Black Midge	12–14	Black	Silver	Black	Medium Blue Dun
Brown Midge	14–16	Dark Brown	Orange	Dark Brown	Medium Blue Dun

cork as the body base and emu feather fibres for breathers produced a fly which not only imitated the natural insect, but performed exactly as intended, a fine example of what I referred to as the holistic approach to fly tying.

There is a very strong case for many of the old traditional wet flies, intentionally or unintentionally, closely imitating midge flies. The old Scots pattern Blae and Black and many of the simple spider patterns cannot help but fairly accurately imitate the midge pupa.

When tying buzzer patterns using the Paraloop Method, there are two moments in the life cycle of the insect that I like to imitate. The first is the pupa sitting upright, under the surface of the water, and the second is the hatching or emerging fly. It could be argued that the emerging midge should be included in chapter 6, but buzzers play such an important role in providing food for trout, they definitely deserve a chapter of their own.

One of the convenient factors in buzzer fishing is that it can almost be brought down to the art of colour selection. Green, olive, brown, red and black are all shades of buzzer. If you can find out which colour of midges are hatching, then you can easily imitate the fly by choosing the appropriate colour. The only other consideration is size. Get the colour and the size right and you will be imitating the correct fly, whichever pattern you choose. Identifying which buzzer the trout are feeding on is not always easy unless you can find a specimen or two. If it is unclear what colour of buzzer the fish are feeding on, then use a multiple-fly cast, one fly on the point and two tied on small droppers coming off the main leader. Using three different-coloured and -sized buzzers can quickly establish which fly the trout currently favour.

The different patterns in this chapter can be used to tie all the different types of buzzers. As I have said all you need to change is the colour and size of hook. It is often the impression that buzzer fishing always uses small flies. This is not the case and many of the flies need to be tied on size 12 and even 10. The table above gives a very general guide to the size and colours used when tying the buzzer Paraloop-style.

There are many more midges than those listed above, but these are the ones I am personally familiar with; they also cover the majority of fishing situations I come across. It may be that where you fish there is a fly not covered by the above; if so, then note the size and colours and tie accordingly. Buzzer fishing is fun and the recognition of what particular colour or size of fly the trout currently prefer is part of that fun.

Tying the Olive Buzzer Pupa

The first fly I would like to use as an example of tying the Paraloop buzzer pupa is the Olive Midge. This buzzer is normally quite large and it can be tied on a size 12 hook. The fly is designed to sit in the water surface, with just a little showing above. The fly is also designed to sit down vertically in the water, rather than horizontally. This position can be seen clearly in the photograph of the fly viewed from under the water. This is similar to the angle of the natural fly pupa prior to entering into emerging mode, and is one of those times when it is particularly vulnerable to fish.

This fly could be classified as a suspender buzzer. If you take the time to watch midge pupae in the water it will soon become apparent that they act in a very specific way. Before entering emerging mode, the insect will often move up and down in the water, suspending itself in the water surface by its tail end. This is the position in which it spends most of its time when suspended in the water surface. When it comes to the actual emergence, it turns, bringing the head section up to the surface. It is from this position that the fly emerges. It could therefore be argued that the numerous patterns of suspender buzzers are inaccurate, the head more accurately should be tied at the hook bend end of the fly and the tail at the hook eye end. This can be done using either CDC or polypropylene as breathers. I have, however, fished the suspender buzzer tied both ways and have found absolutely no difference in the number of takes or successful hook-ups. Therefore I make no rec-

ommendation about which way the buzzer is tied; head up or head down, it appears to make no difference to the trout.

Materials

hook: Kamasan B100 size 12
thread: 8/0, own choice
body: olive rayon floss
hackle: small fibre light blue dun
rib: cream floss waxed
post: GSP floss
thorax: polypropylene dubbing olive Fly-Rite #10 or #34 and coloured foam

The buzzer, a midge pupa, is designed to float vertically in the water to imitate the natural fly more closely.

Tying the Olive Buzzer Pupa

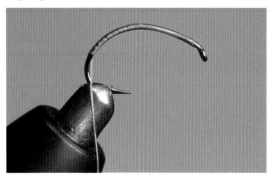 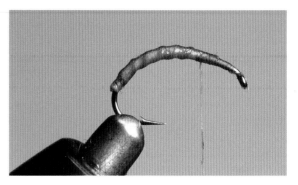

1. Fix the hook in the vice and test it for soundness. Offer the waxed thread to the hook and wind it flat to halfway around the hook bend. If an indicator is required, wind the thread to a point one-third of the way along the hook shank, then wind it back towards the hook eye and tie in a small bunch of the white polypropylene floss. Using the loose-loop/pinch-and-loop method (4/5), tie in the floss onto the top of the hook shank directly behind the hook eye. Return the thread to halfway round the hook bend, cutting off any excess floss. I do not include a floss indicator in the example.

2. Tie in the cream floss, immediately followed by the olive floss under the hook shank (4/11). Wind the thread, continuing to tie in the two flosses under the shank, back to a point beyond the halfway point on the hook shank, cutting off the excess floss, if any, along the way. Wind on the olive floss up to the thread and form a slightly tapered body (4/10), tying it in under the hook shank. Return the thread to where the body begins. The olive floss is best wound flat. Now wind the cream floss over the body as a rib, making five or six turns and again tie it in under the hook shank. Cut off the excess floss. Do not wind the rib on flat, but tighten up the twists.

3. It can be beneficial at this time to varnish the body and to allow it to dry. In the photograph I have varnished the body. This makes the fly more durable but more importantly it allows the rear of the fly to cut through the surface of the water efficiently. This makes the fly sit in the water in a vertical manner, as it was designed to do. If you are tying a few flies, it is tedious to have to wait for the varnish to dry. There are two options. The first is to lock the thread with half hitches, cut it off and remove the semi-tied hook from the vice. When you have tied all the bodies required, varnish each one, allow the first coat to dry then varnish again. When they are dry reintroduce the bodied hooks to the vice, reconnect the thread and continue tying. The other option is to wait until the fly is finished and then varnish the body. But there is always the chance that materials added later will get in the way, so I seldom use this method.

4. Tie in the floss post at this point, loose fibres to hook eye, loop end over the hook bend. Cut off any excess floss and return the thread to the base of the post. Cut a small diamond shape out of a foam sheet (4/13). I normally use white sheet previously coloured using permanent ink pens. Tie in one of the long ends of the foam, directly in front of the floss post. If it is coloured, tie in with the coloured side facing down. Place the post loop into the hook of the gallows tool. Attach the hackle at the base of the hook. The fibres on the hackle must be smaller than those normally used, e.g. size 12 hook = size 14 or 16 hackle. Wind the hackle up the post, for a distance equal to that from the post to the hook eye. Then wind back down again, making a few turns of thread around the hackle end and the hook shank. Pull the hackle brush and post back to help give access to the hook shank. This now forms the hackle brush. Unhook the gallows tool and attach the neck-breaker.

5. Complete tying in the hackle, cut off any excess and return the thread to the post. Wax the thread and dub it with the polypropylene dubbing for the thorax. Wind on the dubbed thread, forming a shaped thorax, wider in the middle, narrower at each end. Remember to leave plenty of space behind the hook eye. Pull the foam over the thorax area and tie in behind the hook eye, cutting off any excess foam. Now unhook the neck breaker, reattach the gallows tool, and compact and slightly double the hackle brush (4/2). Pull the hackle brush over the foam and tie it in behind the hook eye.

6. Cut off any excess floss, form a small head and complete with a whip finish. The foam can be coloured if required. That completes the tying of the Olive Buzzer Pupa. If an indicator is included then it is always best to use a down-eyed hook, as the indicator covers the hook eye and makes it difficult to tie onto the leader.

Tying the Brown Midge Emerger

Another stage of the buzzer's development that can be fairly accurately imitated is the emerging midge. The techniques described in chapter 6 can be applied. To illustrate the tying of an emerging midge, a Brown Midge is used as an example. The hook is different from that used in the tying of the midge pupa; the emerging midge is tied so that it sits more towards the horizontal, in the surface of the water. The pattern is tied at the 'early' position using the open loop method (4/3) and imitates the fly well into the emergence sequence.

1. Place the hook in the vice and test it for soundness. Attach the thread to the hook and wind it in flat turns (4/12) to around the hook bend. Tie in the Antron tail using the loose-loop/pinch-and-loop method (4/10). The tail should be about ¼ in (0.5 cm) long. Tie in the bright orange thread rib (I have used Gudebrod 6/0 BCS77, but a good alternative would be Globrite), followed by the brown polypropylene body floss (4/11). Wind it to the halfway point on the hook shank, tying in the Antron floss on the top of the hook shank and

the rib and body floss on the underside. Cut off any excess material before reaching the point where the body starts. Wind the brown floss in flat turns to the halfway point on the hook shank, and form a slightly shaped body (4/10). Tie the floss in under the hook shank. Now wind on the thread rib, making six turns around the body and again tying it in under the hook shank. Cut off any excess material.

2. If you wish, you can now varnish the fly body, although this can be time-consuming and is probably better left until the fly is completed or done as described in the tying of the Olive Buzzer. For illustrative purposes I have varnished the body with two coats of quick-drying varnish. If you choose to varnish now, have a cup of tea and prepare the hackle-tip wings whilst the varnish is drying.

3. Take the thread to directly behind the hook eye and tie in the prepared light blue dun hackle-point wings. Leave a small section of the prepared stalk showing at the base of the wings when tying them in. Now return the thread to the body start position, cutting off the excess hackle stalks as you go. Tie in the post loop with the loose ends pointing towards the hook eye, cutting off any excess material as you do so.

4. Return the thread to the base of the post and attach the post to the gallows tool. Tie in the prepared medium blue dun hackle at the base of the post. Cut off any excess hackle stalk and return the thread to the base of the post. Wind the hackle up the post for a distance in excess of that from the post to the hook eye (about half the distance again is perfect). Wind the hackle down through the previous windings and tie it in on the hook shank.

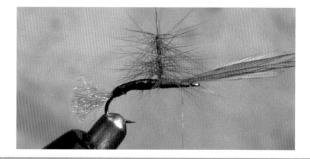

Materials

hook: Partridge Oliver Edwards nymph/emerger
size 14
thread; 8/0 own choice
body: brown polypropylene floss
hackle: medium blue dun cock

wing: light blue dun cock
rib: bright orange thread
tail/shuck: cream Antron floss
post: GSP floss
thorax: brown and orange (or Fly-Rite #30 or #36)
polypropylene dubbing

5. Remove the post from the gallows tool and attach the neck breaker. Complete the tying in of the hackle, cutting off the excess as you go. Return the thread to the base of the post. Wax and dub the thread with the polypropylene dubbing. Wind the dubbed thread to form a shaped thorax, leaving enough space behind where the hackle tips have been tied in to form a small head.

6. Without compacting or doubling, pull the hackle brush over the thorax and tie it in behind the hackle-tip wings. Cut off the excess floss from the post.

7. Now pull the wings backwards over where the hackle brush has been tied in. Bring the thread in front of the wings and make a few turns to set the wings into the correct position. Form a small head and complete the fly with a whip finish.

8. The position of the wings after they have been set into position.

The fly is designed to imitate the natural as it struggles out of the nymphal sac, so the hackle imitates the actual fly, with the body imitating an extension of the shuck.

Locked Wing

I sometimes add an additional form of wing, which I refer to as the 'locked wing'. To tie the fly using this wing the following instructions should be followed, using the same materials.

1. Take the thread down to the end of the body position around the hook bend and tie in the shuck, followed by the rib and body material.
2. Wind the body material to where the post will be tied in, form a shaped body and tie it in under the hook shank. Then wind on the rib using six turns. Tie in the rib and cut off any excess.
3. Tie in two light blue dun cock hackles by the tips, stalks facing back over the hook bend, on either side of the post and on each side of the hook shank, good sides out. Do not be concerned about tying in too many fibres, tie in the tips exactly as the hackles come off the cape. Then tie in the post, attaching it to the gallows tool.
4. Tie in the medium blue dun hackle at the base of the post as per normal. Wind up and down to form the hackle brush. Tie it in on the hook shank.

5. Unhook the post from the gallows tool and attach the neck breaker, and then complete the tying in of the hackle, cutting off any excess. Dub the hook shank with polypropylene dubbing and pull the hackle brush over, using the 'open loop' method (4/3). Tie it in behind the hook eye, leaving plenty of room to tie in the remaining materials.
6. Bring both of the blue dun hackles over the hackle brush angled out to each side, remove any excess fibres and tie them in behind the hook eye. Cut off any excess.
7. Form a small head and complete with a whip finish.

I often fish either the pupa or emerger midge as a bob fly, that is as the top fly in a two- or three-fly cast, the one nearest the fly line. In conjunction with one or two sinking buzzer patterns, it can be a highly effective method of seeking out fish. The Paraloop pupa or emerger not only acts as a fly in its own right, but also as a bite indicator for when a fish takes the sunk fly. Very simple epoxy buzzer flies are ideal for providing the sinking buzzers of this set-up. The method covers a lot of water very quickly and efficiently.

A locked wing Brown Midge Emerger.

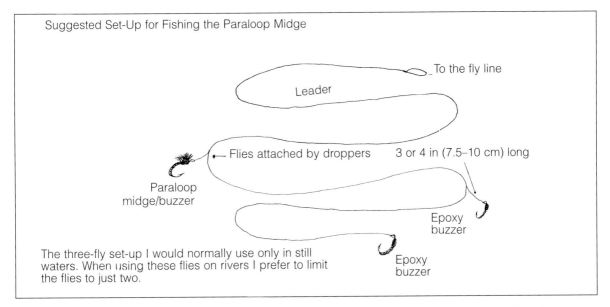

Suggested Set-Up for Fishing the Paraloop Midge

To the fly line

Leader

Flies attached by droppers   3 or 4 in (7.5–10 cm) long

Paraloop
midge/buzzer

Epoxy
buzzer

The three-fly set-up I would normally use only in still
waters. When using these flies on rivers I prefer to limit
the flies to just two.

Epoxy
buzzer

In still waters just let the flies drift with the wind or in the minor currents most still waters have. Only retrieve line to stay in touch with the flies. When fishing a river I would normally only use these flies in the deep, slow-moving waters, especially where the bottom is muddy. A pupa or emerger used with one single sinking buzzer is very effective. I would not usually use more than two flies in a river, owing to the high chance of getting caught up on a snag when fighting a fish, either on the point or dropper fly. I do know many very successful anglers who fish with a three- or four-fly cast when on the rivers and seem to have no problems, but having lost a few good fish due to snagging the other flies, I personally am extremely wary of using any more than two flies when fishing a river.

The flies in this chapter.

8 Tying Spent Winged Flies Using the Paraloop Method

The spent winged fly often appears to be the poor relation of artificial flies. Take a look in the fly boxes of any number of fly fishermen and you will find plenty of perky upright wings and straightforward hackled flies, but few, if any, tied with the wing imitating the spent spinner on the water. There are exceptions, of course. Some fly fishermen love the spent spinners and understand the importance of these imitations when fishing for trout, and you will find the fly boxes of these anglers filled with many different patterns imitating this important stage in the life cycle of the upwinged fly. The angler who uses the spent fly pattern knows about the enthusiasm with which fish feed on them. In recent years the spent winged fly seems to have lost out in the popularity stakes to the emerging fly. This is a mistake as they both provide excellent opportunities. There is little point in fishing the

spent fly if the only flies that are on the water are emergers, and the reverse applies if spent flies are predominant. It is a case of 'horses for courses'; use what is right at the right time. Not fishing the spent fly is truly a lost chance; it is the one time the fly is on the water going nowhere, it would appear that the trout know it.

I described two methods for imitating spent winged flies. The first has been covered when describing the Lunn's Particular in chapter 5. In the case of these flies the wing can be set at any desired angle from upright to spent. It provides an excellent spent winged fly and personally, I would not be without a few in my own fly boxes. The second method is the one covered by this chapter. From a technical fly-tying point of view it could be viewed as the more important, offering as it does a viable alternative to any other method. I have been using it for nearly three

An upwinged fly.

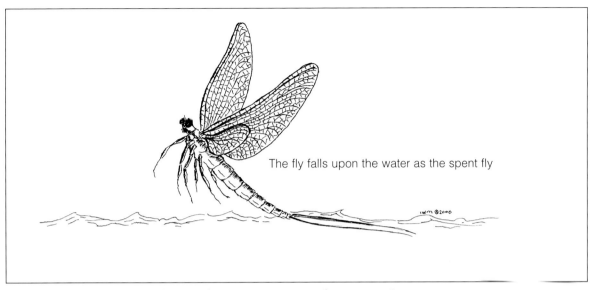

The fly falls upon the water as the spent fly

After mating and depositing the eggs the spinner falls upon the water to die.

years and find uses for it which go far beyond the tying of spent winged flies.

The technique is an adaptation of a few other techniques regularly used by fly tyers, brought together to create what could be a new style of fly. I have never seen the method before, nor have I seen flies tied this way. I expect that the publication of this book will lead a few anglers to inform me that they have been using the method for years. If this is so, I look forward to seeing how the technique has developed in their hands. The following is a description of my own development of the method. The basic technique is very simple. I find, however, that it is in the completion of the detail that the best results are obtained. The compacting (4/1) and doubling (4/2) of the hackle brush are essential when using this technique. In both cases there is little subtlety in their application; they are both taken to the extreme.

When tying any artificial fly intended to directly imitate a specific natural one and, sometimes more importantly, a particular stage in its life cycle, it is necessary to understand exactly what it is that is being imitated. In the case of spent winged flies, we should be fully aware of what the spent winged artificial fly is imitating and when it is best to fish with it. Not all flies become spent winged. This particular stage in the life cycle is limited to the upwinged flies and

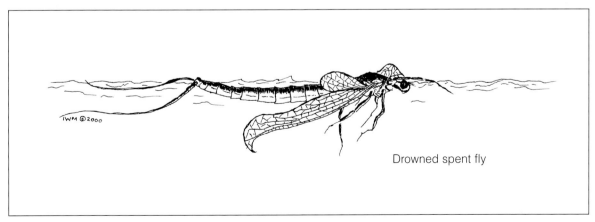

Drowned spent fly

The drowned or drowning spent upwinged spinner.

then only certain members of that large family. Upwinged flies are referred to in scientific circles as Ephemeroptera. These include such favourites of fly fishers as the mayflies, the March brown, olives and caenis (angler's curse), amongst many others, although not all flies in this order become spent winged and of interest to the fly fisher.

The spent winged spinner is the dying fly, usually the female but not always. Its life cycle is complete, mating and egg laying has been fulfilled. The fly falls upon the surface of the water, the wings outstretched, and it becomes easy pickings for trout. It is this factor of 'easy pickings' that makes the spent fly so attractive to fish. In all predators there is a balance between the effort required to obtain sustenance and its food value. If the effort is too great for the nutrition received, then there is little point in attempting to obtain the food. It is this factor that makes the spent fly so attractive. At all other stages of the life cycle of the fly, the insect is instinctively doing its best to avoid being eaten, and is therefore moving as quickly as it can. Even when

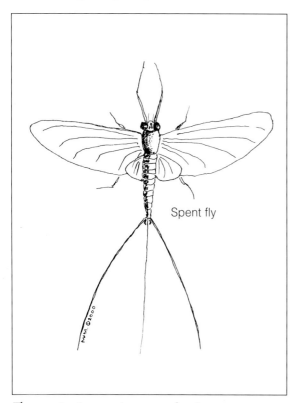

The spent spinner, wings spread out.

going through the procedure of emergence, the process at its best takes just a moment. The spent fly is exactly what it says: spent, finished, dying or dead. It is going nowhere, except maybe downstream with the flow of the water. Fish therefore need to spend little energy to enjoy a feast of spent winged flies, as compared to the other stages of the life cycle.

This is the time when the fish have easy access to the adult flies. The only other times the fish have access to adult upwinged flies is when the female dips the water to lay the eggs, when the adult fly actually emerges and when certain flies climb down under the water, using objects like fence posts to lay their eggs. The spent fly presents the trout with a food opportunity requiring the least expenditure of energy, as can often be seen in the leisurely way trout graze the water surface, feasting on the dying or dead insect. There are times when, after a large hatch of flies, the water is covered in spent flies, and in still or slow-moving water, the fish cruise around sucking down dead and dying insects. In faster-flowing water they will normally let the current bring the spent flies to them.

The spent fly can be imitated in sizes from the tiny caenis right up to the real mayfly. These would involved a hook size ranging from about size 26 to size 8. When tying Paraloops the smallest hook I normally use is size 18. Tying Paraloops smaller than that does not seem to be advantageous. It is doubtful whether the technique makes very much difference and I believe that other methods are less complex and just as effective. Having said that, there are some fly tyers and fly fishers I know of who tie Paraloop flies down to size 22.

When tying spent winged flies using the Paraloop Method, the fly sits very low in the actual skin of the water. This imitates the profile of the real fly far more accurately than a traditionally hackled fly, which would remain off the water. Even if it is partially sunk, the wing profile is lost to a great extent within the hackle.

The Fly Fishing Club in London has as its motto, 'There is more to fishing than catching fish' and for many anglers this is true. I am sorry for those anglers who find little or no satisfaction in a careful and considered pursuit of fish, whether or not it results in capture. The chattering parrot of the mind separates them from what is going on around them. The ability of a fisherman to step into and become an integral part of his surroundings is one of the very great gifts fly fishing has to offer, perhaps the greatest. As I said the last chapter I was recently reading a wonderful book on fly fishing written in 1913 called *Fly Fishing: Some New Arts and Mysteries*. The author Dr Mottram, had some very innovative ideas, and if you think the way you fish is new, then have a look at this book and you may have to think again. Mottram was designing flies in the earlier part of the last century that would not be out of place in the modern angler's fly box. His buzzer imitation is as good as any

Spinners in flight

Spinners in flight prior to mating – a wonderful sight on summer days.

available today and has inspired me to tie similar patterns, all of which have proved very effective.

In one of the chapters Mottram describes his experiences in New Zealand. I must admit to having a chuckle when I read that he did not consider the New Zealanders to be fly fishers, albeit the local fishermen used the same tackle and tied flies on the end of their leaders. To be classified as fly fishing, Mottram believed, the angler must be imitating actual insects upon the water. My chuckling was due to a vision of what Mottram would make of fly fishing today, not only in New Zealand but throughout the world. And although I do not entirely agree with his views, I do sympathise. The eyes to see the life around the water and how it affects the fish, and the ability to respond accordingly are amongst the skills of the fly fisher. The decisions, such as choice of fly, made as a result of such observations, give a greater satisfaction than just choosing any old fly which comes to hand and hoping for the best. That is not to say every fly fisher needs to become an expert entomologist – in fact it can be an impediment. The trout will take or refuse a March brown with as much panache as it will a *Rhithrogena germanica*; Latin and English were never part of its education. But a general understanding will pay dividends and add greatly to the pleasure experienced. To be able to recognise when the fish is feeding on the spent fly and to pick a suitable imitation is a part of this knowledge and understanding.

The sight of adult spinners weaving their flight upwards and downwards, as if to some unheard music has always fascinated me, and I can spend hours watching and checking to see what flies they may be. My partner Nina has had to put up with this fascination when we walk along our local riverbank for many years, and if not exactly encouraging, she is at least tolerant. The numbers of flies involved can at times be awesome. Even today, when we are told that numbers are much reduced compared to yesteryear, the air can at times be thick with their flight. As the flies return to the water to lay their eggs, they die and the water can at times appear pebble-dashed with the dead and dying insects. Soon a trout will rise, then two, then three, until it appears that every inch of water is broken with the rings of rising fish. Where have all the fish come from? Earlier that day the water seemed empty of all but a few conspicuous and nervous trout. Both the spent and the emerging fly have the power to awaken in trout this almost frenzied instinct to feed.

When tying a spent winged fly using the method in this chapter it is advisable to choose a hackle with fibres that are longer than those normally chosen for a particular hook size, and that are stiff and springy. The hackles chosen for parachute flies will often be suitable and those taken from a neck cape are better than those from a saddle. Spade hackles will often provide a suitable feather, but I find that one of the large feathers from the lower end of the cape can provide the ideal hackle. The web must be very narrow if these feathers are used, and the fibres stiff. The reason for this is that the hackle fibres themselves form the spent wing and therefore must be of a suitable length.

The technique effectively changes the Paraloop hackle into a left and right wing and in doing so makes the fly non-hackled. To counteract the lack of a hackle it is important that the fly is tied using floating materials. The hook choice is important in that it must be light; the Partridge Captain Hamilton fine wire dry fly hook is ideal, adding the minimum amount of weight to the fly. The tail should be tied with two or three tails, depending on the fly being imitated. Any suitable material can be used to form the tails, but my preferred choice is micro fibbets. They are light, very strong and do not absorb water to any degree. The strength of the micro fibbets is especially important when tying the tail long; it can be a little disheartening to tie a fly carefully with two or three carefully positioned tails, only to find that, after a few casts, it only has one left intact. Micro fibbets eliminate this problem.

Most of the procedures used when tying the spent winged fly Paraloop style are similar to the previous tyings, but there is an additional element. Before the post is tied in and in a position directly behind (hook bend side) where the post will be tied in, another material is added. This is usually polypropylene or foam, but sometimes I use feather fibres. Originally all my tyings of this fly used feather fibres, but the floatability of polypropylene and foam is better.

As I have said, compacting the hackle is very important and in addition it should be wound up and down the post in close turns, closer than normal. Of no less importance is doubling the hackle brush. This is one of the few times that doubling the fly excessively will benefit the overall tying. In fact the best result can be obtained if the hackle brush is doubled from both sides. There are many flies that can be imitated using this technique; in fact it can be used for any spent winged fly. Changing the colours, the hook size and the number of tails will cover all the flies required.

Tying the Detached Body Spent Winged Sherry Spinner

My first example is the Sherry Spinner, *Ephemerella ignita*. This is a fairly large fly and it can be tied on a large hook – a size 12 is not too big. This example, however, uses a detached body and so a smaller hook is being used, a size 14. This reduces the weight of the fly and maximises the amount of floatable material included. The sherry spinner is the female of the blue-winged olive (BWO) that most loved and prolific of olives. The sherry red colour, from which its name is derived, varies considerably, even within the same area, from fairly pale to a bright red. When tying the body I mix a red claret thread into a fine brown polypropylene dubbing. When twisted and allowed to twist back on itself (4/9), it produces a very realistic mottled effect. If more red is required then double up the thread before twisting.

Materials

 hook: size 14 Partridge Captain Hamilton dry fly fine wire
 thread: 8/0, own choice
 body: light brown polypropylene floss with red thread (furled)
 hackle: blue dun cock
 tail: dark dun or brown micro fibbets
 post: white GSP fine floss (6 in – 15 cm)
 thorax: fine rusty or brown polypropylene dubbing mixed (or Fly-Rite #28)
 thorax cover: foam sheet; colour on one side using permanent marker pens, first with brown and after drying, red

1. First it is necessary to create the detached body. In this case, take the polypropylene floss, I have used Tiemco Aero Wing; a piece approximately 8 in (20 cm) long is more than enough. Then take a piece of red tying thread, preferably polyester or polypropylene, the same length as the floss, and lay both materials together. Then follow the procedure described in chapter 4, section 9. The result of twisting the floss and thread will be a mixed red and brown tapered body, when it is allowed to twist back on itself. In this tying I prefer to take this procedure a little further, which is why the longer length of floss is recommended. After completing the initial twisting of the materials and forming what is normally used to supply the detached body, repeat the exercise again, following the existing twist in the materials. The materials will twist back on themselves again, forming a more compact and stronger body. Effectively the procedure has been repeated, doubling up on the materials contained in the detached body. The inclusion of the red thread adds a mottled effect.

It is optional, but if you wish to add tails then now is the time. Separate three micro fibbets from the bunch and cut them off using scissors near the base, keeping the tips level. Sometimes micro fibbets can be pulled away easily from the base that holds them together; do not do this, use scissors to remove them as this makes it easier to thread them into the eye of a needle. Feed the fibbets, cut end, into the eye of a fine wire needle, which is far easier to do than to explain. If the fibbets have been cut off together they will normally stay together and go through the eye together. When they are through the eye, push just over ¼ in (0.5 cm) through and twist them back from the needle.

Now feed the needle from the top of the tail through the detached body. It is not necessary to be too careful, and you can push the body over the needle. Leave enough of the fibbets outside the body to give the required tail length. If the body has been formed correctly it will resume its correct shape, after the needle has been removed. Remove the fibbets from the needle and place the completed body somewhere safe.

Place the hook in the jaws of the vice and test it for soundness. Wax the thread and wind it to the halfway position along the hook shank. Take the detached body and offer it to the top of the hook shank at the thread position. The body length should be at least twice the distance that the thread has been wound along the hook shank and no more than one and a half times the length of the total hook shank. Using the loose-loop/pinch-and-loop method (4/5), tie in the body and the ends of the tail fibres on the top of the hook shank, using ten turns of touching flat thread moving towards the hook eye. Keep the materials on the top of the hook shank.

2. Cut off the excess body material and return the thread to where the body was first tied in. Cut the foam into a small diamond shape and colour the edges the same as the top. Offer the foam to the hook and tie it in, coloured side down, at the point where the body was tied in, using three or four turns of thread. Return the thread to where the foam was first tied in and tie in the post. There should not be any space between the body-foam and the post. Complete the tying in of the post and return the thread to its base, having cut off any excess floss on the way. Attach the post to the gallows tool.

3. Choose a hackle with long, stiff fibres. Ideally the length of the fibres should be equal to the length of the hook. Prepare and tie in the hackle at the base of the post. Wind it up and down the post in closer than normal turns, forming the hackle brush. Tie it off as usual, unhook the gallows tool and attach the neck breaker. Finish tying in the hackle, cut off any excess and return the thread to the post.

4. Wax and dub the thread with the polypropylene dubbing. Wind it on to form a shaped thorax, leaving enough space behind the eye to tie in the remaining materials and to form a small head. Unhook the neck breaker and reattach the gallows tool to the post loop.

5. Compact the hackle brush (4/1), making sure the height above the hook shank is reduced to less than the distance from the hook eye to the post, less enough room to tie in the additional materials. This usually makes the hackle brush height about three-quarters of the distance from the eye to the post.

6. Double the hackle brush (4/2), to the extent that the side facing the hook eye is mainly placed to the opposite side of the hackle brush, as in the photograph.

7. Place the tip of the first finger of your right hand (left hand if left-handed) against the doubled hackle brush, as in the photograph. Now double the hackle in the opposite direction, bringing the fibres towards the hook eye against your finger. This forms a predominantly flat hackle brush, crossing the hook shank.

8. Pull the flattened hackle brush over the thorax and tie it in behind the eye, leaving enough space to tie in the foam and form a small head. Cut off the excess GSP floss.

There you have the Sherry Spinner Paraloop-style. This fly uses the Paraloop hackle in a completely different way from all the other tyings in this book and which lends itself to future development. The fly will not sink and after a fish has been taken, it can be washed down, removing any slime. After a couple of false casts to dry the hackle, hey presto, you can fish it again!

9. Pull the foam over the hackle brush to form a thorax, and tie it in behind the hook eye. Pull the excess foam tight and cut off the excess. Form a small head, tying in any loose ends of foam, and complete with a whip finish. Pulling the fibres into place and then pressing them between your fingers will alter the angle of the wings. I prefer the wings to sit slightly angled downwards as this presents a particularly attractive profile on the water. It is also the way the hackle sits naturally when tied in without any adjustments. Put a drop of superglue on the end of the body to hold the tails in place. As the glue dries hold the outer tails in a suitable V shape. This procedure is normally sufficient to fix the tails in the desired position.

Tying the Spent Winged Blue Winged Olive

As I have said, it is not necessary to use foam for the thorax cover, although it does provide an excellent profile and obviously maintains the floatability of the fly. Other materials can be used, including floss, feather slips and plastic film; the options are only limited by our imaginations. The next pattern, which demonstrates the technique, uses floss for the thorax cover. The fly being imitated is the male of the sherry spinner, the blue-winged olive spinner. The imitation uses a conventional body and tail. As many of the techniques used in tying this fly have been included in other patterns, the tying sequence

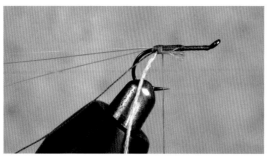

1. Set the hook in the vice jaws and test it for soundness. Wax the thread and wind it to the start of the bend on the hook shank. Tie in the three micro fibbets using the loose-loop/pinch-and-loop method (4/5) and then the thread loop method of splitting the tails (4/4). Tie in a piece of bright orange thread (8 in – 20 cm – is enough), followed by the cream floss (4/11).

2. Wind the thread to the halfway position on the hook shank, tying in the fibbets, floss and orange thread as you go. The fibbets should be tied in on the top of the hook shank and the floss and thread on the underside. Cut off the excess materials. Wind the floss flat, forming a shaped body, and tie it off on the underside of the hook shank. Now wax the orange thread and dub it very lightly with the brown and olive polypropylene dubbing (4/7).

3. Wind the dubbed thread to the other end of the body, allowing the cream floss to show through. This is like winding a very close rib. Tie it in on the underside of the hook shank, cut off the excess dubbed thread and return the thread to the start of the body.

4. Tie in the brown polypropylene floss, which will be used to pull over the hackle brush; the short end of the floss should be facing the hook eye. Make one or two turns of thread to hold it in position and then add the post loop. Tie both materials in tightly, cutting off any excess as you go. Return the thread to the base of the post.

will only detail those areas not previously covered.

Materials

hook: size 14 Partridge Captain Hamilton dry fly fine wire
thread: 8/0, own choice
body: cream polypropylene floss underbody; thread lightly dubbed with orange, brown and olive polypropylene dubbing
hackle: medium blue dun cock
tail: three dark dun or brown micro fibbets
post: GSP fine floss (6 in – 15 cm)
thorax: brown polypropylene dubbing (Fly-Rite #20)
thorax cover: brown polypropylene floss (2 in – 5 cm), Tiemco Aero Dry Wing

5. Attach the post to the gallows tool and tie the prepared medium blue dun hackle in at the base. Wind the hackle up the post for a distance equal to that from the post to the hook eye. Then wind it down, working it through the fibres from the previous windings. Tie it onto the hook shank.

6. Remove the post from the gallows tool and attach the neck breaker. Complete the tying in of the hackle, removing the excess, and return the thread to the base of the post. Wax and dub the thread with the thorax dubbing and form a shaped thorax. Make sure enough space is available behind the hook eye to tie in the remaining materials and form a small head. Remove the hackle brush from the neck breaker and reattach the gallows tool. Compact the hackle to the maximum (4/1) and double it (4/2), as in the tying of the Sherry Spinner, from both sides of the hackle brush. Pull the hackle brush over the thorax and tie it in behind the hook eye, leaving sufficient room to tie in the thorax cover and form a small head. Cut off the excess floss post. Pull the brown polypropylene floss over the hackle brush and tie it in behind the hook eye. Cut off the excess floss. Form a small head and complete with a whip finish. The flat floss used to pull over the top of the hackle brush splits to either side of the tied in post. This pushes the fibres downward, producing a wonderful profile for a fly. This pattern and style of tying is one of my personal favourites and has proved highly effective when the spent spinners are on the water.

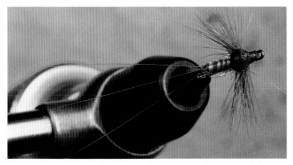

7. The effect of pulling the floss over the top of the hackle brush is shown clearly. The hackle fibres have been forced out and down, forming an excellent spent fly imitation.

8. The effect of the technique from a different angle, showing the downward slope of the hackle fibres.

Tying the Daddy-Long-Legs

Although the spent winged Paraloop Method is specifically designed for tying imitations of the dying spinner, the technique can be applied to other types of fly. One group for which the technique is eminently suitable is the crane-flies, also known as daddy-long-legs. These flies are blown onto the water in great numbers at some times of the year. Once on the water, they become victims of the surface tension, unable to break away from its grip. Trout can become accustomed to them as a relatively substantial source of food. When fishing using this fly, pick a bank where the prevailing wind blows it onto the water naturally; you can be sure that the fish will recognise them and takes can be sudden and quite violent.

One thing I have noticed when fishing the 'Daddy' is that fish will often attempt to drown the fly prior to taking. If you find that you keep getting takes but fail to hook the fish, or even sometimes foul-hook them, then it is quite likely that the fish are initially not taking the fly by the mouth. They are actually splashing onto the fly in an attempt to sink it. If this is the case, just leave the fly after the initial splash and the fish will come around with a genuine take. It can take a little self-discipline, but it will pay dividends.

Tying the fly with a detached body is very similar to tying the Sherry Spinner, the only differences being the omission of the fibbet tails, the use of different-coloured materials, and the inclusion of six knotted legs. When tying this pattern follow the instructions for tying the Sherry Spinner using the following materials, and when you come to

1. Prepare the six legs. Take a complete male pheasant tail feather, one that has equal-length fibres on either side of the stem. Separate three fibres on one side of the stem and using a basic overhand knot, place a knot in each fibre. This is done by having the good side of the feather facing you, bringing the end of one of the chosen fibres round in front of the main part of the fibre, then over the top and under through the loop formed, and pulling tight. This places an overhand knot in the fibre. Repeat for the remaining two fibres on one side and then the three fibres on the other side of the stem.

2. Complete the fly as explained in the description of the Sherry Spinner and, with the hackle brush placed in the neck breaker, wax and dub the thread with the thorax dubbing but only enough to complete one full turn around the hook shank. Make one turn of dubbing immediately in front of the post. Now take the three legs from the right-hand side of the pheasant tail and cut them off the stalk using scissors; do the same with those from the left side. Place the cut ends from the right-side fibres together and offer them to the hook in front of the single turn of dubbing and on the side of the hook shank facing you. Make one turn of thread to hold them in position. Repeat using the three fibres from the left side of the feather, offering them to the far side of the hook shank. The legs should be extended beyond the length of the detached body. Tie in the legs using flat thread and return the thread to the single turn of dubbed thread. Cut off any excess leg material.

the winding of the dubbing for the thorax follow the instructions given here.

The legs in this pattern are tied trailing. There seems to be a trend in photographs of crane-fly patterns in angling publications to have the legs splayed out as in the free and wandering fly, and very pretty they are too. When in, or on the water, however, the crane-fly is anything but free and wandering, in fact it is totally helpless, with the legs tending to trail backwards. It was Richard Walker who first noted this and his later crane-fly patterns all included trailing legs. I agree completely with his observations and tie the legs trailing in all my own patterns.

I am very aware that this chapter is dedicated to spent winged flies, but I would ask your indulgence for including the pattern for the Daddy-Long-Legs. The spent winged method is ideally suited to tying this fly and is so effective it would be a missed opportunity not to include it.

Materials

hook: size 12 Partridge Captain Hamilton dry fly fine wire
thread: 6/0 or 8/0, own choice
body: brown polypropylene floss with cream thread
hackle: blue dun, red cock or furnace
tail: none
post: white GSP fine floss (6 in – 15 cm)
thorax: fine brown polypropylene dubbing mixed (Fly-Rite #39)
thorax cover: foam sheet; colour on one side using permanent marker pens, brown
legs: six knotted male pheasant tail fibres, three from each side of the stem.

3. Dub the thread again and complete the fly as per the instruction for the Sherry Spinner. There you have the completed Daddy-Long-Legs Paraloop-style.

The Daddy-Long-Legs can be tied using other Paraloop methods; the hackle-point wing method works wonderfully. Just tie the legs in after the first turn of thorax dubbing. This allows the legs to splay out slightly from the body.

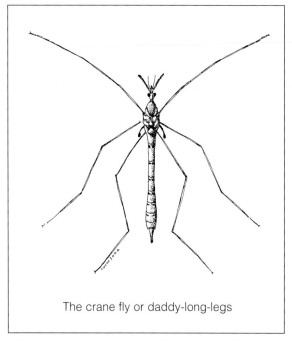

The crane fly or daddy-long-legs

The mayfly

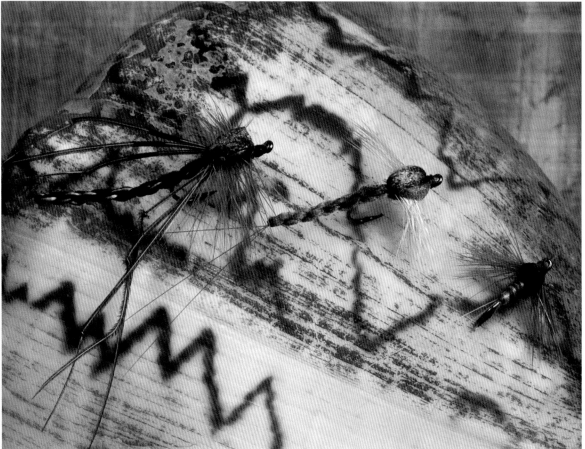

The flies in this chapter.

9 Tying Wet Flies Using the Paraloop Method

When I first started fly fishing it was with my converted 6 ft 6 in (2 m) solid fibre-glass spinning rod, centrepin reel and peelable plastic-coated, so-called level floating line. I had no idea whatsoever that there was such a thing as a wet fly. The only flies I had ever come across were all dry and I therefore assumed that fly fishing consisted only in presenting the adult fly to a rising fish. It cannot be said that my ignorance in any way reduced the pleasure I derived from the incompetent presentations I usually made – quite the opposite. I would have been happy to spend all my fishing days in the bliss of ignorance, profoundly happy with the few flies I kept in a matchbox or tobacco tin. Oh how times have changed – although in my heart of hearts I will probably always remain that young boy splashing his way through the shallows, cracking the fly off the line and occasionally, admittedly just occasionally, tempting a fish to take my fly.

All my flies had wings, simply because I liked the look of them. It made sense: the flies I was imitating had wings and so all my patterns had wings. In the end I became fairly successful at picking trout out of streams and rivers using the half dozen or so patterns that I was familiar with. My skills and knowledge of fly fishing were practically zero which, growing up in the part of the country I came from, was hardly surprising. I was the only fly fisher I knew, my little knowledge gleaned from Mr Crabtree. I must have been a strange sight, a twelve-year-old boy with this strange tackle casting little flies to the carp, roach and dace on the local ponds.

It was not until much later in my fly fishing life that I became aware of other fly patterns, patterns that did not float, in fact flies that did not imitate what I thought of as flies. I must admit to some initial confusion over this. It was quite some time before I was able to come to terms with the fact that when fly fishing, we do not always try to tempt the fish by imitating a fly. Over time I began to accept that I could use other types of what were known collectively as flies.

It was at this time that I was introduced to patterns such as lures, nymphs, shrimps, corixa, and traditional-style wet flies – in fact a whole brave new world of alternatives to the few patterns I had, up until that time, been conscious of. Now, if I wished, I had many new toys to play with when pursuing my sport. Some aspects of this new world did not appeal to my nature. Standing on the banks of some waterhole, casting and pulling back a miniature Christmas tree, in the hope that some recently stocked, pellet-overfed, denizen of the nets might grab my lure failed to fire me with any enthusiasm whatsoever, no matter how many fish there were to be caught, or how large. Fishing the nymph or wet fly on a moorland stream or lowland river was different, very different, and a whole new experience opened up for me. This has given me much pleasure over the years.

I am not a great lover of boat fishing; it is something I enjoy in small bites. But there are times when, given a wild Highland loch or Irish lough, a wind throwing up waves to rival the sea, a good solid boat and a skilled boatman, I have experienced an exhilaration in fishing the wet fly to compare with the best.

The Paraloop Method is not ideally suited to tying wet flies – or at least I have, as yet, only found one way in which it can be used to tie them successfully. It incorporates the open loop technique (4/3) and it creates a fly with a substantial amount of movement. The flies tied this way should be used as top droppers in teams of flies. The bushiness and movement make them perfect for dibbling through the surface of the water.

Tying the Bibio

The fly I have chosen as the example of this technique is the Bibio, because it is well known to most anglers who fish using the wet fly, and especially those who fish the lochs and loughs of Scotland and Ireland with a team of flies. Many an angler feels deprived if the Bibio is not one of the flies on his cast, and it is as popular today as it has ever been.

Materials

hook: Kamasan B110
thread: 8/0, own choice
body: black seal's fur front and rear, claret seal's

1. Fix the hook in the vice jaws and test it for soundness. Attach the thread and using flat turns wind it to the bend of the hook. Tie in the post, loose ends towards the hook eye, by winding the thread back along the shank and then back to the post. Cut off any excess floss if necessary. Attach the floss post to the gallows tool and tie in the prepared black cock hackle at the base. Wind the hackle up the post for a distance equal to the length of the hook shank and then half again. Now wind the hackle back down again. Tie in the hackle with three carefully positioned turns of thread. This will produce a particularly long hackle brush.

2. Unhook the post from the gallows tool and attach the neck breaker. Complete the tying in of the hackle and cut off the excess. Return the thread to the base of the post. Then tie in the rib on the underside of the hook shank.

3. Wax the thread and dub it, using the black seal's fur. Dub enough to be able to wind it short of the halfway position on the hook shank. Remove any excess black seal's fur dubbing and dub with the claret seal's fur. Wind the claret dubbed thread over the central section of the hook shank. Remove any excess claret dubbing and again dub the thread with the remaining black fur. Wind this towards the hook eye, leaving enough space to form a small head and tie in the remaining materials.

fur centre (or substitutes)
hackle: black cock
rib: silver tinsel
post: GSP

That completes the Bibio Paraloop-style, using the open loop technique. The open loop helps to create additional movement in the fly, especially when it is dibbled through the surface of the water. As with all Paraloop flies, the lack of material in front of the hook point assists in the solid hooking of fish.

This is the only Paraloop technique I can recommend for tying wet flies at present. It has been well used and has proved very successful. Sedges, midges and upwinged flies can all be imitated using this technique and I have found that, if it is allowed to swing round on a river or stream causing a wake, it will also bring fish to the fly.

4. Wind on the silver tinsel rib, tying it in behind the hook eye, and cut off any excess rib material.

5. Unhook the hackle brush from the neck breaker. Do not compress the hackle or double it in any way. Pull the released hackle brush over the dubbed body, forming an open loop (4/3) and tie it in behind the hook eye. Cut off the excess floss post, form a small head and complete with a whip finish. If you are in any-way sensitive about the colour of the head of the fly and you have used neutral-coloured thread, then you can colour the thread black, using a permanent ink pen, prior to completing the head.

The finished Bibio.

10 The Paraloop in the Hands of Others

As I have said, I originally thought that the Paraloop was my own invention, but it became clear fairly soon after I first started tying flies this way that this was not the case and that there was a whole wealth of knowledge and experience of the method. I could not find a tyer in the UK who could demonstrate a usable knowledge of the method, but in the USA there were quite a few. I am delighted to have had the opportunity to communicate with a few of these tyers, and have found their uses of the method, no matter what name they have for it, to be ingenious and inspirational. I am extremely honoured to have had the co-operation of two of them, Jim Cramer and John (Ned) Long, both of whom provided unique ways in which the Paraloop hackle can be used.

When I first started tying Paraloop flies I thought the technique was so useful that it merited being publicised. The most natural way of doing this is obviously to tell everyone you know who has a keen interest in fly tying. One of the first people I told was a young fly fisher and fly tyer living in Edinburgh called Brian Cornwall. Brian has a methodical approach to fly tying and he took to the technique with enthusiasm. He has also contributed a section, based on his own use of the method. He is, I am sure, one of those young tyers we will hear at lot more from in the future.

Jim Cramer

Jim was the first fly tyer I became aware of who used a form of the Paraloop Method in some of his tyings. It was Hans Weilenmann from the Netherlands who put me in contact with him. He has used what he calls the Pullover Method for

many years, and, although he admits he is not the originator of the method, he has added considerably to its usefulness. Jim does not use a gallows tool in his tyings because of his professed dislike of the tool and he does not wind the hackle back down through the up windings to form a hackle brush. He winds it up the post

Jim Cramer.

and then pulls the post and hackle over, tying both in at the same time. Using the Paraloop Method in this way dispenses with the need for a gallows tool. This is what Jim says:

My first attempts to tie a trout fly occurred in 1944 when I was nine years old. Living on a wheat farm in the Oklahoma panhandle put me about as far from the fly fishing fraternity as one could get. I had seen some of my great-uncle's snelled wet flies and my efforts to duplicate them consisted of tying chicken feathers to hooks with my mother's sewing threads and embroidery floss. I had no idea that a vice was used to hold the hook, or how they managed to have all those little legs on the finished fly! Two years later an uncle changed my life for ever with a fabulous gift of a fly tying kit and a book by George Herter. During my high school and college years in Albuquerque, I was paying for my fishing habit by selling flies to the local sports shops. Fly tyers were few and far between in those days and what I knew I learned from the few books then available. Even in those early days being able to tie a fly quickly was a point of pride and gave a sense of accomplishment. Now, some fifty-odd years later, the same feelings remain but now the flies are of much high quality. I tie and fish everything from size 26 extended body parachute dries to large salt-water patterns. I am now a retired engineer living in Bodega Bay, California and spending as much time as possible either with rod in hand or in my fly tying room.

During the past two decades we have seen an explosion in the popularity of fly fishing. Thousands of new fly fishermen, and women, have embraced the sport and taken up fly tying as a part of it. During this same period we have had a proliferation in new tying materials; and new magazines abound espousing and rehashing the many nuances of tying. After fifty-plus years of fly tying, I am always amused by tyers who purport to have discovered a brand new technique. Truth be told there seems to be little that is truly new in the fly tying world. Claims of hot new patterns consistently appear that are nothing more than recycled variations or modifications using new materials on an old, forgotten

fly. Having said all that, let me say that I truly believe fly tying is equal to any of the other arts in providing an outlet for the flow of creative juices from creative minds. Just because your new invention at the tying table was a technique in vogue forty or more years ago makes little difference to the level of satisfaction that you experience. The feeling of self-discovery and accomplishment remains. That is the glory and lure of fly tying.

I do recall an early Pullover technique from forty or fifty years ago, when most of the available hackles had thick stems. A section of the bare hackle stem was used as the post for a parachute hackle. The stem was then pulled over and tied down, further securing the hackle. Modern thin-stemmed hackles are not suitable for posts and this method is seldom seen today. While the method was primitive compared to the techniques offered in this book, the concept was similar.

Developing and fishing new patterns is one of the joys of fly tying. My boxes are always full of new flies with which to tempt the fish. I cannot really say when I added the Paraloop or Pullover hackle technique to my arsenal. It is a method available for those occasions when a special effect if needed for a new creation. One of the first patterns on which I recall using the approach was the Adult Damsel Pattern shown here. While this appears to be a complicated pattern, with its extended body, it is really quite a simple quick tie. This is certainly not one of the 'must-have' patterns with which I fill my boxes. It is just a pretty fly that is fun to tie and pleasant to view.

Adult Damsel Pattern

hook: any short shank dry fly hook
thread: white
extended body: 20 # test-braided monofilament
under thorax: bright blue dry fly dubbing
over thorax and post: white Z-Lon or Antron yarn
wings: Z-wing material (a thin soft plastic film-like material)
hackle: cream (large hackle with extra-long barbs)
felt tip pens: bright blue and black

Tying the Adult Damsel

1. Tie in several inches of the braided monofilament, extending it to the rear of the hook. With the blue marking pen, colour the braid and with the black pen add the black bands. Cut the braid to the proper length and singe the end with a flame to seal. Note: Tying in an excess length of braid gives the tyer something to hold taut while applying the felt tip markers.

2. Tie in a strip of Z-wing material with X wraps in the centre of the strip, then fold both sides (wings) to the rear end and trim to body length. Tie in a 3 in (7.5 cm) piece of Z-Lon on the top of the hook shank directly in front of the wings. Pull the section extending to the rear into a vertical position and form the post. Colour the Z-Lon and post using the blue marking pen. Next tie in the hackle next to the

post, but, do not wrap the hackle at this time. Now form a small thorax with the blue dubbing material, covering the section of Z-Lon that is extending forward. Leave the thread hanging forward near the eye of the hook.

3. Wind half a dozen wraps of hackle around the posted Z-Lon and then pull the post forward and tie off the Z-Lon and the hackle near the eye of the hook. Cut off the hackle but not the Z-Lon. Now take the thread back to the rear behind the posting point. Fold both ends of the Z-Lon back over the top of the fly, dividing the hackle equally to both sides. Tie down and whip finish the Z-Lon at that point. Trim the Z-Lon, leaving a short stub extending to the rear.

Above: The finished Adult Damsel.

Note: Use the blue marking pen to occasionally colour the tying thread as you tie the fly for a consistent colour throughout.

Left: The finished fly from above, clearly showing the wings and the pulled over Z-Lon.

Midge Cluster pattern.

A second fly on which I use a Paraloop technique is a simple midge cluster pattern. The pattern itself is fairly common, consisting of a peacock body with a Paraloop hackle folded over the back of the body from rear to front. The only difference is the method of forming the Paraloop, a tip shown to me by my best friend, Bob Norman. For those who have difficulties tying parachutes or Paraloops this approach may be of real help. A 3 in (7.5 cm) long loop of 2X or 3X tippet material is tied in at the rear of the hook. I am not a fan of gallows tools and having a loop of monofilament allows the tyer to control the post easily with one finger while posting and wrapping hackle.

Furled Extended Bodies and Furled Hackles
[Although the following contribution is not directly concerned with the tying of a Paraloop

fly, the technique is so useful and impressive that I have included it. It links well with the furled detached bodies used throughout the book, taking the technique that little bit further in its development. It can also be linked with the forming of hackle brushes using hair and other materials, which can then be used as the hackle in a Paraloop fly, examples of which are included in the gallery. The possibilities offered by this method are many.]

A completely different technique from the hackle-formed Paraloop is a technique that allows me to use hair or synthetics such as Krystal Flash to produce a similar effect. Many years ago I tried to duplicate the woven-hair hackle techniques of Franz Potts and George Grant. For two decades, starting in the early 1920s, Franz Potts, a barber and wig maker, produced the popular Mite series of woven-hair flies, which were very popular in the west United States, despite being priced at three times the cost of other flies of the time. In 1939 George Grant received a US patent for his method of weaving hair hackle. I found their methods produced excellent results but were very time-consuming, and they were put on the shelf. In 1995 I started making furled leaders, and ideas always seem to propagate other ideas. Applying the furling technique to fly tying allowed me to produce a very long, extended dubbed body. The Vertical Worm, the Limp Leech, the Bonefish Worm and other patterns quickly evolved from these long extended bodies.

To the best of my knowledge this technique has never been described in print and represents a new technique for fly design. Having said that, I must acknowledge that there is little that is new in fly tying and I certainly do not profess to know it all. A few flies are currently tied with extended furled bodies, but none that I know of incorporates dubbing, and most of the bodies are quite short. Taking the technique one step further allowed me to produce a preformed hackle with hair and/or synthetics. The spun deer hair bass fly shown is my Scaredy Cat. (page 175) A single length of preformed hackle is tied in for the tail at the rear of the hook, after the deer-hair body is spun and clipped into shape.

The technique for making the preformed dubbed bodies or preformed hackle is shown in the accompanying photographs. When first starting to attempt this technique, I recommend that you use a heavy thread such as Kevlar and apply a good coating of very tacky wax, as it will make your first attempts that much easier. I also suggest that for your first attempts you use a soft dubbing such as marabou. Making the hair hackle requires a bit more dexterity than the plain dubbed bodies; however, with practice the effect is quite striking.

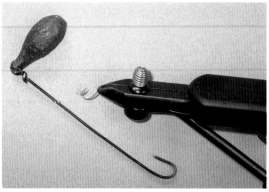

1. Clamp any large hook in your vice by the shank so that you can loop the thread around its bend. This is just a convenient way of working and has nothing to do with the actual tying of the fly. Note the long wire shank on the whorl, which facilitates the spinning.

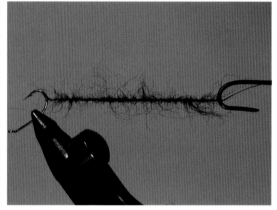

2. To form a 4 in (10 cm) finished body which can be used for several patterns, start with 19 in (48 cm) of Kevlar, RTS Dynacord or other strong thread. Knot the ends together to form a loop. Place the knot at either the top or the bottom of the loop so that it will not end up in the middle of the finished body. The first part of this technique is exactly the same as dubbing via the dubbing loop method except that a longer loop and a tighter twist is employed. Trap chopped or short pieces of dubbing material between the threads for a bushy effect. Do not roll the dubbing on the thread. The dubbing loop has been considerably shortened in the photograph for clarity. Spin the whorl slightly to trap the material in the loop, then pluck out any oversized lumps of dubbing to achieve a uniform strand. Continue spinning until the loop begins to shorten and spinning becomes more difficult.

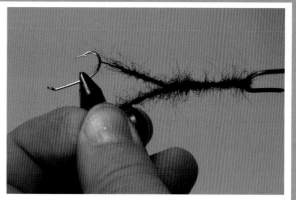

3. Grasp the bottom of the loop with your left hand and remove the whorl, keeping tension on the loop at all times. Place the whorl at the mid-point of the dubbed section, and pull the bottom end up towards the top end such that the two legs are about 20 degrees apart.

4. Spin the dubbing hook in the opposite direction to that in which it was initially spun, allowing the two legs to progressively twist together. It is important to keep the legs equally angled away from the centre line of the strand to achieve the best results. Remove the dubbing hook when finished and let the body hang free for a couple of seconds to come to equilibrium. It may untwist slightly but this is normal. Cut the thread from the hook and the body is ready to use.

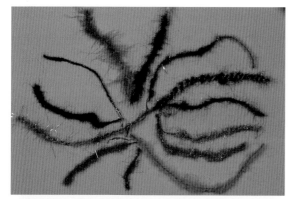

5 & 6. Other dubbing such as marabou, craft fur or even deer hair can be used for a variety of different effects. Using different colours and selectively placing them in the dubbing loop before twisting can yield variegated and two-tone bodies. Let your imagination be your guide.

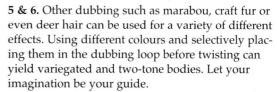

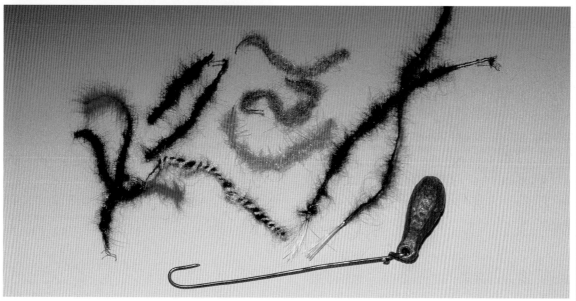

John 'Ned' Long

I am very grateful for the following contribution from Ned Long. Ned ties Paraloop flies by using a gallows tool and forming a hackle brush. There is no difference between his basic technique and that which I employ in my own tyings. Ned has, however, developed some very interesting techniques using different materials.

He was born in Delaware, Ohio, on 8 December 1922. His nickname of 'Ned', was chosen by his mother before his legal given name; she had wanted a son with that nickname. When aged four, his family moved to Glendale, California. He attended college at the University of Southern California and obtained a Bachelor of Arts degree. It was while he was in college that he met his wife Betty on a blind date and on 12 August 2000 they celebrated their fifty-second wedding anniversary. Ned and Betty have three children and live in Tahoe City, California. He worked as an insurance broker for thirty years before retiring.

Ned was taught to fly fish by his older brother

Ned Long.

Jim when he was ten years old. They would fish around Mammoth, California, for rainbow and brown trout. Fly tying started at the urging of Don Martinez of West Yellowstone and Woolly Worm fame. Needless to say he became an addict and took fly tying classes to improve his skills. Ned's wife Betty says that he probably has every book written about fly fishing and fly tying. Brother Jim, who first introduced him to fly fishing, was also talked into fly tying, but he never jumped into it with the same enthusiasm.

In 1996 Ned won the prestigious Federation of Fly Fishers' Buz Buszek Memorial Fly Tying Award. Although he feels he was lucky to win the award, everyone who knows him will agree that he deserved it. He has been innovative and taught extensively before he lost an eye to a melanoma. Extended bodies and Pullover flies (Paraloops) have been two of his specialities. Ned says that he did not invent the Pullover Method, but he did change materials and improve on the general concept. One of his most popular patterns is his extended body Damselfly Nymph.

Commercial fly tying has not been his bag, because, he says, 'it is too boring'. But, as a demonstrating fly tyer at shows, he always attracts a large crowd. He joined the Federation of Fly Fishers in the late sixties and was one of the founding fathers of the Tahoe Truckee Fly Fishers. He served as President and has held every other office possible. The club has been active in conservation issues and extremely helpful to the California Department of Fish and Game by completing surveys and helping wherever and whenever possible.

One of the honours Ned and Betty had was fishing with Buz Buszek. Betty says that she got cross with Buz one day when she hooked a steelhead and he would not help her land it! His attitude was; you hooked it, you can land it – which she eventually did.

Today, Ned's favourite stream is Hat Creek and he has two favourite lakes in the Tahoe area: Martis Lake and Milton Lake. Favourite flies for the lakes are Calebaitis and his Damselfly Nymph. Like all the Buszek winners before him, Ned is a credit to the award. He is a prototype Buszek winner, an excellent fly tyer and a fine gentleman.

Ned has chosen to describe the tying of one of his own flies, Ned's Emerger. This fly imitates the emerging midge (family Diptera), also known as the emerging buzzer. It is first class when this most prolific of all fly types is entering into the adult phase of its life cycle. Ned's Emerger is a very specific tying, but the methods he uses could be applied across the board for all types of midge emergers, with only the colours of the materials and the hook size being changed; the chart in chapter 7 suggests sizes and colours for different midges.

In his tying Ned uses Superfloss to create the post, which is stretched over the gallows tool and the hackle wound around the stretched floss. After the hackle has been initially tied in, the Superfloss post is released, automatically compacting and expanding within the hackle brush, a method that I find fascinating.

Ned's Emerger

hook: sizes 12–16 Tiemco #2487 or equivalent
thread: 8/0 Uni-thread, brown
shuck: Z-Lon dyed with coffee
body and post: Superfloss, red
thorax: SRI Fine & Dry dubbing, reddish brown
hackle: Hoffmann Super Saddle, dyed brown
head: tying thread

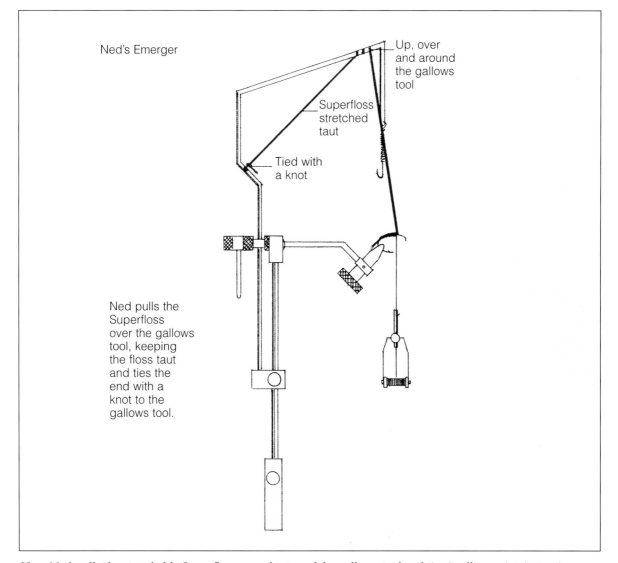

Ned's Emerger

Up, over and around the gallows tool

Superfloss stretched taut

Tied with a knot

Ned pulls the Superfloss over the gallows tool, keeping the floss taut and ties the end with a knot to the gallows tool.

How Ned pulls the stretchable Superfloss over the top of the gallows tool and ties it off to maintain tension.

1. The emerger pattern that I developed can be tied in various colours and using various dubbing materials, depending on the fly to be imitated. It is best tied on a scud hook. I use a Tiemco hook, #2487 size 12–16, but any hook of this type will work. I wrap the hook using the 8/0 Uni tying thread, and I space the thread slightly to hold the materials better. The thread is wrapped partially around the bend of the hook, then back towards the eyes about two-thirds of the way. At that point I tie in the Z-Lon to emulate the shuck. The Z-Lon should be laid out towards the bend of the hook, and tied in with the thread wrapped back around the bend of the hook. Cut the Z-Lon to equal about the length of the body. Return the thread to the tie-in point. Now melt the Z-Lon tip with a cigarette lighter.

2. For the body, I use Superfloss. This is a material similar to latex, but much more durable and does not deteriorate like latex. It is Lycra, nylon-based material that stretches 6 times its length, has zero memory and is slightly plus on buoyancy. It easily takes a dye. A strand of the red Superfloss is tied in at the tie-in point on top of the shank of the hook and wrapped back to the bend of the hook. As I wrap the thread over the Superfloss, I leave the floss slack for the first few wraps, and as I continue to wrap I stretch the floss more and more till I reach the bend of the hook. Bring the thread back to the tie-in point. The floss is then wrapped forward, very tightly at first, loosening slightly as I come forward to the tie-in point, thus giving me a tapered body that is slightly segmented and translucent. [Note: Ned's tie-in point is not at the tail, but where the body starts.]

3. At the tie-in point I make about four wraps of thread over the Superfloss. Then I stretch the floss very tightly, up over the gallows tool, creating a post from the floss. At this point I tie in the dyed light-brown dry-fly-quality saddle hackle.

4. Then I dub the thorax with dubbing to match the body and return the thread to the base of the floss post. The hackle is then wrapped, parachute-style, around the floss post. I wrap the hackle up about eight wraps and then down through the wrapped hackle, spreading out the wraps as I go down, about four wraps. Tie off the hackle at the base of the post with two or three wraps, then bring the thread forward to the eye.

5. At this point I release the Superfloss post and bring it forward down over the shank of the hook and tie it off just behind the eye. Cut the floss and whip finish.

There are quite a few advantages to using Superfloss. Not only does it give you a translucent body and excellent segmentation. When stretched tightly it makes a very thin post that when released compacts the hackle and also swells up inside the hackle wraps, securing even better. (See the appendix for suppliers of Superfloss.)

Brian Cornwall

Brian was born on 3 May 1974 in Peebles in the Scottish Borders, and like many of the young boys in the area, started fishing when young, at around the age of six. Living in Peebles made access to good water easy, as the famous River Tweed runs through the heart of the town. Brian is especially keen on trout fishing and started dabbling in the tying of flies at the age of ten. Nymphs and dry flies are his speciality, especially those patterns that aim to imitate the natural fly accurately. Currently Brian is manager of the Sportfish shop in Edinburgh, where he can often be found tying flies or demonstrating to interested onlookers a new or interesting technique. He has fished in exotic locations but always finds his way back to the Borders rivers. These days he will more usually be found on the tributaries of the Tweed rather than the main river, preferring the challenge and variety offered by the smaller streams.

Brian became one of the youngest candidates to qualify for the Scottish Game Angling Instructor's Certificate, which he passed in the discipline of trout. He has been tying Paraloop flies for at least a couple of years and has become

Brian Cornwall.

an ardent advocate of the method. He describes his experience with the Paraloop fly and the tying of two flies. The first is a Paraloop version of the Klinkhamar, and the second uses a CDC loop wing. Unlike me Brian uses the Paraloop method to tie flies down to size 20 and has had much success with them.

How the Paraloop changed my approach to tying dry flies

Brian Cornwall

I first met Ian Moutter about five years ago whilst working in a small tackle shop in Edinburgh. My first impression was that he took a very matter-of-fact approach to fly fishing and fly tying. He talked a lot of sense and, more to the point, he practised it. As anyone who has held station behind a tackle shop counter will know, guys like Ian are a breath of fresh air!

A few months after we first met, Ian made one of his frequent visits to the shop, during which he started to bang on and on about a thing he called 'the Paraloop', which at the time he believed he had invented. It was all very interesting, but, I did not have a clue what he was talking about and I just kept nodding and smiling as he enthused about what he believed was a revolutionary technique. After a few more conversations on the subject, however, I realised what he was getting at, and when I saw the flies, I knew that he was on to something very interesting. Also, the flies fished brilliantly, and importantly (for me, at least) they *looked right*!

I began to retie most of my dry fly collection as Paraloops, and the results were immediately noticeable. On my native River Tweed and its tributaries, I began to deceive trout with alarming regularity, and I remain convinced that this was mostly due to the new flies I was using. On a number of occasions, I would attach a traditionally hackled Greenwell's Glory and present it to a trout three or four times in a row, only to have it ignored. If I returned later and showed the same fish a Paraloop Greenwell, the result would almost always go my way.

It made me wonder why the fish preferred one fly to another, especially when they were so similar in terms of colour, size and silhouette. Then

I remembered another style of fly which had produced such a dramatic difference in results: the Klinkhamar. I had read a magazine article in which Hans van Klinken described how one of the key elements of the Klinkhamar was the fact that the abdomen sank while the hackle supported the thoracic area in the surface film. This factor, combined with the shape of the hook, ensured that the abdomen would be clearly visible to the fish, and proved to be a highly effective way of imitating an emerging caddis fly.

I began to think about combining the Klinkhamar shape with the Paraloop technique – not so much to copy emerging caddis flies, but to imitate upwinged flies, of which several species abound on the Tweed and her tributaries. The olives were my first goal. I remembered an old Tweed angler who had told me to snip off the hackles that protruded beneath the horizontal plane of my traditional Greenwell's Glories, and indeed this proved to be very effective in a fall of spinners. But the clipped hackles did not provide much floatability, and the flies were easily 'drowned'. It was a very easy job to tie olive patterns using the Paraloop and spent wings, and they are still some of the most effective flies I know during a fall of olive spinners. Furthermore, they float *in* the surface all day long! But that still left me pondering the application of Ian's Paraloop to emerging dun patterns.

I have often read the theory that trout, being simple creatures, will always go for the easiest meal, and that equates to spent flies, 'stillborns' and crippled emergers. I am certain that, in a hatch of upwinged flies (or indeed any aquatic species), trout will always go after these 'dead certs', rather than run the risk of rising to a dun that may well take off before the trout can add it to its calorific intake. This made sense to me, so I experimented, and eventually came up with a pattern incorporating a Paraloop hackle and a folded CDC 'loop' wing. It was intended to look like an emerging dun that had become stuck halfway through its metamorphosis, trapped in the surface film of the water. I went through my usual rigmarole, dropping examples of the fly in a pint glass of water, trying to see it as a trout might, then dropping them in a bath and splashing around to simulate the quick, choppy flows I often fish through (I'm not insane, honestly!). It floated through even the roughest 'simulated chop' and so I decided to try it on the trout.

It worked then, and it still works now. I went on to use this technique to imitate other species, and it works equally well with them. I have tied imitations with and without tails, with and without wings, with varying degrees of success. Whether or not these features make the flies any better or worse I am unsure. However, I remain absolutely convinced that a fly tied using the Paraloop technique will allow the fish to get a better look at the body of an emerging fly. I am equally certain that it is a more durable and effective way of imitating a spent spinner than other popular techniques such as the parachute hackle. Once learned, it is also an easier, faster method than the traditional parachute hackle.

One of the things that struck me while I was experimenting with this new technique was that it became possible to tie very small flies with quality saddle hackles – something I had always struggled with when it came to parachute patterns. I found that the amount of hackle required to support a traditional parachute fly effectively was rather more than the amount I could tidily apply to a small hook. Finishing a tiny parachute fly neatly was also something I found extremely difficult, and yet again the Paraloop has been the answer to my prayers.

These days, I tie Pale Watery Duns down to size 20, and the Paraloop hackle means that I am confident in their ability to float well, but without a heavy hackle.

Rivers like the Tweed are often prone to low water throughout the summer months, and this means that the imitations I offer the trout must be light, wispy and sparse. These are properties easily provided by the Paraloop, and I have now been able to obtain the right density without sacrificing floatability. A dry fly is of no use to me if the hook pulls the dressing beneath the surface, and I have always hated the oil slick left by our modern floatants. A little floatant applied sparingly the night before a fishing trip should suffice – if it does not, then the hook is too heavy for the dressing, or as some might argue, the dressing is too light for the hook. Now, I've been called awkward more than a few times, but I want my dry flies to look as natural as possible,

without having to use a hook that a good-sized minnow can straighten out! Ian's Paraloop has allowed me to produce just such flies.

To me the Paraloop provides the tyer with endless opportunities to improve their dry flies. Cast your mind back to all those finicky trout and fussy grayling, and then tie a few Paraloop patterns. I promise you this: learning to tie the Paraloop will unlock more than a few doors of opportunity. I cannot claim any of the techniques or innovations as my own, but I have found my own combinations, and remain delighted with the results. Experiment and find your own.

My future dabbling with the Paraloop is going to focus on still-water flies. There are only a few upwinged flies which occur in any real numbers on the still waters I fish, but then there are the sedges, the buzzers, and the terrestrials. I have already mentioned that I find the Paraloop an easy fly to tie in small sizes, and as far as imitating chironomids goes, this can only be a bonus. I have never been keen on using bits of polystyrene or closed-cell foam for very small flies, because I believe that it makes the fly awkward and clumsy in the water. Expecting a size 18 buzzer pattern to behave naturally with a polystyrene bead stuck on its head is, I believe, asking too much! Try using the Paraloop technique to suspend the body of the fly in the water, and you will find that the soft wispy hackle does not restrict the tiny, subtle motion of the imitation. A stiff breeze will pass more easily through the hackle barbs, and you will reduce the chances of unnatural drag on the fly. Even a CDC 'shuttlecock' style of fly seems to catch the wind like a sail when compared to a lightly dressed Paraloop buzzer. The experiments continue apace!

Almost all of my Paraloop flies are tied on Partridge hooks, principally GR12ST and K14ST patterns. I bend these to suit the angle of hang required for any particular pattern. I do not heat the hooks prior to bending, and I have never experienced a broken hook while playing fish. There are proprietary Klinkhamar hooks available on the market, but I like to vary the angle at which I bend the hooks for different patterns, and the Partridge hooks are ideal.

I would like to take the opportunity to describe a couple of the patterns I regularly use

The Paraloop Klinkhamar Medium Olive Emerging Dun.

which incorporate the Paraloop hackle. Most of the tyings I use are based on the Klinkhamar pattern. I find the Paraloop method of providing the hackle is superior to the normal parachute hackle and ideal for patterns like the Klinkhamar. Since the Paraloop hackle is far more substantial than the parachute hackle, I find I have no trouble keeping the fly afloat, yet I still manage to let the fly sit very low in the water with the abdomen underneath the surface.

Paraloop Klinkhamar Medium Olive Emerging Dun

The first pattern is my Klinkhamar-style Medium Olive Emerging Dun, a big name and a very successful fly for me. The fly is tied on a size 18 hook. Kevlar thread is used for the post, due to its strength.

> hook: Partridge YK12ST (black finish) size 18
> thread: Benecchi 12/0 light dun
> abdomen: dark hare's mask blend
> hackle: Hoffman grade 3 grizzle saddle hackle, dyed blue dun
> wing: Benecchi CDC Deveaux, grey

> tails: brown partridge hackle fibres
> rib: single-strand floss (Globrite #10)
> thorax: dubbed CDC fibres (yellow-olive)
> post: Kevlar

Paraloop Klinkhamar Large Dark Olive Emerger

> hook: Partridge GR12 ST size 14
> thread: Benecchi 8/0 pale yellow
> abdomen: Superfloss, Dark Olive and Medium Olive wound over Globrite #10
> hackle: olive dyed Hoffman saddle grade 3 (this example is tied slightly 'loose loop' style)
> wings: dyed blue dun hackle points
> thorax: mink underfur mixed with dark hare's mask, treated with Watershed before tying in
> post: Kevlar thread

Brian ties all his flies by first taking the thread to the tail position and working back, applying the different materials as required. When a fly includes a hackle-tip wing he adds it after tying in the hackle brush, by bringing the thread forward towards the hook eye and tying in the prepared wings at the required position. When he

The Paraloop Klinkhamar Large Dark Olive Emerger.

includes a loop wing he adds it before tying in the post, at the same point on the hook shank at which the post is to be tied in.

Tying Procedure

1. Take the thread to the tail position.
2. If required add the tail, followed by any rib and then the body material.
3. Return the thread to the post position, tying in the body and rib materials as you go onto the underside of the hook shank. Remove any excess material.
4. Wind on the body and then the rib, tying it on the underside of the hook shank. Cut off any excess. If a loop wing is to be included it is tied in at this point.
5. Tie in the Kevlar loop post and complete the hackle brush, tying it onto the hook shank. Remove any excess hackle.
6. If a wing is required it is at this time that the thread is taken to the correct position on the thorax and the prepared hackles tied in. The thread is returned to the post.
7. The thread is dubbed to provide the thorax and wound on, creating a shaped thorax.
8. The hackle brush is pulled over the thorax and tied in behind the hook eye. Any excess Kevlar is removed. If hackle-tip wings are included, the hackle brush is pulled over between the two wings. If a loop wing is included then this is pulled over the hackle brush after it has been tied in behind the hook eye and tied in when forming the head.

11 Adding a Little Sparkle to Paraloop Flies

The fly tyer of today is spoilt in comparison with those of yesteryear in the choice of materials available. Although we do not have many of the natural materials used in days gone by, there are products available today which would leave the tyers of even just a couple of decades ago amazed, as well as enthused and inspired to try them out on a fly pattern. These products tend to be synthetics.

As I have said, for many years I never used any materials other than natural ones: silk, feather and fur and that was all. I even went to the lengths of deliberately shunning any man-made materials, looking on them as an intrusion into my little world of fly tying. Even my thread needed to be cotton or silk. Do not ask me why I acted this way; maybe it was a desire for all things natural, on the water and off.

Happily those days are long gone and, looking around my fly tying room today, amongst the labels for such things as cock genetic black, hen capes red, arctic fox dyed and partridge breast, are strange names like Lite Brite, Holographic Tinsel, SLF and Crystal Hair – a bit like *Star Trek* meets *Little House on the Prairie*. Many of these materials would at first glance appear to have more to do with decorating a Christmas tree than tying flies. However, used sensibly and judiciously, they can be used not only to tie lures and fancy flies, but also to enhance imitative flies. The real trick in using them is to make a little go a long way. Their over-use in imitative flies will usually tend to frighten fish.

We have already seen the importance of some of these man-made fibres; Antron, polypropylene in its many forms, the myriad of proprietary dubbing such as SLF, foam sheet and micro fibbets all add something special to the treasure chest of fly tying materials. In this chapter we will be looking at some of the more sparkling materials available and how they can be used to add life to even the most drab of flies. After a lot of thought I decided to limit these to only three. That is not to say that these are the only materials suitable for the flies in this book; there are lots of other materials available, many of which I will not personally be familiar with, and some of these may indeed be superior to those I have chosen. The three chosen, however, really do a good job. They are materials that I am familiar with and well used to using, and they are easily obtainable. If any other material is preferred, then using it in place of one I have chosen should not present a problem. The methods used to include these materials in the fly can easily be adapted for others. The names used for these materials are also fairly international and as such easier to source.

The experienced tyer will, I am sure, be familiar with these materials, and will probably use them regularly, usually when tying fancy patterns such as lures, streamers and bait fish, which require sparkle and reflection. When included in imitative patterns the materials are used to give the impression of wings, gas and air bubbles, movement and an overall indication of life, all acting as attractions to the trout. The use of such materials can greatly enhance the overall look of a fly and add that little extra magic sometimes required.

Flashabou

This is a flat mylar tinsel-like material which is normally sold in small hanks. It is often used as a winging material when tying streamer and baitfish patterns. I only use it in the pearl colour

Flashabou

nature makes it ideal to use mixed with other forms of dubbing. It adds very little bulk when included in a fly pattern and adding just a few strands can make a real difference to the overall look of the finished fly. It can also be incorporated as a wing tied in the same way as Flashabou. I have also found this material marketed as Angel Hair, although I am aware of another product which uses that name and which is very different in nature and unsuitable for our purposes.

Holographic Tinsel

This comes in various colours and is available in hanks or on a thread bobbin. Whatever the base colour is, the reflective colours are myriad. This material appears to reflect back light with all the colours of the rainbow. Its use in Paraloop flies has been fairly limited to date, but its inclusion as a rear body material on buzzer patterns, or a couple of strands used as a wing, sometimes combined with Flashabou, can be most effective.

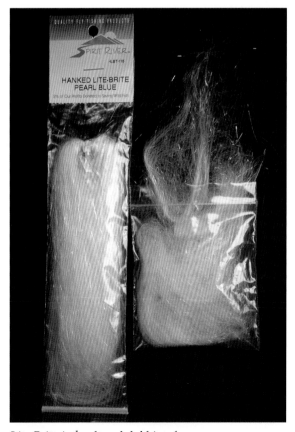

Lite Brite in hank and dubbing form.

when including it in Paraloop flies. The reflective qualities are quite amazing; the intensity of reflective light seems to be magnified many times compared to the ambient light, the reflected light taking on an ultraviolet-like hue. When tying some Paraloop flies I include Flashabou as a wing, tied either behind the hackle brush or in the centre of the thorax area; three or four short strands on either side of the fly suffice to produce a good effect. It can also be used in forming bodies; for example the rear body of the Grey Midge can be enhanced by including Flashabou as a rib or body material.

Lite Brite

This is available in either hanks or as a dubbing, and in a multitude of colours. Its reflective qualities are very similar to Flashabou, although it is more fibrous. When using Lite Brite I tend to stick again to the Polar Pearl colour. Its fibrous

Holographic tinsel in hank form. It is also available wound on bobbins.

Wings

When used as wings the above materials can add that little extra something that makes a good fly great. As I have said, they must be used very carefully and sparingly; the fly, rather like a good meal, is not to be spoilt by over-cooking.

When tying the Paraloop fly the wing can be included at two different points. The first point is directly behind the hackle brush. Any of the above materials can be used, but my favourites are Lite Brite and Flashabou. Lite Brite adds a very wispy wing, whilst Flashabou provides a more solid look, although due to the thinness of the material and its reflective qualities, this does not come over as bulk but rather as light.

When adding additional wings it can sometimes be advisable to tie the fly in a different order, by tying the rear first. The reason for this is to keep the additional materials off the hook whilst tying the rear of the fly so they do not get in the way. I find, however, that if plenty of wing material is added it can easily be held out of the way and on completion of the fly the wing can be cut to the desired length. I prefer the length of the wing to be enough to let it sit at the same height as the hackle when set in position.

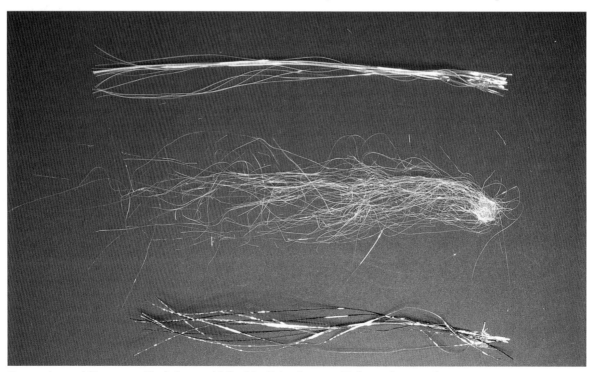

Comparison of fibres: top; Flashabou, middle; Lite Brite, bottom; Holographic tinsel.

1. The wing, in this case Flashabou, is added prior to tying in the post. Six strands are sufficient, keep them long, so they can be pushed out of the way when tying the rest of the fly. Complete the fly as normal.

2. When the fly is complete, cut the wing so that it reaches the same height as the hackle.

Adding a wing within the hackle brush area or thorax area is very useful when tying emerging flies, giving as it does, the impression of a fly struggling out of the shuck. The following method can be used with either the normal hackle or better still the open loop hackle (4/3). Instead of using Flashabou, the wing in the following example is made from Lite Brite.

3. Complete the fly up to and including attaching the hackle brush to the neck breaker. Dub the thread with sufficient dubbing to do half of the 'thorax' area. Now tie in the wing, remembering to keep the fibres long. Cut off the excess wing material at the tying in end.

4. Return the thread to the initial point at which the wing was tied in. Complete the dubbing of the 'thorax' area and complete the fly. Make sure that, when the hackle brush is pulled over, an equal amount of wing material is placed on either side of the hackle. Now give the wing material a hair-cut to the right length.

5. The wing has been split either side of the hackle brush.

The above methods can be applied to any Paraloop fly, I would normally use six or eight fibres of Flashabou or a small bunch of Lite Brite fibres, enough to give a similar effect to the Flashabou. Both the above methods can be used using holographic tinsel in place of Flashabou if preferred.

Body, Thorax and Tail

The body of a buzzer, either the suspender type or the emerger, can be enhanced using holographic tinsel as the main body material, or as a ribbing. The holographic tinsel is tied in at the tail section either as a body or rib and then wound on accordingly. The resulting fly is most attractive and is now a well-proven method of tying buzzer patterns. My good friend Jimmy McBride of the Craftye Fisherman in Edinburgh has been one of the pioneers in using holographic materials when tying buzzer patterns and the method is extremely effective when applied to Paraloop flies. When tying

sinking buzzer patterns the body section can first be created using holographic materials and then covered in either epoxy resin glue or a couple of coats of quality varnish.

When tying a dubbed body or thorax the inclusion of a little Lite Brite can be useful. Before the dubbing is applied add a pinch of Lite Brite to the dubbing material and mix it in well. Although the addition of the Lite Brite is not obvious, the apparent translucence of the fly is increased considerably. Any movement results in reflections of light from different parts of the body or thorax.

1. Suspender and emerger buzzer patterns using holographic tinsel in the body.

2. Mix the Lite Brite thoroughly with the main dubbing material before applying to the waxed thread.

3. In using Lite Brite mixed with Antron as an alternative to SLF, the same procedure is followed and the tip of the shuck is singed and pressed as explained. The shuck can be brushed with a dubbing brush to bring out the fibres and if necessary a dubbing needle can be used to tease out individual fibres.

Tails and shucks can benefit from a little Lite Brite added to the floss or spun dubbing material. I think it is extremely useful to add this material to a shuck, as it helps give the impression of the emptying nymph skin. Where SLF has been used as an added material to the Antron base in the flies described in this book, Lite Brite can be added as an alternative.

It will be obvious that it is easy to add these materials into imitative patterns and enhance the look of the fly. Although it is not always advisable to use these materials, there are times when they can be of great benefit, often making all the difference to the response of the fish.

12 The Paraloop and Its Future

More often than not a method of fly tying is limited to one or two applications; only in rare cases does the usefulness of a technique go very far beyond this. It will be clear that the method I call the Paraloop is one of those rarities. Adaptable by design, it is made even more versatile by using different materials. Ned Long's technique of using a stretch material is a case in point; the material itself becomes involved in the mechanics of the tying, to the enhancement of the fly. The introduction of open loops and the spent fly techniques are further examples of the flexibility of the method.

The parachute fly first came to light in the earlier part of the last century. It was Alex Martin's of Edinburgh and Glasgow who registered their copyright of the name. That is why, originally, the parachute fly was marketed by other fly dressers and fly fishing supply companies under different names, such as Ride-rite. One of the original techniques employed by the tyers at Alex Martin's was pulling over the post and tying it onto the hook shank behind the eye. This technique is very similar to the basic Paraloop, but without the creation of the hackle brush. When I first started demonstrating the Paraloop, I was approached by one of the old stalwarts amongst Edinburgh fly tyers. He was able to describe to me the first time he saw the technique of pulling over the loop and even gave me the name of the lady tyer, which I have unfortunately forgotten. It transpired that she was Alex Martin's head fly tyer and apparently at one time she used the Pullover Method in all her parachute flies. From the method used at that time for tying parachute flies it is a very small step forward to the creation of the Paraloop fly.

Parachute flies have gained in popularity over the last couple of decades, and for very good reasons. The myth that they are difficult to tie has been well and truly quashed and most tyers these days can tie a parachute fly as easily as they can a traditionally hackled fly. The method has evolved into innumerable techniques to produce the parachute style hackle, and this, in itself, is testament to how effective the flies tied this way are. I have lost count of the number of techniques I have seen for creating the post and securing the hackle.

I have tried to establish who was the first person to start tying what I have named as Paraloop flies and what others refer to as Pullovers or Hackle Stackers. The task has proved almost impossible; small transition from the parachute to the Paraloop can probably be traced back to the pulled-over post used by some of Alex Martin's tyers. The only references I can find to this style of tying the loop in by pulling it over, is in one of John Veniard's books. His reference to the parachute style hackle being wound around the post and the post then pulled over to be tied in, is exactly the same as the process used by some of the tyers at Alex Martin's. The nearest I can find to the Paraloop is in a book called *Chauncy Lively's Fly Box* (1980, Stackpole Books) and I am grateful to Bob Quigley and Ally Gowans for pointing me in its direction. There is no doubt that Mr Lively uses the basic technique in a number of the patterns, including what he refers to as a Parachute Sedge, the Coffin Fly Spinner and the Isonychia Spinner. As far as I can see, the basic Paraloop Method differs from Mr Lively's patterns only in the number of turns of hackle taken up and down the post and the overall length of the hackle brush. Other than these differences the method he describes is, for all practical purposes, the same as the basic Paraloop. The Paraloop/Pullover Method would appear therefore to have been around for quite some time in one form or another.

There have been a few USA-based tyers who have been using the method in some way or another regularly since the 1970s, including Jim Cramer, Ned Long and Bob Quigley. Mr Quigley published an article highlighting an excellent pattern, using what he refers to as the Hackle Stacker and what I call the Paraloop, in *Fly Fisherman Magazine* in, I believe, 1998. This pattern incorporated a foam ball as a thorax, with the hackle brush pulled over the ball. Coincidentally, this article was published in the same month that I had my first article on the method published by *Fly Fishing and Fly Tying* in the UK. A few days after the publication of both articles, I received a phone call from a friend asking me if I was now writing in the USA under an alias, as the methods described were almost exactly the same. This was confirmation that the method was being used by various groups of tyers throughout the USA.

Having said all that, what I refer to as the Paraloop Method has, with a few exceptions, failed to make its mark amongst the majority of fly tyers. This, I believe, can be put down to a lack of awareness of the method and its usefulness and adaptability. The publication of this book is an attempt to rectify that, and to promote what I believe to be an important fly tying method. In the UK I have found only one tyer who claimed to know of the method, but when asked to explain it to me, he was unsure how to go about using it. In fact, if the truth was known, he really had no idea at all. Beyond that single claimant, I have never known anyone else who claimed to know anything about the method, other than perhaps a recognition of the flies tied using it.

What I have found, however, is a tremendous interest whenever I have demonstrated the Paraloop Method, indeed a fascination, and a genuine enthusiasm to learn the techniques involved. An example of this is the Fly Dresser's Guild in Edinburgh. In the last couple of years I have demonstrated at their Wednesday evening meetings on at least four occasions. Each time I

have done so, the Paraloop Method has been amongst the requested tyings and once started nothing else seems to hold their interest to the same degree, even though most of the audience has seen the method demonstrated on various occasions.

I hope that you will take the time to try out some of the patterns here. I am positive that you will recognise the potential the method offers for most forms of imitative fly tying. Applying the Paraloop to your favourite flies spices up old friends and is the sure way to test the effectiveness of patterns tied this way. The method continues to be developed and I hope that this book will inspire a few tyers to take it further than I have been able to do to date. The ingenuity of fly tyers never ceases to amaze me and when the Paraloop Method becomes part of the mainstream of fly tying we are sure to see some wonderful flies.

I have not, as yet, found that nymph patterns are enhanced by the use of the Paraloop, but if anyone has found a way in which the method can be applied to them, I would be most interested.

Throughout the book, I have tried to help readers appreciate that the Paraloop Method is worthy of inclusion in every fly tyer's repertoire of techniques. Like many experienced fly tyers, I am not always willing to take on board any method which is claimed to be new and revolutionary. The Paraloop is neither new nor revolutionary; it is simply relatively obscure and subsequently undervalued. We are always on the look-out for a different approach or method to add to those we already use. When fishing the imitative fly, the Paraloop offers this different approach and one that thinking anglers and tyers can use to their own advantage.

One of the factors involved in fly tying which we sometimes take for granted is the sequence used in tying a fly. Very often the tying sequence is not the best for that particular pattern. The tying of the Olive Buzzer described in chapter 7 is a case in point. The inclusion of the foam overthorax makes it sensible to tie the body, then add the post and hackle brush prior to tying in the foam overthorax. This sequence makes tying the fly easier than adding the post, hackle and overthorax first, as these elements limit access to the rear of the hook. Some tyers may prefer to use a different sequence to the one I have recommended; please feel free to do so, it could well be better than mine. I am always learning better ways to tie flies and one of the ways I learn is by appreciating the reasons for the order in which materials are applied to a fly pattern. The sequence of material application is often the key to a well-tied fly. My own sequences for tying Paraloops have changed since I first started tying them and I expect that they will continue to do so.

The nights are getting much longer and the days a lot shorter, as I bring the writing of this book to its conclusion. Here in Scotland the autumn heralds the late salmon runs, and I will be spending much of my time on the great River Tweed, hoping that the days will not be too cold and the winds not too cutting. If the fates allow, I may enjoy a little success as a reward for my frozen fingers and dripping nose. The trout season here has ended and all thoughts of fishing Paraloop flies are locked away for the time being. The trees are spread in a richness of gold, red and yellow, a splendour that will soon fall to the earth to be shared with the soil, leaving the branches empty, stark and pointing to the snow-promising sky. As sure as the day turns to night and the summer to autumn, the snows and frosts will soon confirm that winter is truly here. The rods, the reels and all the paraphernalia we collect in the name of fishing will be carefully put away, to await a new year and yet another season. If I am feeling brave enough to face the cold winds of December or January, one rod may be dusted down and a day or two, perhaps even three, fishing for grayling may settle the restless spirit. There is much delight and pleasure to be found fishing for the 'lady of the stream', especially when the grass cracks under your boots and the fingers of ice creep into the fringes of the water. The days are short from breakfast to fireside dinner, short but filled with winter's puritan beauty, a special time and one that seems less distracting for the soul.

The nights are often spent at the tying bench, the house warmed from the heat of a roaring fire, with welcome thoughts of fishing to come. Soon the seasons will turn and once again, as they have for many thousands of years, the trout will rise to the fly and we anglers will again cast our carefully tied attempts at imitation gently upon the waters. Let us hope we may continue to do so.

Gallery

The following gallery of flies is here to provide additional information on the adaptability and range of the Paraloop Method. The flies are explained in an order based on the type of Paraloop technique used in their tying, and each has a subheading describing its type. The main purpose of the gallery is not to display yet another selection of pretty flies, but rather to be an extension to the other chapters within the book. Each method described in earlier chapters is further demonstrated by the patterns included and in some cases the techniques are extended.

Each fly has a list of materials used. As I have said, unless there is a good reason for changing them, it is better to stay with those materials.

All the patterns shown are either variations of well-known flies or patterns of my own design. There is little doubt in my mind that, where patterns are attributed to me, some readers will recognise them as similar to patterns they use. It is unfortunate but inevitable, I believe, that with so many active and ingenious tyers around the world, such coincidences will occur. You only have to look at the so-called new patterns being published in fly fishing magazines, which are similar to those that have been used for years, to see that it is impossible to avoid. I can say, however, that where a pattern is knowingly based on one developed by another tyer, then acknowledgement is given.

To further assist with the tying of the patterns included in the gallery, each is provided with any special instructions that may be needed to complete the fly successfully.

I have tried to provide as varied a selection of flies as possible, to ensure that each technique is covered and, hopefully, most fishing situations. That said, the greatest value that any book of this genre has is as a source of inspiration for fly tyers. When a method of tying flies finds its way into the mainstream, in a single country or around the world, the possibilities offered by that method begin to be realised. It is my own belief that individuals or small groups of tyers can extend the development of a method only so far. It is only when the method is thrown out into the hands of innumerable tyers throughout the world that its full potential can be realised.

The ingenuity of tyers both old and young is amazing and it is this ingenuity that highlights what a fine pursuit fly tying is. The tying and designing of flies is a never-ending process, a process in which we are always learning. Even as we get older, new ideas flow from us to others and from others to us. It is this flow of information and development that keeps the frontiers of fly tying moving forward.

Enjoy the patterns shown in the gallery; I hope they inspire you to develop the Paraloop Method in your own way, with your own flies. I do not believe it is necessary for me to sing the praises of the method any more than I have already done, and I trust that thinking fly tyers and fly fishers will recognise where the Paraloop Method can be applied in their own circumstances.

Experienced tyers will find the methods described fairly easy to understand and apply. Some less experienced tyers may find some of the techniques difficult and thus frustrating to use. If this is the case, do not worry, just keep trying, and suddenly you will find that it is easy. With every single fly pattern attempted, your skills are developed and knowledge increased. It does not take long to become reasonably proficient at fly tying.

I have always maintained that fly tying is easy and can be learned by anyone who wishes to do so. It does not matter if the flies being tied are micro trout patterns or fully dressed Atlantic salmon flies. Each one can be approached by using simple techniques which, when learned and practised, will produce the required result. There is no area of fly tying that cannot be learned by anyone who wishes to do so, and this to me is one of the wonders of the pursuit. There is also no fly pattern which, when the simple techniques required to complete the tying are learned, cannot be tied by any aspiring fly tyer. So do not be put off if your experience is currently limited. All fly tyers have been there at some time or another and we are all still on a learning curve, one in which we cannot help but progress if we continue to try.

Unless otherwise indicated, the following flies are tied by the author.

The Wickham's Fancy

(Tied by B. Cornwall)

Basic Paraloop

Materials
    hook: Kamasan B170
    thread: black silk
    body: flat gold tinsel
    hackle: red cock
    tail: red cock
    post: Kevlar
    wing: blue dun hackle points
    rib: gold wire
    thorax: fiery brown seal's fur

Special Instructions
Basic Paraloop tying. Start by tying the tail in first.

The Harlequin Olive

Basic Paraloop

Materials
    hook: Partridge Captain Hamilton dry fly
    thread: own choice
    body: mixed bright olive and brown polypropylene not fully mixed
    hackle: dyed olive cock
    tail: dyed light olive cock
    post: GSP
    wing: none
    rib: none
    thorax: dark olive polypropylene dubbing

Special Instructions
Tied exactly like the Olive Dun. The Harlequin Olive takes its name from the body colours and the bright tail and hackle. A sunshine fly to be used when all else has failed. Tied in sizes 12–16.

The Grey Duster

(Tied by B. Cornwall)

Basic Paraloop

Materials

hook: Kamasan B170
thread: black silk
body: grey/blue rabbit's underfur
hackle: badger cock
tail: none
post: Kevlar
wing: none
rib: none
thorax: grey/blue rabbit's underfur

Special Instructions

Apply the body first, then complete the rest of the fly

The Kite's Imperial

(Tied by B. Cornwall)

Spent paraloop style

Materials

hook: Kamasan B170
thread: purple silk
body: heron herl or substitute
hackle: honey dun cock
tail: honey dun cock
post: Kevlar
wing: none
rib: none
thorax: heron herl or substitute / cover the same

Special Instructions

This fly is tied as per the basic pattern but with heron herl or substitute tied in before the post. After the hackle is tied in the herl is pulled over the thorax and hackle brush.

The Ready Sedge

Open Loop Paraloop

Materials

hook: Partridge Oliver Edwards sedge/emerger
thread: own choice
body: olive Antron behind hackle, olive/brown polypropylene under hackle
hackle: red game cock
shuck: olive Antron melted and squashed
post: GSP (dark)
wing: red game cock
rib: none
thorax: as per front body

Special Instructions

Tie the wings as normal, leaving a generous section of prepared stalk. When setting them into position fix them facing slightly downward to the horizontal. This imitates the emerging sedge about to take off over the water. It can be fished with the occasional retrieve to imitate a skating fly.

The Hair Wing Medium Sedge

Hair-winged

Materials

> hook: Partridge Captain Hamilton dry fly
> thread: own choice
> body: olive and brown polypropylene dubbing
> hackle: grizzle
> tail: none
> post: GSP
> wing: natural grey squirrel hair
> rib: none
> thorax: as body but slightly darker

Special Instructions

Tie the body, then add the wing. Now tie in the post. A fine fly when the sedge are on the water. Tied in darker colours the pattern has been useful as a stone-fly imitation.

The Greenwell's Glory

(Tied by B. Cornwall)

Basic Paraloop

Materials

> hook: Kamasan B170
> thread: primrose silk (Pearsalls)

> body: primrose silk darkened with cobbler's wax
> hackle: red cock
> tail: red cock
> post: Kevlar
> wing: none
> rib: fine brass wire
> thorax: leave as it is, with just the hackle brush pulled over

Special Instructions

This pattern is unusual in that there is no build-up of the thorax. In tying this fly Brian has duplicated the method I first used when tying Paraloop flies. Originally I never included a dubbed thorax, but these days I prefer to do so. However, if a lighter-built fly is required this method will fit the bill.

The Tup's Indispensable Variation

(Tied by B. Cornwall)

Basic Paraloop

Materials

    hook: Kamasan B170
    thread: primrose silk (Pearsalls)
    body: rear primrose silk; front yellow, fiery brown and crimson seal's fur mixed with a pinch of buff-coloured hare's fur
    hackle: blue dun cock
    tail: blue dun cock
    post: Kevlar
    wing: none
    rib: none
    thorax: as body

Special Instructions

Brian Cornwall uses his own tying for this fly and although I prefer to see the colours more defined in the thorax and the fly more squat in appearance, his version has proved most successful.

The Red Hatching Buzzer

Winged buzzer

Materials

    hook: Kamasan B100 size 12
    thread: own choice
    body: red Superfloss
    hackle: dark ginger
    tail: cream Antron
    post: GSP
    wing: light blue dun
    rib: none
    thorax: orange and claret polypropylene dubbing

Special Instructions

Tie in the wing with plenty of prepared stalk showing and set it into a downward position when completing the head.

The Hair-Tailed Hopper

Basic Paraloop with legs

Materials

    hook: Partridge Captain Edwards dry fly size 10
    thread: own choice
    body: grey/black mixed polypropylene dubbing
    hackle: grizzle
    tail: natural grey squirrel tail
    post: GSP
    wing: none
    legs: pheasant tail, two fibres each side knotted to form legs
    thorax: slightly darker than body

Special Instructions

Make the upper fibre on both legs slightly shorter than the lower fibre. This opens the legs out. Tie in the legs halfway along the thorax.

Large Dark Dun Winged

Open loop with slip wings

Materials

hook: Partridge Captain Hamilton dry fly size 10
thread: own choice
body: grey polypropylene dubbing
hackle: brown or red cock
tail: natural grey squirrel
post: GSP
wing: 2 slips grey mallard
rib: none
thorax: as body

Special Instructions

Tie in the slip wings first, complete the fly and pull the hackle over using an open loop. The open loop allows the wings to sit in a semi-upright position.

The Claw Wing Dun

Open loop with slip wings

Materials

hook: Partridge Captain Hamilton dry fly size 10
thread: own choice
body: olive and grey polypropylene dubbing
hackle: red cock
tail: feather fibres
post: GSP
wing: mallard slips
rib: none
thorax: as body

Special Instructions

Complete the fly as per the Large Dark Dun. The hackle can be pulled over and left slightly open as in the example, or with no space as per the basic

Paraloop. The wings are then lightly waxed and the thumb and first finger pulled up each slip separately, with the nail of the finger pressed against the inside of the slip. This places a curve in the wing which, when repeated, can start to resemble a claw, hence the name. The wing will hold up surprisingly well when fished.

The Badger Hackle

Basic Paraloop with hackle over the whole body

Materials

hook: Partridge Captain Hamilton dry fly
thread: own choice
body: flat silver tinsel
hackle: badger
tail: red cock
post: GSP
wing: none
rib: none
thorax: none

Special Instructions

There are many variations of this fly; this is one that I find very effective. Tie in the tail first, immediately followed by the post, then form the hackle brush. If you are using metal tinsel, tie it in at the point that the post is tied in; if you are using lurex tinsel, wind the thread to the point where the head will be formed and tie the tinsel in there. With the metal tinsel, carefully wind to the head position in touching turns, taking care not to overlap. With the lurex tinsel, wind it to the post and then back again. Pull the hackle brush over the whole body and tie it in at the head position.

Fan-Winged Mayfly

Slightly open loop Paraloop with fan wings

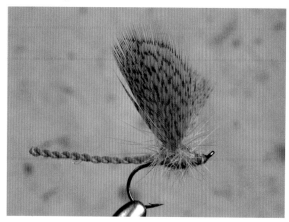

Materials

hook: Partridge Captain Hamilton dry fly
thread: own choice
body: cinnamon Aero Wing floss furled
hackle: light blue dun cock
tail: none
post: GSP
wing: partridge dyed orange
rib: none
thorax: orange and grey polypropylene dubbing

Special Instructions

Single-furl the body. Tie in the wings after the hackle brush has been attached to the neck breaker.

The Poly-Winged Spinner

Basic Paraloop with polypropylene floss wings

Materials

hook: Partridge Captain Hamilton dry fly
thread: own choice
body: stripped hackle stem, red cock
hackle: light blue dun cock
tail: medium blue dun Aero Wing floss
post: GSP dark
wing: medium blue dun Aero Wing floss
rib: none
thorax: brown and grey polypropylene dubbing

Special Instructions

Tie in the tail and body, and complete the body. Tie in the post and complete the hackle brush. With the thread, figure-of-eight the wing floss in the centre of the thorax area, with the hackle brush in the neck breaker. Return the thread to the post, dub it and form the thorax figure-of-eight wing with dubbed thread.

The Paraloop Klinkhamar Iron Blue Dun Emerger

(Tied by B. Cornwall)

Basic Paraloop

Materials

hook: Partridge YK12ST (black finish) size 18
thread: Benecchi 12/0 light dun
body: tying thread
hackle: dyed blue dun grizzle, Hoffman saddle grade 3
tail: filoplume stripped from the base of a partridge feather
post: Kevlar
wing: none
rib: none
thorax: dubbed CDC fibres (grey)

Special Instructions
Follow the instructions for Klinkhamer patterns in chapter 10.

The Adams Irresistible

Basic Paraloop deer-hair body

Materials
> hook: Partridge Captain Hamilton dry fly
> thread: own choice
> body: natural deer hair
> hackle: grizzle cock
> tail: elk (moose) hair
> post: GSP
> wing: none
> rib: none
> thorax: mixed grey, black and brown polypropylene dubbing

Special Instructions
A variation of one of the very great patterns. Tie in the tail, then form the deer-hair body, cutting it into shape. Tie in the post and form the hackle brush. Dub the thorax, shaping it to match the body. Pull over the hackle brush and form the head.

The Pond Olive

Basic Paraloop with detached body

Materials
> hook: Partridge Captain Hamilton dry fly (size 16 or 18)
> thread: own choice
> body: green and claret tinsel body wrap and olive

> polypropylene floss, single-furled
> hackle: dark ginger
> tail: none
> post: GSP dark
> wing: none
> rib: none
> thorax: mixed grey and claret polypropylene dubbing

Special Instructions
Tie in the body first, followed by the post. Complete as normal.

The Large Dark Olive

Single hair-wing Paraloop

Materials
> hook: Partridge Captain Hamilton dry fly
> thread: own choice
> body: brown and olive polypropylene dubbing mixed
> hackle: grizzle cock

tail: natural grey squirrel tail hair
post: GSP
wing: white polypropylene
rib: none
thorax: as per body

Special Instructions

Tie in the tail and then complete the body. Tie in the wing leaving a small tag extending over the body, followed by the post. After completion cut the wing and tag to size.

The Lost at Sea Dun
Double thorax with foam Paraloop

Materials

hook: Partridge Captain Hamilton dry fly
thread: own choice
body: stripped stalk
hackle: ginger cock
tail: a few natural squirrel tail fibres
post: GSP (light)
wing: none
rib: none
thorax: rear grey and brown polypropylene dubbing; front as rear with olive polypropylene and foam pulled over

Special Instructions

Tie in the tail, followed by the body. Tie in the post and complete the hackle brush. Dub the rear of the thorax and then add the foam cover. Dub the front of the thorax and return the thread to the centre of the thorax. Pull the hackle brush over, tying it in behind the foam.

Lightly dub the thread and return it to the head position. Again tie in the hackle brush. This fly is designed to imitate a medium to large dun fly which has failed to take to the air and is at the mercy of the water currents and hungry trout.

The Wulff-Style Olive
Single hair-wing Paraloop

Materials

hook: Partridge Captain Hamilton dry fly
thread: own choice
body: dark olive polypropylene dubbing
hackle: red cock
tail: natural grey squirrel tail
post: GSP dark
wing: natural grey squirrel tail
rib: none
thorax: dark olive dubbing, as body

Special Instructions

Tied as normal. The wing can be either single or split. In the photograph it is tied single.

The Paraloop Klinkhamar Greenwell
(Tied by B. Cornwall)
Winged Paraloop fly
Materials

hook: Partridge GR12ST size 12
thread: Benecchi 8/0 olive
body: 2 strands of Veniard's super-stretch floss (1 light olive, 1 dark olive) wound over an underbody of Globrite single-strand floss (shade #10)
hackle: coch-y-bondhu, Hoffman saddle grade 3
tail: none

post: Kevlar
wing: blue dun (dyed) cock hackle tips
rib: none
thorax: fiery brown baby seal's fur, treated prior
to tying in with Watershed proofing

Special Instructions
As per previous instructions.

The Emerged March Brown
Detached body winged basic Paraloop
Materials
hook: Partridge Captain Hamilton dry fly
thread: own choice
body: dark brown polypropylene furled
hackle: medium blue dun
tail: none
post: GSP
wing: 6 strands of Flashabou

rib: none
thorax: light olive polypropylene dubbing mixed
with chopped Flashabou

Special Instructions
Tie the wing within the thorax section. A good pattern
when large upwings are on the water, it has also had
some success when stone-flies are emerging in the
summer, more by chance than intent though.

Rubber-Legged Creature
Basic Paraloop

Materials
hook: Partridge Captain Hamilton dry fly
thread: own choice
body: yellow and orange mixed polypropylene
dubbing
hackle: medium blue dun
tail: none
post: GSP
wing: none
rib: none
thorax: as body
legs: rounded rubber band

Special Instructions
Complete the fly up to and including the hackle brush
and attach it to the neck breaker. Tie in the legs using
figures of eight with thread. Complete the thorax and
then tie in the hackle brush. This is a non-specific
attractor pattern. It can be tied in infinite variations,
both sinking and floating.

The Paraloop Klinkhamar Pale Watery Emerging Dun

(Tied by B. Cornwall)

Loop-winged basic Paraloop

Materials

    hook: Partridge K14ST Oliver Edwards nymph emerger size 20

    thread: Benecchi 8/0 tobacco colour

    body: light olive super-stretch floss, wound over tying silk. Dorsal surface is coloured with a medium brown Pantone marker

    hackle: natural red game, Hoffman saddle grade 2

    tail: none

    post: Kevlar

    wing: Benecchi CDC Deveaux light olive

    rib: none

    thorax: mink underfur (mix of yellow, olive and dun shades), proofed with Watershed before tying in

Special Instructions

Follow the instructions for Klinkhamar patterns in chapter 10.

The Red Surface Buzzer

Basic Paraloop

Materials

    hook: Kamasan B100

    thread: own choice

    body: red holographic tinsel

    hackle: medium blue dun short fibre

    tail: none

    post: GSP white

    wing: none

    rib: none

    thorax: grey polypropylene dubbing

Special Instructions

Keep the thorax short. The hackle fibres should be suited to a hook two sizes smaller than the one used. This fly will float fairly well but will eventually start to sink, which seems to make it more attractive. Leave it without retrieving and after it has sunk, recast and dry off with a couple of false casts, then start again.

The Crippled Sedge

Basic Paraloop

Materials

hook: Partridge Captain Hamilton dry fly
thread: own choice
body: cinnamon polypropylene dubbing
hackle: furnace cock
tail: none
post: GSP dark
wing: none
rib: none
thorax: as body, covered by foam coloured light
brown
head: black polypropylene dubbing

Special Instructions

Complete the body around the bend of the hook. Tie
in the post and foam at the start of the hook bend and
complete the hackle brush. Complete the thorax, then
pull over the foam, followed by the hackle brush. Dub
the thread with black polypropylene dubbing and
form a large head. This fly is fished when sedges are
rising from the water surface and is intended to imitate a fly unable to take to the wing.

The Foam Body Mayfly

Basic Paraloop with foam detached
body

Materials

hook: Partridge Captain Hamilton dry fly
thread: own choice
body: white foam cylinder coloured brown, red
and olive wrapped with thread

hackle: medium blue dun cock
tail: none
post: GSP dark
wing: none
rib: none
thorax: olive and claret dubbing
head: coloured red or claret

Special Instructions

Tie in the body first, winding the thread up and down
the foam to create the segmentation. Tie in the post
and complete the hackle brush. Dub the thorax and
complete the fly. Finally colour the head slightly red
or claret with thread or a permanent ink pen.

Black Midge

Basic Paraloop

Materials

hook: Partridge Captain Hamilton dry fly
thread: own choice
body: black polypropylene dubbing
hackle: light blue dun cock, tied slightly open
tail: none
post: GSP
wing: none
rib: none
thorax: grey polypropylene dubbing

Special Instructions

None.

Titanic (Red Spinner)
Foam thorax basic Paraloop

Materials
    hook: Patridge Captain Hamilton dry fly
    thread: own choice
    body: cinnamon and black polypropylene dub-
    bing
    hackle: furnace cock
    tail: ginger cock hackle fibres
    post: GSP dark
    wing: none
    rib: none
    thorax: foam ball, first coloured brown and then
    red with permanent ink pens

Special Instructions
A hole is put through the foam ball with a dubbing
needle and it is then fed over the hook eye.

Bonny Boy
Foam thorax basic Paraloop

Materials
    hook: Partridge Captain Hamilton dry fly
    thread: own choice
    body: brown and white polypropylene dubbing
    hackle: furnace cock
    tail: natural red deer
    post: CSP dark
    wing: none
    rib: none
    thorax: foam ball, first coloured brown and then
    red with permanent ink pens

Special Instructions
As the Titanic. An unspecified fly but a proven attractor pattern.

Spent Spinner
Hackle-tip winged Paraloop

Materials
    hook: Partridge Captain Hamilton dry fly
    thread: own choice
    body: brown polypropylene dubbing
    hackle: medium blue dun cock
    tail: grizzle cock hackle fibres
    post: GSP dark
    wing: light blue dun set in horizontal position
    rib: none
    thorax: dark brown polypropylene dubbing

Special Instructions
As per hackle-tip winged flies.

Scaredy Cat

(Tied by Jim Cramer)

Deer-hair detached hackle Paraloop

Materials

    hook: dry fly

    thread: brown

    body: deer hair

    hackle: detached furled deer hair

    tail: as hackle

    post: none

    wing: none

    rib: none

    thorax: deer hair

Special Instructions

Complete the body of the fly, then trim and shape it. Then cut a groove along the back and tie in the detached hackle/body at the rear, pull it down into the groove and tie it in at the head. This fly has been included as it clearly shows the use of the furling technique described by Jim Cramer. I personally believe that the method can be developed to produce detached hackles for use with Paraloop flies.

Common Problems Encountered When Tying Paraloop Flies

Q. When I wind the hackle down through the previously wound hackle to form the hackle brush, lots of hackle fibres are caught under the down windings. How do I stop this?
A. The sure way of stopping this problem is to work the down windings of the hackle through the previous windings. Wiggling the hackle up and down through the windings will normally rectify this problem. Some hackles have fibres that are excessively curved from front to back, which can be problematic, however, and careful manipulation will solve even the worst of these.

Q. When I come to tie in the hackle brush behind the hook eye it is always too long and I end up tying in some of the hackle fibres. How do I stop this?
A. Compacting the hackle will solve this problem and will allow you to form a hackle brush of the exact length required. If you find the hackle brush is a little too long when you come to tie it in, slightly compact it and then tie it in.

Q. When I pull the hackle brush over the thorax most of the hackle fibres on the front edge are crushed between the post and the thorax. How do I ensure that all the fibres are standing out from the post and some are not crushed under the tied-in post?
A. Doubling the hackle will solve this problem, but as explained it should be done with care and only in rare cases done to excess.

Q. When I am tying winged emergers and I am pulling the hackle-tip wings back to set in position with the forming of the head, a lot of the fibres on the lower part of the wing splay out, spoiling the wing shape. What can I do to stop this?
A. This problem occurs when not enough prepared hackle stalk is left free when the wing is tied in, and when positioning and tying in the wings the turns of thread go over the lower part of the wing fibres. To solve this make sure enough prepared hackle stalk is left free at the base of each wing.

Q. When winding the hackle up the post it insists on turning onto the side no matter what I do. This produces a messy hackle brush.
A. Two things here. First, sometimes pulling the hackle towards you and for one turn around the post in the opposite direction, then bringing it back round and winding as normal will sort out the problem. Secondly, a few hackle feathers have a stalk which is unsuitable for winding straight, and the tendency for these hackles is to wind on flat or in the opposite position to that required. This is the fault of the hackle and cannot be rectified easily. Try a new source of hackles.

Q. When I use the loose-loop/pinch-and-loop method my materials still pull over to the other side of the hook. How do I stop this?
A. Two possible problems. The first is that the pressure between the thumb and finger is insufficient. The other, and the more common, is that the thumb and finger do not have the hook shank between them as the thread is pulled tight. This has the effect of initially bringing the material down straight towards the hook shank, but as the material reaches the shank it is pulled over to the far side. For the first problem increase the pressure between the finger and thumb. Moving the thumb and finger down to incorporate the hook in their grip solves the second problem.

Q. When tying in the thorax, although I use the neck breaker, I still tie in some hackle fibres. I also experience this problem when tying the hackle brush in behind the hook eye and when forming the head. Can this helped?

A. When tying flies it is not necessary to be very gentle; if the fly cannot take some pushing and pulling, it will not survive long in the real world. Pull all the fibres and wings back with your thumb and forefinger before tying it in. When released they will return to their original position.

Q. I find it difficult to cut GSP. How do I do this easily?

A. Cutting GSP is a problem, especially if tension cannot be applied to the material. The same applies to some extent when cutting Kevlar. The fine fibres often make using scissors impossible. When cutting off the excess GSP used for the post, place a sharp blade at the point there it has been tied in and pull the material upwards. This will normally cut it easily.

Q. I do not have access to all the materials used in this book. What should I do?

A. Do not worry, just use what you have. Tying Paraloop flies is like trying any other flies; the materials recommended are what I believe to be the best for that particular fly. A different material might not allow the fly to float as well as intended, but it will be quite functional.

Q. When winding the hackle up the post, the post moves around, making it difficult to keep control of the hackle windings. How do I stop this?

A. This is caused by the post being held too loosely by the gallows tool. Although some methods of tying the Paraloop do not require a gallows tool, the length of the hackle brush makes it advisable and in many circumstances essential. Tighten up the post by adjusting the position in which the gallows tool is fixed on the vice.

Q. When I pull the hackle brush over the thorax to tie it in behind the hook eye, a lot of hackle fibres are pushed over the hook eye, making it difficult to tie in the hackle without tying in fibres. How do I stop this?

A. This is a problem that can be experienced when tying any Paraloop fly. The trick is to brush the lower fibres gently downwards before tying in the hackle brush, using the thumb and forefinger. This will place the fibres out of the tying-in zone.

Q. When I compact the hackle I sometimes break the hackle stalk. What can I do to stop this happening?

A. This is a common problem when the technique of compacting is first tried. The way I get around this is to use a dubbing needle or my finger to push the hackle down. These days I tend to just use my finger, as it also pushes any wayward hackle fibres into place.

Glossary

Adams: Very popular and successful US fly

Aero Dry Wing: Proprietary brand of polypropylene floss made by Tiemco

Angel hair: Synthetic hair, sometimes the name used for Lite Brite but also used for another material

Antron: Synthetic floss or dubbing material, non-floating

Badger hackle: Light hackle with a black central strip

Barb: Part of hook

Basic pattern: The simplest forms of a Paraloop fly; a simple hackled fly

Bend: Section on hook between shank and spear

Black Gnat: Artificial fly imitating a flat-winged fly

Blue-Winged Olive: Prolific upwinged fly

Bobbin holder: Tool used to hold thread bobbin

Body: Section of fly between the tail and the thorax

Braided nylon: Used to make detached fly bodies, backing on reels and loops to attach to the end of the fly line

Brown Sedge: A caddis fly

Bucktail: Tying material used for wings and tails

Buzzer: Midge pupa

Caddis fly: Sedge fly, roof-winged fly

Cape: Source of feathers for hackles

Captain Hamilton: Name of fisherman whose designs of hooks are used by Partridge

CDC: Cul-de-canard feathers from the rear end of a duck, highly floatable

Chinese cape: Type of cape imported from China

Classic patterns: Well-established fly patterns

Claw wing: A Paraloop Method wing

Compacting: Paraloop technique where the hackle brush is shortened

Continuous bend: Design of hook where the hook bends from the eye to the point

Crippled flies: Flies that fail to emerge correctly and damage wings etc.

Debarbed hook: Hook with barb removed

Detached body: Body of artificial fly which is separate from the hook shank

Doubling: Paraloop technique whereby the hackle fibres are reset

Down-eyed hook: Hook with eye bent down in relation to hook shank

Dry fly: Fly that floats on the surface of the water

Dubbed body: Body formed by using dubbing

Dubbing: Material and technique for applying the material to the thread

Dun: The first adult stage in the life cycle of the upwinged fly

Early: When used with reference to the Paraloop, refers to the position the post is tied on the hook shank, before the halfway point

Emerger: Transitional stage of insect from nymph or pupa to fly

Entomology: The study of insects

Ephemeroptera: Upwinged flies, mayflies, olives

Exoskeleton: Outer shell of an insect

Eye: Part of the hook

Feather-fibre wing: Wing formed from feather fibres; different from slip wing, as the fibres are separated

Flashabou: Synthetic material, Mylar-like ribbon, very reflective

Filoplume: Light fluffy fibres at the base of a feather

Floating yarn: Usually polypropylene products

Floss: Yarn used for tying flies: many different materials

Fly-Rite Inc.: US company supplying fly tying materials, especially polypropylene products

Foam sheet: Material used in fly tying; when tying Paraloop flies, closed-cell is used

Furnace hackle: Brown hackle with black centre

Gallows tool: Tool originally designed to tie parachute flies, also used to tie Paraloops

Gape: Part of hook, closest point between point and shank

Genetic breeding: Selective breeding of birds to obtain the best feathers

Green Drake: Upwinged fly, a mayfly

Grey Wulff: One of the many Wulff patterns

GSP: Gel-spun polypropylene, used for post loops in Paraloop flies

Guard hair: Stiff, larger hair from fur

Hackle: Feather from bird

Hackle brush: Term used for the hackle on Paraloop flies before tying in

Hackle pliers: Tool designed to hold hackle feathers when winding on the hook

Hackle-tip wings: Wings formed using the tips of hackles

Hackle fibre: Single fibre protruding off the stalk of the hackle

Hair wing: Wing formed from hair fibres

Half-hitch: Knot used to lock thread

Half-hitch tool: Simple tool used to create a half-hitch knot

Halford, Frederick: Influential fly fisher, advocate of dry fly

Hard hair: Hair which is hard and difficult to tie in, e.g. squirrel

Henny cock: Hackles which are between a cock and hen feather

High wing: Form of wing, normally on emerger patterns

Holistic fly tying: The author's approach to designing and tying flies

Holographic tinsel: Synthetic material, tinsel-like ribbon, highly reflective

Imago: The adult upwinged fly

Imitative pattern: Artificial fly designed to imitate the natural fly

Indian cape: Type of cape imported from India

Indicator: Normally an addition to a fly to make seeing it easier

Jorgensen, Poul: USA-based Fly tyer. Very influential especially on salmon flies

Kamasan: Hook manufacturer

Larva: Stage after egg and before pupa in the life cycle of some insects

Late: When used with reference to the Paraloop, refers to the position the post is tied on the hook shank, three-quarters to all the way along the hook shank

Lite Brite: Synthetic material, highly reflective

Loose loop: Method of applying material to the hook

Lunn's Particular: Traditional hackle-tip winged fly

Lure: Non-imitative fly pattern

Marryat, George Selwyn: Greatest influence on Frederick Halford

Mayfly: Member of Ephemeroptera family of flies

Medium: When used with reference to the Paraloop, refers to the position the post is tied on the hook shank, just after the halfway point

Micro fibbets: Synthetic tailing material

Microthread: Proprietary name of thread used by the author

Midge: Member of the Diptera family of flies; flat-winged

Mottram, J. C.: Unusual fly fisher, very innovative

Multistrand thread: Thread formed by twisting many fine strands together

Mylar: Flat, tinsel-like ribbon material

Neck breaker: Tool used to tie Paraloop flies

Neck cape: Source of hackles from bird from neck and upper back on the skin

Olive dun: Upwinged fly. Sub-imago

Open loop: Paraloop technique for hackle

Orvis: Tackle and fly tying material supplier

Oval tinsel: A tinsel wrapped around a thread

Parachute: Style of tying the hackle of a fly

Partridge: UK hook manufacturer owned by Mustad

Pinch and loop: See loose loop

Plecoptera: Stone-flies

Point: Tip of hook

Prewaxed thread: Thread waxed by manufacturer

Pupa: Stage in insect life cycle, after larva, before adult

Quill: Hollow lower section of a feather

Quill body: Body made from stripped feather or herl stem/stalk

Rooster: Source of feathers

Rotary vice: Vice with jaws that rotate, keeping the fly on the same plane

Saddle cape: Feathers from rear of back on the skin

Salmon iron: Large hook traditionally used to tie salmon flies

Sedge fly: Caddis fly, roof-winged fly

Shank: Straight section between the eye and bend on a hook

Shuck: The exoskeleton of a nymph or pupa during emergence, which is discarded

Silicon spray: Spray used to treat materials; helps to resist water

Skues, G. E. M.: Highly influential UK fly fisherman; helped develop nymph fishing

SLF: Synthetic living fibre, a dubbing material

Slip wing: Method of forming a wing using feather fibres

Spade hackle: Feather from shoulder of neck cape, good source of tailing fibres

Spear: Section of hook from the end of the bend to the point

Spent fly: Dying upwinged fly

Spent wing: Style of tying the wing of an upwinged fly; the dying or dead fly

Spinner: The adult upwinged fly; the imago

Split wings: Wings formed by splitting either hair or feather to form two

Stalk: Centre stem of feathers

Stem: Central stalk from which feather fibres extend

Stillborns: Flies that fail to emerge and die during the emerging process

Stripped stalk/stem: Feather stem/stalk stripped of fibres

Superfloss: Lycra-based stretch floss

Superglue: CA Cement fast-drying glue

Synthetic: Man-made materials

Terrestrials: Flies blown onto the water by the wind etc., not linked to the water in their life cycle

Testing for soundness: Checking that the hook is not flawed before tying a fly on it

Thorax: Section of fly between the body and the head

Tiemco: Fly-tying tools and materials manufacturer in Japan

Tinsel: Metal or plastic ribbon, usually used in bodies or as ribbing material

Trichoptera: Sedge or caddis flies

Tying flat: Method of untwisting thread and winding it flat on the hook which has less bulk

Tying tight: Opposite to tying flat; the thread is wound tighter so more compression may be applied when tying

Underfur: Soft fur at the base of the pelt

Up-eyed hook: Hook with eye bent up in relation to the shank

Up winged fly: Member of the Ephemeroptera family of flies, olives, mayflies

Upright: Style of tying a wing

Varnish: Used to bond and seal when tying flies, especially the head

Web: Soft central portion of feather running either side of stem

Wet fly: Fly designed to sink

Whip finish: Final locking of thread onto a fly pattern

Wulff, Lee: Very influential US fly fisherman

Z-Lon: Synthetic fibre material

Z-wing: A thin plastic film used for producing semi-translucent wings

Appendix IV

Materials Used

This list is to be read in conjunction with the suppliers listed in Appendix V. I have given each product a code, which is shown under the suppliers which can provide it. Only the products used in the actual tyings or in the flies in the gallery are listed, except threads and hooks, where all the recommended brands are listed. The code is not the official number of the product but is given to enable readers to ascertain which supplier stocks which product. If a supplier has not been allocated any code numbers, this is because the information is not available at the time of going to press. The likelihood is that they will stock most if not all of the products used in this book.

Material	Code Number
Genetic capes	
Hoffman	HGC
Metz/Umpqua	MUC
Other	OC
Polypropylene products	
Tiemco Aero Dry Wing	ADW
Fine fibre floss	PFF
General floss	PGF
Siliconised floss	PSF
Dubbing	PDG
Thread	
Benecchi	BTH
Dynacord	DTH
Gudebrod	GTH
Gutemann	GUTH
Uni-thread	UTH
Kevlar	KEV
Feathers other than genetic capes	
Chinese capes	CC
Indian capes	IC
Bronze Mallard	BM
Benecchi CDC Deveaux	CDC
Partridge hackles	PH
Fur and hair	
Squirrel tail	SQT
Squirrel fur	SQF
Hare's mask	HM

Material	Code Number
Mink Fur	MIN
Synthetic fibres excepting polypropylene	
Antron floss	AF
Antron dubbing	AD
SLF	SLF
Lite Brite	LB
Flashabou	FB
Holographic tinsel	HT
Superfloss/Superstretch floss/	
Flexifloss	SF
Globrite	GB
Wax	
Cobbler's wax	CW
Beeswax	BW
Hooks	
Partridge	PH
Kamasan	KH
Tiemco	TH
Daiichi	DH
Orvis	OH
VMC	VH
Miscellaneous	
Micro fibbets	MF
Foam sheeting closed-cell	FS
Tinsel and wire	
Silver oval tinsel	SO
Stainless steel wire	SS

APPENDIX V

Useful Addresses

Web Sites

www.Ianmoutter.co.uk. Author's web site.
E-mail: Ian@Ianmoutter.co.uk. **Paraloop web site**:
www.Ianmoutter.co.uk/paraloop.

www.danica.com/flytier. Hans Weilenmann's web site.

www.flyshop.com. More than just a commercial site; covers most aspects of fly fishing and fly tying.

www.apgai.co.uk. Web site of game angling instructors, mostly in United Kingdom.

www.fishandfly.co.uk. Online magazine, including up-to-date information.

www.connect4free.net/home/arthurfoxon/materials.html. Commercial site with good information pages.

www.martex.co.uk/eftta/pr014.htm. Information on European tackle suppliers.

www.angling uk.net. Information and an immense list of links world-wide. Direct links address: **www.anglinguk.net/links/flytying.html.**

www.f-deans.freeserve.co.uk/default.htm. Good general fly fishing site.

www.flyfishing-and-flytying.co.uk. Web site of UK's leading fly tying magazine.

www.sana.org. Web site of the Scottish Anglers' National Association, the governing body for game angling in Scotland.

www.brucepub.com/sata/index.htm. Web site of the Salmon and Trout Association, the governing body for game angling in England.

www.fedflyfishers.org/indexmst.htm. Federation of Fly Fishers (USA).

fff-e-tripod.com/index. Federation of Fly Fishers (Europe).

Suppliers

United Kingdom
Wholesale. The companies below are probably in the position to supply all of the materials in the list in Appendix IV. Not all of the companies will supply direct to the public. Some materials are supplied exclusively to a particular company; if this is the case the supplier is marked as such.

Craftye
60A Inverleith Row
Edinburgh
EH3 5PX
Tel: 0131 551 1224; fax: 0131 551 1226

Lureflash
Victoria Buildings
Victoria Street
Kilnhurst
Mexborough
South Yorkshire
S64 5SQ
Tel: 01709 580238; fax: 01709 586194

Tiemco products in UK

Orvis
Bridge House
High Street
Stockbridge
Hampshire
SO20 6HB
Tel: 01264 810017

Partridge of Redditch Ltd
Mount Pleasant
Redditch
Worcestersthire
B97 4JE
Tel: 01527 543 555; fax: 01527 546 956
E-mail: hooks@partridge-of-redditch.com

Tom Saville
9 Nottingham Road
Trowell
Nottingham
NG9 3PA
Tel: 0115 930 8800
Fax: 0115 930 3336

E. Veniard Ltd
Paramount Warehouses
138 Northwood Road
Thornton Heath
Surrey
CR7 8YG
Tel: 020 8653 3565; fax: 020 8771 4805

Retail and Mail Order: The following businesses are either retail, mail order or both. In each case this is indicated: **R = Retail M = Mail Order**

Carillon UK (R/M)
Maple House
North Road
Torworth
Retford
DN22 8NW
Tel: 0800 917 0898 and 07967 635713

OC ADW, PGF, CDC, SQT, SQF, HM, AF, AD, LB, FB, HT, SF, GB, FS, SO, SS, CW, BQ

The Craftye Fisherman (R/M)
60A Inverleith Row
Edinburgh
EH3 5PX
Tel: 0131 551 1224; fax: 0131 551 1226

HGC, ADW, GUTH, KEV, CC, IC, BM, CDC, PH, AF, AD, LB, FB, HT, SF, GB, MF, FS, SO, SS, CW, BW, KH

Fishtec (M)
Tel: 01874 612 600
Web site: www.fishtec.co.uk

HGC, MUC, PGF, UTH, KEV, SQT, HM, MIN, AF, AD, SLF, LB, FB, HT, SF, GB, MF, FS, SO, SS, CW, BW, KH

Gordon Griffiths Fishing Tackle (R/M)
Units 1/8
Lifford Way
Binley Industrial Estate
Coventry
CV3 2RN
Tel: 024 76 440 859; fax: 024 76 635 694
Web site: www.gordon-griffiths.co.uk
E-mail: fishingtackle@gordon-griffiths.co.uk

Gows (R/M)
12 Union Street
Dundee
DD1 4BH
Tel: 01382 225 427
Web site: www.scotland-fishing.co.uk
E-mail: gows@sol.co.uk

HGC, MUC, UTH, CC, IC, BM, CDC, PH, SQT, SQF, HM, AF, AD, SLF, LB, FB, HT, SF, GB, MF, FS, SO, SS, CW, BW, PH, KH, TH

Mikes Tackle Shop (R/M)
46 Portobello High Street
Edinburgh
EH15 1DA
Tel: 0131 657 3258; fax: 0131 669 0672
Web site: www.mikestackleshop.co.uk
E-mail: sales@mikestackleshop.co.uk

SF, OH, KH, PH, SO, SS, FS, AF, AD, HT, SF, SQT, SQF, HM, PH, BM, CC, IC, HGC, MGC, OC, GTH, UTH, KEV

Niche Products (R/M)
1 White Mead
Broomfield
Chelmsford
Essex
CM1 7YB
Tel/fax: 01245 442041
Web site: www.nicheflytying.com
E-mail: niche.fly@virgin.net

HGC, MUC, ADW, PFF, PSF, PDG, UTH, CDC, SQT, SQF, HM, MIN, SF, HT, GB, MF, SF, CW, TH

John Norris (R/M)
21 Victoria Road
Penrith
Cumbria
CA11 8HP
Tel: 01768 864211; fax: 01768 890476
Web site: JohnNorris.co.uk
E-mail: sales @johnnorris.co.uk

Orvis (R/M)
Bridge House
High Street
Stockbridge
Hampshire
SO20 6HB
Tel: 01264 810017

Orvis also have shops in Harrogate, Bath, Exeter and London

HGC, KEV, CDC, AF, AD, LB, FB, HT, GB, MF, FS, BW, OH

Sportfish (R/M)
Winforton
Hereford
HR3 6SP
Tel: 01544 327111; fax: 01544 327093
Web site: www.sportfish.co.uk
E-mail: sportfish@sportfish.co.uk

George Street
Edinburgh
EH2 2LR
Tel: 0131 225 7225; fax: 0131 220 5110
E-mail: sportfish-edinburgh@sportfish.co.uk

Haywards Farm
Theale
Reading RG2 4AS
Tel: 0118 930 3860
E-mail: sportfish-reading@sportfish.co.uk

13 Pall Mall
London
SW1Y 5LU
Tel: 0207 839 9008; fax: 0207 839 9010
E-mail: sportfish-pallmall@sportfish.co.uk

HGC, PGF, BTH, UTH, KEV, CC, BM, CDC, PH, SQT, SQF, HM, MIN, AF, AD, SLF, LB, HT, SF, GB, MF, FS, SO, SS, CW, PH, KH

Canada
Country Pleasures
Bow River Shop 570
10816 Macleod Trail Street
Calgary
Alberta
T2J 5N8
Tel: 403-271-1016

Howard's Super-Natural Hackle
Box 1
Site 5
R.R.2
Didsbury AB
T0M 0W0
Tel: 403-335-9155; fax: 403-335-9155

Ruddick's Fly Shop Ltd
3726 Canada Way
Burnaby
Vancouver
British Columbia
V5G 1G5
Tel: 604-434-2420; fax: 604-681-3747
Web site: www.rudfly.com
E-mail: ruddicks@rudfly.com

Europe
Roman Moser
Kuferzeile 19
A-4819 Gmunden
Austria
Tel: 07612-5686; fax: 07612-5633

Hero-Jacht & Vliegvisshop
Leuvensestraat 134
3300 Tienen
Belgium
Tel: 0168-14581
Web site: www.mouche.com/heronl.htm

Go Fishing
Brogade 6–8
DK-5000
Odense C
Denmark
Tel: 666-12-1500; fax: 66-14-0026

Mouches de Charette
Les Guillets
Montracol
01310
France
Tel: 4.74.24.22.73; fax: 4.74.24.30.88

Fly Fishing Brinkhoff
Auf der Liet 1
D-59519 Mohnesee-Delecke
Germany
Tel: 02924-637; fax: 02924-332

Giorgio Benecchi's Products
Via Giotto 279
Modena
41100
Italy
Tel: 059.341.190
Fax: 059.243.627

Fly Fishers Tackle Shop
Weiswampach 30 A
L-9990
Luxembourg
Tel: 97225; fax: 979382

Kelson Collection
Rijksweg Zuid 142
6161 BT Geleen
Netherlands
Tel: 046-4749197; fax: 046-4757774

Streamside Service
Postboks 2092
Hasle 3202 Sandefjord
Norway
Tel: 33-453445; fax: 33-453344

Julius Sport
Caunedo 32
28037 Madrid
Spain
Tel: 091-304-2257; fax: 091-327-2696

Lennart Bergvist Flugfiske
Box 5194
200 70 Malmo
Sweden
Tel: 031-26-9890; fax: 031-26-9870

A & H Hebeisen
Schaffauserstrasse 514
CH-8052 Zurich
Switzerland
Tel: 01-301-22-21; fax: 01-302-06-38

United States of America
American Angling Supplies and Services
23 Main Street
Salem NH 03079
Tel: 603-893-3333; fax: 603-8988141

Anglers Choice
PO Box 466
Custer
WA 98240
Tel: 360-366-5894; fax: 360 366-5894

BT's Fly Fishing Products
560 Willow Wood Lane
Delta
CO 81416-3036
Tel: 888-243-3597; voice: 970-874-7033;
fax: 970-874-6960
Web site: www.btsflyfishing.com
E-mail: gbeatty2@aol.com

Cabela's
812 13th Avenue
Sidney
NB 69160
Tel: 800-237-444; fax: 308-254-2200
Web site: www.cabelas.com

Clouser's Fly Shop
101 Ulrich Street
Middle Town
PA 17057
Tel: 717-944-6541

Dan Bailey's Fly Shop
PO Box 1019
Livingstone
MT 59047
Tel: 406-222-1673; fax: 406-222-8450
Web site: www.dan-bailey.com
E-mail: info@dan-bailey.com

E.A.T.
PO Box 8885
New Fairfield
CT 06812
Tel: 203-746-4121; fax: 203-746-1348

Evets & Co.
5825 Dover Street
Oakland
CA 94609
Tel: 510-652-9387
Web site: www.roundrocks.com/others/dist/evets-co.html

Feather Craft
8307 Manchester Road
PO Box 19904
St Louis
MO 63144
Tel: 800-659-1707; fax: 888-963-0324
Web site: www.feather-craft.com

Fly & Field
560 Crescent Boulevard
Glen Ellyn
IL 60137
Tel: 800-328-9753
Web site: www.flyfield.com

Fly-Rite Inc.
7421 S. Beyer
Dept. FT
Frankenmuth
MI 48734
Tel: 517-652-9869; fax: 517-652-2996

Hook and Hackle Co.
7 Kaycee Loop Road
Plattsburgh
NY 12901
Tel: 800-552-8342; fax: 518-561-0336
Web site: www.hookhack.com
E-mail: bob@hookhack.com

Longhorn Flies & Supplies
Route 4
Box 139A
McKinney
TX 75070
Tel: 214-562-9542; fax: 214-542-4558

Umpqua Feather Merchants
17537 N. Umpqua Highway
PO Box 700
Glide
OR 97443
Tel: 503-496-3512; fax: 503-496-0150
Web site: www.umpqua.com
E-mail: umpqua@umpqua.com

The importers of Tiemco products in the USA

Whiting Farms Inc.
PO Box 100.
Delta
CO 81416
Tel: 501-425-9500; fax: 800-425-9599
Web site: www.whitingfarms.com
E-mail: info@whitingfarms.com

Hoffman genetic capes

Yellowstone Angler
Highway 89 South
PO Box 629/5256
Livingston
MT 59047
Tel: 406-222-7130; fax: 405-222-7153
Web site: www.yellowstoneangler.com
E-mail: staff@yellowstoneangler.com

UK Fly Tying Instructors

The instructors listed below are qualified Fly Tying Instructors to APGAI (Advanced Professional Game Angling Instructor) level, who are familiar with the Paraloop method of tying flies.

Gary Champion
1 Higher Terrace
Ponsanooth
Truro
Cornwall
TR3 7EW
Tel: 01872 863551

Gary Coxon
Dinglevale Cottage
Off Forest Road
Cuddington
Cheshire
CW8 2ED
Tel: 01606 882891

Donald Downs
The Mead
Hosey
Westerham
Kent
TN16 1TA

Vic Knight
16 Freshwater Drive
Lakeside
Amblecote
Brierley Hill
West Midlands
DY5 3T

Ian Moutter
South Wing
Borthwick Hall
Heriot
Midlothian
Scotland
EH38 5YE
Tel: 0131 557 8333

Ken Muter
70 Longdean Park
Chester-le-Street
Co. Durham
DH3 4DG

Peter Scott
8 Janetta Street
Clydebank
Dunbartonshire
Scotland
G81 3EB

Ken Smith
18 Beaumaris Drive
Gedling
Nottingham
NG4 2RA
Tel: 01159 617939

UK National Angling Associations

The Salmon & Trout Association
Fishmongers' Hall
London Bridge
London
EC4R 9EL
Tel: 020 7283 5838; fax: 020 7929 1389

The Salmon & Trout Association (Scotland)
The Caledonian Club
32 Abercromby Place
Edinburgh
EH3 6QE
Tel: 0131 558 3644; fax: 0131 557 6269

The Scottish Anglers National Association
Caledonia House
South Gyle
Edinburgh
EH12 9DQ
Tel: 0131 339 8808

Bibliography

Ord Clark, Barry and Spaight, Robert (1996), *International Guide to Fly Tying Materials*, Merlin Unwin Books.

Goddard, John (1991), *Trout Flies of Britain and Europe*, A & C Black.

*Halford, F. M. (1897), *Dry Fly Entomology*, Vinton & Co.

Lively, Chauncy (1980), *Fly Box*, Stackpole Books.

Martin, Darrel (1994), *Micropatterns: Tying and Fishing the Small Fly*, Swan Hill Press.

*Mottram, J. C. (1913), *Fly Fishing: Some New Arts And Mysteries*. The Field Press.

*Skues, G. E. M. (1910), *Minor Tactics of the Chalk Stream*, A & C Black.

*These books are very difficult to obtain in their original editions. It is possible to obtain reprint editions; the best source for these that I know of is:

Paul Morgan
Coch-Y-Bonddu Books
Machynlleth
Mid-Wales
SY20 8DJ
Tel: 01654 702837; fax: 01654 702857
Web site: www.anglebooks.com
E-mail: orders@anglebooks.com

Paul Morgan offers a full international mail order service, which, having used it for a number of years, I can recommend.

Index

A

Anatomy of the fly   15
Adult Damsel pattern   141–2
Adams Irresistible   169
Antron   40
Anatomy of the hook   48

B

Badger Hackle Fly   167
Basic Paraloop   52
Black Gnat   84
Black Midge   173
Blue Winged Olive   112–13, 128,
                             132–3
Bobbin holder   23
Bobbin threader   27
Bodies   40, 76, 158
Bonny Boy   174
Borders, the   9
Braided monofilament   42
Bronze Mallard   36
Brown Midge Emerger   120–21
Brown Sedge Emerger   105
Buszek, Buz   146
Buzzer patterns   114–23

C

Caddis   102–105
Chinese cape   29
Cigarette lighter   27
Claw Wing Dun   167
Compacting the hackle   61, 125
Cornwall, Brian   149–53
Cove, Arthur   115
Craft knife   27
Craftye Fisherman, The   50
Cramer, Jim   10, 42, 140–45
Crippled Sedge   172

Cul-de-canard   37, 150
Cutting a cape   32

D

Daddy Long Legs   134 5
Datam   45
Deane, Peter   92
Defined body   72–3
Detached bodies   75–6, 96
Detached Body Green Drake   96
Deveaux, Aimé   13, 14
Diptera   103
Doubling the hackle   62, 125
Dry Fly Entomology   102
Dubbing brush   23
Dubbing needle   23
Dubbing the thread   71–3
Dynacord   50

E

Early, Medium, Late   65
Emerged March Brown   171
Emerger life cycles   101
Emerger patterns   100–113
Emerger shucks   75
Epoxy buzzer   114–15

F

Fan-Winged Mayfly   168
Feather stalks   41, 90
Flashabou   154–8
Flat-winged flies   103
Flexifloss   42
Floatability   59
Floss   40, 76
Fly-Rite Inc.   34
Foam   42, 81–2, 119, 130
Foam Body Mayfly   173

G

Gallows tool — 12, 19
Genetic hackles — 29–31
Giorgio Benecchi — 37, 50
GloBrite — 44
Glue — 50
Green Drake — 96–9
Greenwell's Glory — 150, 165
Grey Duster — 164
Grey Wulff — 91–6
GSP — 27, 34, 45
Gudebrod — 50
Gutemann — 50

H

Hackle brush — 56, 61
Hackle colour chart — 30
Hackle pliers — 22
Hackle stacker — 10
Hackle-tip wings — 33, 70–71
Hackles — 28
Hair stacker — 25
Hair-Tailed Hopper — 166
Half hitcher — 27
Halford, Frederick — 102
Hard hair — 34, 73
Harlequin Olive — 163
High-Winged — 112
Hoffman — 29
Holographic Tinsel — 154, 156–8
Hooks — 46
Hunter, Richard — 109

I

Indian cape — 29
Iron Blue Dun Emerger — 168

K

Kamasan hooks — 47
Kevlar — 27, 45, 144
Kite's Imperial — 164
Klinkhamar — 13, 150, 152–3
Klinkhamar Greenwell — 170

L

Large Dark Dun — 166
Large Dark Olive — 169
Large Dark Olive Emerger — 153
Lighting — 27
Lite Brite — 155–8

Lively, Chauncy — 159
Locked Wing — 122
Long, Ned — 10, 140, 146–9
Loose Loop — 68
Lost at Sea Dun — 170
Lunn's Particular — 88

M

Martin, Alex — 159
Medium Olive Emerging Dun — 152
Medium Sedge, Hair Wing — 165
Micro fibbets — 39, 65–7, 128
Microthread — 49
Midge Cluster — 143
Midges — 114–16
Mohican hairstyle — 63
Mottram, J. C. — 115, 127

N

Neck breaker — 12, 21
Ned's Emerger — 147–9
Niche Products — 34

O

Olive Buzzer Pupa — 116–19
Olive Dun — 53
Open loops — 64

P

Pale Water Emerging Dun — 172
Partridge Hooks — 47
Petitjean Fishing Equipment — 37
Pinch and Loop — 68
Polypropylene — 34, 39, 41
Poly-Winged Spinner — 168
Pond Olive — 169
Posts — 45
Preformed dubbed bodies — 144–5

Q

Quigley, Bob — 10

R

Ransome, Arthur — 13
Ready Sedge — 164
Red Hatching Buzzer — 166
Red Spinner — 174
Red Surface Buzzer — 172
Removing feather fibres — 42
Ribs — 44

Rubber Band Fly   115
Rubber-Legged Creature   171

S
Scaredy Cat   175
Scissors   22
Sherry Spinner   128–31
Shucks   75, 158
Single Wing hair   95
Skues, G. E. M.   102
Spade hackles   39
Spent Spinner   174
Spent Winged Flies   124–36
Squirrel Tail   33, 39, 73
Stainless steel wire   44
Superfloss   42, 45, 147–9
Suspender Buzzer   46

T
Tails   38, 65–7, 158
Thorax   40, 41, 158
Thread   44, 49, 79–80
Three Fly set-up   123
Tiemco   25, 34
Tinsel, Oval   44, 76–7, 138
Titanic   174
Traditional Dry Flies   83–99
Tup's Indispensable Variation   165
Tweed, River   84, 150

U
Undefined Body   72–3
Uni-thread   50
Upward swimming buzzer   52

V
Varnish   50
Vice   17
View Board   26

W
Walker, Richard   135
Wax   45
Weilenmann, Hans   10
Wet Flies   137–9
Whip finish   24
Whiting Farms   29
Wickham's Fancy   163
Wings   32, 157
Wulff, Lee   91
Wulff-Style Olive   170

Y
Yellow May Dun   109–111

Z
Z-Wing   38
Z-Lon   142, 148